THE CHELSEA WHO'S WHO

The OFFICIAL Chelsea books

THE CHELSEA WHO'S WHO

CHELSEA'S HEROES AND ZEROES FROM ABRAMS TO ZOLA

RICK GLANVILL

BOXTREE

First published in 1998 by Boxtree, an imprint of Macmillan Publishers Ltd,
25 Eccleston Place, London, SW1W 9NF and Basingstoke

Associated companies throughout the world

ISBN 0 7522 2493 X

9 8 7 6 5 4 3 2 1

A CIP catalogue record for this book is available from the British Library

Typeset by SX Composing DTP, Rayleigh, Essex
Printed by

Photographs:

Sporting Pictures: Celestine Babayaro, Peter Bonetti, Ed de Goey, Kerry Dixon, Ruud Gullit,
Ed McCreadie, Pat Nevin, Eddie Newton, Peter Osgood, Dan Petrescu, Graham Roberts,
Ken Shellito (1979), Clive Walker; Empics: Charlie Cooke, Steve Clarke, Roberto Di Matteo,
Tommy Docherty, Jimmy Greaves, Ron Harris, John Hollins, Brian Laudrup, Terry Venables,
Gianluca Vialli, David Webb, Dennis Wise; PA News: Tommy Lawton, Joe Mears, Ken Shellito
(1965), David Webb and Alan Hudson; Hulton Deutsch: Roy Bentley; Popperfoto: Vic Woodley;
Action Images: Gianfranco Zola

To the same old Chelsea of Robertson, Drake, Docherty, Sexton, Gullit and Vialli.

'Bring back The Cat!'
'Never mind that – bring back
the greyhounds!'

ACKNOWLEDGEMENTS

Grazie mille...

To my researchers Yael Cohen and Peter Collins. Respect is due to Jenny Olivier and Boxtree, and of course my lovable agent Cat Ledger. Gratitude is owed to the many people who contributed indirect or off-the-cuff, sometimes oblivious ways, including fellow matchgoers – Neil, Steev, Frannie, Gary, Giles, Ciaran, Chris – members of the Chelsea Internet Mailing List – especially Roald Aune, Roy Boston, Claire Boyes, Brewster Bob, Chris Carver, Carlo Capelli, Jamie Crampton, Patrick Davies, Peter Davis, Lawrence Evans, John Fisher, Roy Foran, Bill Fordham, Martin Freshwater, Will Hartje, Jax, David 'Furry' Kettle, Steve Lloyd, John Macleod, Anthony McGarrigle, Peter McIntyre, Alec McKay, Solomon Malcolm, Paul Mason, Steve Millington, Nick Moon, Andy Morley, John O'Connell, Graham Parley, Richard Price, Andy Sennitt, Matt Sheehan, Ketil Tellevik, Nick Waddell – and others who have helped me shape opinions of players for this book over the years. This was vital if I was to present a more rounded view of a footballer than the one framed by my own favouritism and prejudices. (That was the theory. It didn't quite work out like that. Write your own book if you disagree.)

My thanks also extend to the club officials past and present who have spared time to share memories and thoughts with me over the years.

LARRY ABRAMS

This steadfast left-half was unlucky enough to begin his Chelsea career at the advent of the First World War. Given that defensive role his record of five goals in thirty-one starts in his first season, 1914/15, was excellent. Unluckily he was overlooked for the "Khaki Cup Final" defeat by Sheffield United at Old Trafford. Although stocky, he was asked to convert to outside-left on resumption of league hostilities in 1919/20, but couldn't hold the place down and consequently drifted off to Cardiff City.

JIMMY ARGUE

The stereotypically combative 'Ginger' Glaswegian lived up to the short-temperedness inferred by his name. A pre- and post-war inside-forward, his ball skills and flair, added to a decent haul of goals between 1934 and 1939 made him a valuable asset to Leslie Knighton's inconsistent side. After the war the competition for places under Billy Birrell's new 'quality-first' regime proved too much for Jim. Although he skippered the reserves for a season, he soon moved on to pastures new. His greatest game was the 5–5 draw against Bolton during the 1937/38 season. The flame-haired Scotsman grabbed a hat-trick of great goals, but Chelsea were still knocked off the top slot in Division One.

KEN ARMSTRONG

One of the few players whose ashes were strewn over the sacred Stamford Bridge turf on his death. Some of those who saw the two in action are keen to compare Ken and his latter-day repro-duction Ron Harris, and not simply in terms of longevity of service. Loyal. Consistent. Hard in the tackle. Rarely beaten or bested. A zesty competitor. As a right-half his style was effective enough to earn an England cap during the 1954/55 Championship season. And when Ken went up front to temporarily replace the mighty Tommy Lawton, in contrast to Chopper he could acquit himself pretty well; top-scoring in 1947/48 for a while.

Off the pitch, again like Ron, he was quiet, gently humorous and liked his golf. Some even said he was better on the links than the pitch. But they didn't teach golf in the army, where Ken had come from in 1946.

You could always count on Ken Armstrong, and not least because he could count pretty well himself. Before the advent of agents, pre-war bank clerk Ken, introduced to the club's assistant manager Joe Shaw, negotiated a move to Chelsea for the princely sum of £10.

His debut came in a 5–0 defeat against West Ham. Suddenly company audits and bankers' draughts must have appeared hugely attractive. But the club Ken joined as a demob-happy pro in 1946 was – eventually – going places under Billy Birrell.

Ken notched important goals, not least three goals in the last four games that retained the team's top-flight status in 1951. His consistency was vital to the mid-50s Chelsea of Ted Drake. And the only surprise for Bridge regulars about his call-up for a solitary England cap against Scotland in 1955 (a 7–2 win) was that it was so long overdue. That same magical year brought the Championship to SW6 for the first time. With Stan Wicks and Derek Saunders, he formed the international class half-back line that drove Drake's Ducklings on to an historic triumph.

For Yorkshireman Ken, another milestone was passed – 300 appearances for the newly re-christened Blues. That put his transfer cost at 3.3p a game – the price of a beer in those days. Even allowing for inflation, that's pretty good going.

He went on to appear 402 times, then a club record, and he

remains high on the Blues' all-time appearances list. In 1957 Ken retired to New Zealand where he was to become national coach, and died there aged sixty in 1984.

TREVOR AYLOTT

Lantern-jawed, mop-headed striker with a lop-sided grin. He was amiable enough. Strong – in a bull-in-a-china-shop kind of fashion – and, in his first few games, he showed enough promise for that regular type of premature ejaculation from Brian Moore that millions of London football fans were all too well acquainted with. In November 1975, Chelsea had, according to Mooro, 'possibly found the new Peter Osgood'. 'Ay-lott, Ay-lott, Ay-ay-lott Ay-lott, born is the ki-ing...' Somehow no. His technique was none too good and he found defences including the likes of Wrexham and Birmingham, impenetrable.

After two goals in twenty-nine appearances, the Bermondsey boy was flogged downwards, surprisingly to Oakwell and Barnsley, for £50,000. (A lot of money in those days.) Half a dozen more moves followed in ten years as he carved a football career for himself. Interesting, isn't it, how some mediocre players make more of their opportunities than infinitely more talented ones. In the end, he got what he wanted out of the game and had paid off his mortgage through signing-on fees. One of his closest pals at Chelsea was Johnny Bumstead; he was godfather to the trusty midfielder's son.

B

CELESTINE BABAYARO

'One-Baba, two-Baba, three-Babayaro... hey, Babayaro!' The Macarena boy arrived as the most expensive teenager in Chelsea's history. The eighteen-year-old Nigerian international was Chelsea's second black African signing after Mark Stein, but the first former Rancher Bees player.

Raised in the suburbs of Kaduna, northern Nigeria, Celestine Babayaro's ascent to the top of European football has been phenomenal and success has come early. He was an Olympic football gold medallist at the 1996 Atlanta Games, but remains modest. 'There are many like me who have tried to get where I am, but it has not been their destiny to make it,' he said during his first season at Stamford Bridge in his quiet, pious way.

Many players of his age at the club had just signed professionally after moving from YTS status. But at 15 he was a winner at the JVC World Championships for Under-17 teams in Japan with the Golden Eaglets, the young Nigeria team. Anderlecht saw him and wanted him. Baba had to leave Africa immediately for Belgium, overcoming the reservations of his parents. Unsurprisingly it was something of a culture – and meteorological – shock. He added layers of clothing under his shirt to keep warm in Brussels. No doubt this was useful when he had to face Tromso inside the Arctic Circle in the Blues' Cup Winners' Cup campaign of 1997/98, though he had never seen snow before and found conditions hard to deal with.

At Anderlecht they soon noted his versatility, lightning pace, balance, positional sense and all-round defensive acumen. He won a championship medal and became the youngest-ever player to appear in a UEFA competition there, turning out against Steaua Bucharest at the age of sixteen in 1994. In the same match he also became the youngest player to get sent off in a UEFA competition, for a trip on Lacatus.

Baba was Belgium's Young Player of the Year in 1995 and a year later picked up the Ebony Boot as the country's best African player.

He also scored a vital equaliser, a diving header, for his country in the Olympic Final against Argentina. Though his penchant for attacking had been noted, followers of the Belgian game hadn't bargained for what happened when he first scored a goal: the very African 'Arab spring'. 'The fans in Belgium loved me for it,' he recalls, 'so they always prayed that I score. They even made a feature of it on a Belgian TV show. No one had seen anything like it.'

But the uncommon celebration was blamed for part of his enforced absence from combat for Chelsea following his move to the Bridge in 1997 for £2.25m.

'I was surprised to read that my injury was caused by a somersault,' he mused, 'because I sustained it in a knockabout during training. I have been doing acrobatic moves since I was a child and there is no way that I am going to change that now, anyhow.'

Baba was lured by Rudi's reputation and personal invitation to join the revolution in SW6. 'Everyone knows that Ruud Gullit is one of the living legends of world football,' he commented, 'so I was honoured to know he was keen on having me in his team.'

Once he'd recovered enough to make his debut Baba looked the part. A natural left-sided player with slick defensive skills, he linked well with Graeme Le Saux and others whether playing at left-back or in midfield, where his initial timidity in going forward looked to be waning. Then disaster. The foot bone problem, one Anderlecht apparently knew about, flared up and Baba needed an operation. He was unable to appear for the rest of the season, recovering just in time to scrape into Nigeria's France 98 squad.

Happily his teammates were very supportive. Steve Clarke had seen enough in Baba's thirteen appearances to comment that with his technique, pace, style and endeavour, the Nigerian was definitely a Chelsea hero in the making. Gwyn Williams has spoken of Baba's ability in the air – already evident – and his excellence as a man-marker.

'I'm happy that people have very good things to say about me,' Baba says, 'but I don't allow it to go to my head. I'm still young and I've got a lot to learn in football. I'm very conscious of my background and how I've had to fight for all I've achieved so far.'

Like many of the 'new Chelsea' Baba settled on a dwelling in the West End, close to Robbie Di Matteo and his new boss, Gianluca Vialli. Presumably his parents approve of the career now.

TOMMY BALDWIN

In truth Balders was something of a mystery to most fans when he joined in exchange for George Graham. The 'average' forward at Highbury – who top scored at every junior level for Arsenal and notched ten goals in nineteen games before the £70,000 switch – was transformed into a hero by Chelsea. Tommy, his Gateshead accent weakening with each pint in a West End boozer, carved his name in the trees around Stamford Bridge. His last game as a Gunner was against Chelsea. The next week-end, he opened his account for the Blues at Maine Road, scoring in a 4–1 win and becoming an overnight star.

Soon after joining, Balders scored again against Manchester United just as he had for Arsenal against the same team, and he was on the scoresheet again when we lost 4–1 at Liverpool. Like Vialli a generation later, there was always a sense that Balders was a grafter, but a 'lucky' player too. His crucial Cup goal against Sheffield Wednesday, a mishit after Hateley's head-down from Eddie McCreadie's cross, was a case in point. 'If I had hit it properly,' he was honest enough to admit, 'Springett (Wednesday's goalkeeper) would probably have got it!'

Until his power began to wane in 1972 he was averaging around a goal every other game.

Dubbed 'The Sponge' for his capacious thirst as much as his equally impressive ability to work hard and withstand pressure from rugged defenders, Tommy was recognised at England Under-23 level. He could be a brilliant battling striker and he knew where the goal was too – when he found a place in the side consistently. Whether through lack of form, favour or, more likely, injury, that wasn't always the case. (His departure in 1974 was precipitated by a three-month bout of jaundice the previous season.)

But it was as the man for the moment that Chelsea fans best remember him, sliding in crucial goals and making things happen. It was Tommy who lunged into the Leeds defenders along with Webby, to clear the way for his mate to get the winner in the 1970 FA Cup replay.

And he was there in Piraeus a year later when the Cup Winners' Cup was won. No surprise then, that a generation of followers still associate medal-winner 'The Sponge' with an excuse for a good old-fashioned knees-up. His ninety-two goals in 228+11 games make him Chelsea's ninth all-time top scorer.

EAMONN BANNON

Danny Blanchflower's first signing as manager was a one-man team, but unfortunately in the least productive sense. Clearly a strong, technically gifted attacking midfielder, with an eye for openings and a knack for creating them, the Scot, signed from Hearts, was too inclined to play the Roy of the Rovers role, going for solo glory rather than team salvation. Despite the evident ability, therefore, he could be a frustrating player to watch. His move to Dundee after barely two seasons in the south heralded the flowering of a substantial talent in the less demanding league north of the border, and perusal of Sunday's paper for some years was tinged with envy at the regularity with which he knocked in goals.

JIM BARRON

David Webb's fond of reminding people that 'in the old days' people made their name at Chelsea rather than arriving with a celebrated past as part of the deal. But there were just as many whose fame came after their departure from the Bridge. Equally, there were those who never amounted to much. Barron was never much of a goalkeeper, but then he had Bonetti to oust. He wasn't a success in his year in London (one first-team appearance) and moved on to Oxford, then Nottingham Forest, clearly harbouring a grudge. Four hundred league appearances proved that he was capable enough with the ball, but it was as a coach that he's best remembered. Under Big Ron at Villa, Jim returned to Stamford Bridge in the early 1990s. Told that he couldn't have something that he wanted by Chelsea staff, he was heard to mutter 'this has always been a poxy club'. Eventually, one hopes, the sour grapes he'd ordered duly arrived.

DAVE BEASANT

'After the Norwich match I made certain comments which I feel have been exaggerated by various elements of the media,' said Ian Porterfield in September 1992. Winning, with two goals on the scoreboard, the Blues snatched infamous defeat from the clutches of victory with an array of goalkeeping errors that allowed the carrot-crunchers to run away with the points. It was an absolute embarrassment and for once there was really only one culprit: poor old Lurch.

The man who saved the penalty for Wimbledon against

Liverpool at Wembley in 1988 made his share of spectacular saves in his spell from January 1989 to 1992. His arrival bolstered the Division Championship campaign up to May 1989 and in his first full season was ever-present as Chelsea finished fifth in the top flight, Bez keeping fourteen clean sheets and going on to become club captain, such was his good influence. With his willowy six-foot 4-inch frame, spindly legs and self-deprecating humour, the Willesden lad took criticism of his lapses in good spirit. Porterfield's treatment of him, which ended his career at Chelsea, but not his association – he helps coach Chelsea youngsters – was unworthy.

ROY BENTLEY

Roy is one of our finest ever players, and we have a lot to thank him for. Firstly, though, let's be grateful to climatic variation round the regions, for that's what prompted our first title-winning skipper's arrival at Chelsea in January 1948. The cold air in Newcastle, where the Bristol boy was plying his trade at the time, didn't agree with his lungs, and doctors recommended a warmer spot. Sunny SW6 was just the ticket, apparently.

Curiously, Roy joined us as an inside-forward (for those too young to remember five strikers in a team formation, an inside-forward was a flashy bloke with a better sense of direction than a winger and less selfishness than a centre-forward) and for months he could do nothing right, seemingly unsettled by London and still troubled by his breathing problem. As he'd run convoy missions during the war, at least he knew what troubled waters were like.

An experimental target man role was not repeated in a first season which saw him score three goals in fourteen games (another striker, Hugh Billington, was even bought as a possible replacement). How matters changed after that! The five-foot ten-inch forward became Chelsea's top scorer for eight consecutive seasons.

LEAGUE EVER-PRESENTS

It hasn't been done for almost ten years and may not be done again in this brave new world of multiple substitutes and rotating squads. But on forty-three different occasions players have started every League game in a season. The closest to the feat since 1990 have been **Andy Townsend**, with forty-one of forty-two in 1992/93, and **Dmitri Kharine**, with forty of forty-two in 1993/94.

The roll-call is:
1989/90 **Dave Beasant, Graham Roberts**
1988/89 **Graham Roberts**
1987/88 **Tony Dorigo**
1984/85 **Nigel Spackman**
1983/84 **Kerry Dixon, Eddie Niedzwiecki, Colin Pates**
1981/82 **Colin Pates**
1980/81 **Peter Borota**
1976/77 **Ray Lewington, Gary Locke, Ray Wilkins**
1975/76 **Ray Wilkins**
1974/75 **Ron Harris**
1973/74 **John Hollins**

In his first full season, 1948/49, he was fit again and, having converted to centre-forward, the goals just kept coming. He had a superb right foot but didn't mind using his left and would leap high in the air for extra control and power so that few missed the man he ostensibly replaced, Tommy Lawton.

Typically of his early career at the Bridge he scored two fantastic goals against Arsenal in the 1950 FA Cup semi-final, but still ended on the losing side. His ability was recognised at international level and he earned twelve England caps. Whisper it, but one of those was for the notorious 1–0 defeat by the USA in

1972/73 **Ron Harris, John Hollins**

1971/72 **John Hollins**

1969/70 **John Hollins, Peter Houseman**

1968/69 **David Webb**

1967/68 **Peter Osgood**

1966/67 **Ron Harris**

1964/65 **Ron Harris**

1962/63 **John Mortimore, Terry Venables**

1958/59 **Jimmy Greaves**

1957/58 **Reg Matthews**

1955/56 **Stan Wicks**

1954/55 **Eric Parsons, Derek Saunders**

1951/52 **Billy Gray**

1947/48 **Ken Armstrong**

1934/35 **Allan Craig**

1932/33 **Vic Woodley**

1926/27 **Willie Ferguson, George Smith**

1922/23 **Tommy Meehan, George Smith**

1921/22 **Bob McNeil**

1910/11 **Bob Whittingham**

1906/07 **Tommy Miller**

Belo Horizonte during the 1950 World Cup.

Needless to say, that didn't figure amongst the choices for his 'Greatest Game'. He rated his late-rallying performance against former club Bristol City in the FA Cup in January 1949 as the best. Roy scored twice in a memorable victory at Ashton Gate. Others might nominate his two goals against Wolves in the last match of the 1950/51 season. The match ended 4–0, and although relegation rivals Sheffield Wednesday won 6–0, the Bentley brace ensured First Division survival on goal average – by 0.044 of a goal.

He was an unorthodox frontman for the time, not unlike the revolutionary 'deep' centre-forward Hidegkuti of Hungary's 'Magnificent Magyars' of 1953. With his elusive mobility and brilliance in the air (despite his height), as skipper and inspiration, Roy held the Championship trophy aloft in 1955. He should have been allowed to keep it, scoring twenty-one of the eighty-one goals struck that season.

Particularly memorable was his performance at title competitors Wolves when Chelsea came from behind to win 4–3 and one of his goals was a charge from the halfway line when he flew past England captain Billy Wright.

One former Chelsea man who was managed by Roy at Reading recalls playing against his boss in the irregular five-a-sides as 'facing the hardest bastard you'll ever play against'. Intemperate talk maybe, but how many times has it been said recently that we need a bit of steel if we're to win the title again?

Roy's all-action style endeared him to fans and it was his determination that dragged Chelsea by the scruff of the neck to our first and only League title (an honour Chelsea still hadn't equalled fifty years later). Having led by example, he raised the League trophy proudly aloft on the penultimate match of the season at the Bridge.

Happily Roy is still a regular and heroic guest at Chelsea, although after his departure he went into management and eventually onto the board of Reading.

WALTER BETTRIDGE

According to his boss David Calderhead, the full-back he signed from Burton United reserves in 1909 was the 'pluckiest little player that ever pulled on a football boot.' An injury to Jock Cameron provided him with a first-team breakthrough, but it was the partnership with Jack Harrow, one of the finest before the Second World War, that stayed in the minds of Chelsea fans. Walter was a tough tackler, but his major legacies to his position were the origination and perfect execution of the sliding tackle – another Chelsea first – and an early awareness of the advantages of making yourself available in attacking positions. Walter passed away in 1931, just ten years after quitting the Bridge.

HUGH BILLINGTON

Eight grand bought an experienced striker in 1948, someone who would, two years later in his first full season, 1949/50, match the prolific Roy Bentley for goals. The former Luton stalwart was thirty-three by then, and once the trademark long-range efforts began to fall away in 1951, Hugh was transferred to Worcester City.

ALAN BIRCHENALL

Birch looked more like he should be advising you on which jumbo collar shirt you should wear with that kipper tie from his swanky boutique than battling with the likes of Jackie Charlton and Frank McLintock for an orange ball on a muddy, frozen pitch.

There was also something of the Jack-the-lad about him that evidently appealed to 'the ladies'.

Pacy for a big man and very useful with his head, his potent runs through on goal, bursting through between defenders were a joy to watch. He wasn't bad at the classic forward's long pass out to the wing either. He wasn't the most skilful of players but for endeavour and quite often effectiveness you couldn't fault him. Birch was a one hundred per cent/ninety-minute man. His finest hour came in a ten-man Rourke's Drift of a performance at West Ham in the 1968/69 season. This was the Hammers of Moore, Peters and Hurst. Birch was a tireless runner that game, playing alone upfront, chasing lost causes, badgering and battling to knock 'the academy' off its rhythm and retain the status quo. He was successful: the result was 0–0. Birch was a sensation whatever he did after that. Especially as his biggest rival was Tony Hateley.

In his first season, he scored in a 2–1 win over Sheffield United, the strugglers we had bought him from, and nabbed two of the three goals that saw off Birmingham in the third round of the FA Cup.

Today Birch is stadium host at Leicester, where he spent most of career. You may recall he got into trouble for barracking the referee for bias over the public address system midway through a game the home side were losing. When Chelsea play there he's frequently joined on the pitch by an old Chelsea mucker (usually Ossie). Banter invariably ensues. At half-time during the dismal match between the two sides at Filbert Street in 1997/98, Birch introduced his old Kings Road playmate and asked him what he thought of the game. 'Not much,' grunted Ossie. He was rewarded with jeers from the Midlands crowd. 'Well,' observed the King of Stamford Bridge, to Birch's stifled amusement, 'I suppose you're used to rubbish like that here every week.'

BILLY BIRRELL

The architect of much that followed his period of management was appointed manager of the Chelsea Football & Athletic Club Co. Ltd. in April 1939. It wasn't his fault that within six months the Second World War had broken out, but the suspension of regular League football delayed his plans drastically.

Despite the club's lack of success the kindly, thoughtful Scot recognized that he had accepted 'one of the most glamorous and responsible posts in the game'. Chelsea, he wrote, 'has always been a popular club with a cosmopolitan, national and international appeal in spite of an indifferent playing record throughout its history.'

Borrowing heavily from other teams' available players Billy brought Chelsea to two consecutive Wembley appearances at the League South Cup Finals of 1944 and 1945. By the time the League was reassembled for 1946 he had recognized that serious changes were required. Only seven of the squad registered before the war were still available. Naturally he had the backing of a young Board, all comprising sons of founder directors.

Billy's 'fundamental change of policy' was twofold. He brought in experienced, preferably proven international players in Goulden, Harris, Lawton, Robertson, Williams, Winter and Walker, all for a bargain basement sum of £30,000. The all-star cast enabled Chelsea fully to capitalize on the postwar turnstile boom.

More significantly, in 1947 he introduced – partly in concern at escalating transfer fees – the youth development system that would reap enormous benefits for decades. Three of the seven wartime long-servers, Albert Tennant, Sidney 'Dicky' Foss and Dick Spence, would take vital crucial roles in coaching youngsters in the years to come. From 1947 onwards, Tennant, Foss and others started the annual task of sifting through hundreds of young players for the few they could nurse and nurture into the first team. There was, vowed Billy, 'no place for second- or third-raters' at Chelsea. He urged patience from the crowd.

Unusually for a manager, the Scotsman took the long-term view while staving off crowd dissent in the short-term. He was building for 'the day Chelsea will be second to none in this great game.' What would he have made of the current squad? Crammed with internationals, but boasting well over a dozen homegrown youngsters, and challenging for the top honours in Europe.

Back in the post-war years, though, maintaining First Division survival was often a struggle. Twice in three seasons between 1949 and 1951 he took us to FA Cup semi-finals at White Hart Lane. Twice Arsenal defeated us after replays. But his legacy will forever be the much-coveted production line of Chelsea youngsters, beginning with Bobby Smith, running through Ron Tindall, Jimmy Greaves, Terry Venables, Peters Bonetti and Osgood, Ron Harris, John Hollins and Alan Hudson, right up to the more recent crops of Eddie Newton, Craig Burley,

BURY MY HEART AT BLACKPOOL

Although Chelsea scored their first-ever goal and secured their first-ever victory in the seaside town (9 September 1905), and the club's best current record against a single club is at Blackpool (six wins in the last six visits), the Seasiders have also played host to three of the worst episodes in Blues history.

It all began on 29 October 1932 when Chelsea faced Blackpool in a first division game at Bloomfield Road. Two weeks in incessant rain had left most of Blackpool flooded and the pitch covered in two inches of water. Fierce protests from the Blues' management came to no avail, however, and the game started with freezing rain still thundering down. Blackpool adapted better to the conditions and led 3–0 at half-time. Conditions worsened and the pitch became a sea of water, but referee Jones resisted pleas to abandon the game.

Only eight Chelsea players resumed in the second period – one retired with severe cramp and two just refused to come out. And although they relented and came back out again after ten minutes or so, they soon trooped off once more.

Despite the advantage in numbers, Blackpool scored just once more – the cue for two more exhausted Chelsea players to shrug their shoulders and slink off, apparently arm in arm for support. The six remaining players held on valiantly for the final fifteen minutes, but the incident remains one of the darker episodes in the club's history. Despite further complaints, the result was allowed to stand and

Michael Duberry, Jody Morris and Jon Harley. Thanks Billy. It was worth the wait.

THE 'BLACKPOOL EIGHT'

Only one Tuesday, in spring 1965, is celebrated in Chelsea

Blackpool retained the two points.

In 1964/65, a young Chelsea team had been chasing a treble all season. The League Cup was secured in April, but the Blues faltered on the other two fronts – the FA Cup semi-final defeat by Liverpool at Villa Park on 27 March was a particular disappointment. However, with four League games to go Chelsea were still in with an outside chance of the Championship. That all faded over seven days in Lancashire. With the last three games away at Liverpool, Burnley and Blackpool, Tommy Docherty took the squad to the Golden Mile for the duration. It all ended in tears. After losing 2–0 at Anfield, Docherty sent eight players home for breaking a curfew – when he checked the players concerned, they appeared to be tucked up in bed, but were in fact wearing their evening gear under the covers. 'I didn't know whether they'd just come in or if they were on their way out again,' Docherty has said since. With reserves thrust in at Burnley, Chelsea duly lost 2–6 to the mid-table Lancastrians. And even with most of the culprits called back for the last game, the Blues succumbed 2–8 to Blackpool and finished six points behind Manchester United and Leeds. A depressing end to an outstanding season.

The cursed run culminated with Peter Osgood's leg being broken by an Emlyn Hughes tackle in a League Cup tie at Blackpool on 5 October 1966. According to the King of Stamford Bridge himself, by the time he returned to the team he'd put on a couple of stone and was never quite the same player again.

circles. It's not a football night. Not even a signing. This was the Tuesday before a Saturday game. As the Blues were visiting title contenders Liverpool and Burnley in the space of a week, the team was booked to stay in a hotel in the north-west for the duration. Chelsea lay third in the League. Victory at Anfield would have confirmed our place in the run-in for the last few weeks of the Championship. Unfortunately, the game was lost by the odd goal. Moody manager Tommy Docherty was furious and scrapped the previously granted Tuesday night out. To no avail, as it turned out. George Graham, John Hollins, Bert Murray, Terry Venables, Barry Bridges, Joe Fascione, Eddie McCreadie and Marvin Hinton decided to implement the plans they'd already laid and sought a drink amongst the bright lights of Blackpool. The only surprise was that Ossie wasn't there! From here on the incident becomes apocryphal. The players returned late, that much is certain. Tommy Doc maintains that he was woken up in the middle of the night by a night porter claiming that some of the Chelsea team had been spotted sneaking in up the fire escape. Finding his players seemingly fast asleep in their beds, Doc suggested to the porter that he was mistaken; it had been a rugby team, also billeted there. However, the truth came out and the ramifications were huge, in the short and the long term. All eight revellers were sent home in disgrace, with the 'scandalous' story ('Football stars drink late' or some such revelation) running for days. The weakened side at Burnley was thrashed. More importantly, the events at Blackpool set Doc's mind on course for demolition. Venables was stripped of the captaincy and, along with Murray, Graham and Bridges, swiftly sold off. A young side that had reached two successive semi-finals, challenged for the League title and won the League Cup was broken up over one night's indiscipline.

DANNY BLANCHFLOWER

In 1978 the former Spurs legend gave up his career as a football writer of sparkling wit and resonance to assume managerial control of a struggling team, in a game he no longer understood. It was one of Brian Mears' worst (and last) decisions. Blanchflower was out of touch, ill, and desperately out of place. When he was replaced by his assistant nine months later, the club was eighteenth in Division Two – it was an undeserving end to a glittering football career.

FRANK BLUNSTONE

A real crowd-pleaser was Frankie B. In keeping with the wing style of the day, he was a head-down, foot-on-the-gas merchant, rarely looking up before crossing. And every time the ball made its way out to him, you could feel the buzz of expectancy surge from the terraces. His crosses were a vital instrument of attack for Chelsea and – in the five games he played – England. A snip at £37,000 when he was signed, aged nineteen, from Crewe in 1953, his misfortune was to be often starring in a weak team. But the demon dribbler earned a special place in the hearts of Chelsea fans, along with the unique honour of that Chelsea 1955 squad – a Championship medal.

He also survived new manager Tommy Doc's purge of the old guard – a little old gem among Docherty's Diamonds. His experience was vital; the young Jimmy Greaves always recalled Frank's lamenting the late 1950s team's defensive frailties after a 6–5 defeat by throwing down his boots and yelling: 'If we scored eight you can bet you lot would let in nine!' Such was his passion.

The left-winger, who shared duties with Jim Lewis in our title-winning year, broke the same leg twice, missing the entire 1957/58 season, but scored fifty-four goals in his 347 appearances. Perhaps his finest strike was the goal (the fourth on the night) he nabbed in the 7–0 destruction of Portsmouth that secured promotion from the old Second Division back to the top flight in 1963. He played a clever one-two and whacked it with more than enough fizz to give the keeper no chance.

The following season he totted up forty-one League appearances, equal almost with Ron Harris and John Mortimore, as the young Chelsea stormed to fifth place in the final table. But another broken leg sustained the following pre-season brought the curtain down on his bright, exciting playing career at the age of thirty.

He became our youth team coach for a while, then quit Chelsea to manage Brentford, and was later youth team coach at Manchester United. He was associated with them for many years, and has now retired and is living in his home town of nearby Crewe.

PETER BONETTI

Christened 'The Cat' by old stager Ron Tindall, for the best part of twenty years Peter was Chelsea's first-choice keeper and hero. During that period he saw off more than thirteen challengers, beginning with England international Reg Matthews. Lord knows who was watching over Catty, but whoever had pretensions to his number one slot was swiftly served with a five-goal dose or an injury. Quite simply Peter is not just Chelsea's finest-ever keeper. He was also an innovator, not simply in his attention to technical improvements such as introducing goalkeeping gloves, or in wishing to sport an all-black jersey (forbidden by the Football League) but in his play. Until he began leaping like a salmon and claiming anything within the eighteen-yard box, keepers had never even considered coming out so far for crosses. In distribution, too, he was an original, often rolling the ball out to build play from the back rather than hoof it randomly forward. (In fact, he was never the world's best kicker.)

An FA Youth Cup winner in 1960, Peter made his debut in April 1960 and never looked back, winning twelve England Under-23 caps and figuring for Chelsea in a then record-breaking 729 appearances, considerably more than Ken Armstrong's previous record of 402.

On his senior international debut in 1966 he made an astonishing close-range reflex save from the Spanish forward Amancio

KEEPING IT CLEAN

Chelsea's top ten goalkeepers in terms of shut-outs include some famous names, with the Cat undoubtedly the bees' knees (if a cat can act as an insect's leg joints)

Bonetti – 208 from 729 games (29%)
Millington – 78 from 245 games (32%)
Molyneux – 77 from 239 games (32%)
Woodley – 60 from 272 games (22%)
Niedzwiecki – 55 from 175 games (31%)
Kharine – 49 from 141 games (35%)
Beasant – 41 from 157 games (26%)
Whitley – 39 from 138 games (28%)
Robertson – 38 from 215 games (18%)
Howard Baker – 36 from 93 games (39%)

Most consecutive clean sheets – 9 by Willie Foulke, November-December 1905
Most clean sheets in a season – 23 in 58 games in 1971/72
Fewest clean sheets in a season – 2 in 47 in 1960/61
Most clean sheets in a season by an individual – 21 in 48 games by Peter Bonetti 1971/72
Worst run without a clean sheet – 31 games from November 1960 to August 1961

Two outfield players have played the full ninety minutes in goal – **David Webb** when Chelsea beat Ipswich 2–0 at home in December 1971, and **Bob Mackie** when Chelsea beat Southern United 1–0 away in the FA Cup, October 1905

(the two would meet again in the 1971 Cup Winners' Cup final) that confirmed him as England's reserve keeper for that year's

World Cup. (Ironically, just as he stifled others' careers, so Gordon Banks smothered his internationally.)

Following the World Cup, and no doubt irked by England's victory, Tommy Doc claimed that Peter's head wasn't right and that he'd been 'tapped up' for transfer by West Ham's England players. Oddly enough, Peter seemed to reserve some of his best saves for the Hammers, including one blinding back-leap and catch (including, no doubt, triple salko and toe-loop) from a superb Martin Peters header.

Alex Stepney was brought in and the two top keepers were supposed to figure in some kind of shoot-out (or shut-out?), alternating in the first team role. 'When Tommy went and signed Alex I clapped my hands,' said Peter later. 'It seemed I was on my way and there was a lot of talk about West Ham at the time. But in the end everything worked out for the best for me.'

Before Catty could organize a move away, the Doc sold Stepney to Manchester United. Chelsea retained the better all-rounder. Doc knew there would have been all hell to pay if the hugely popular man, who went on to become Chelsea's first official Player of the Year in 1967, had been sold. In 1969, a programme poll elected him Chelsea's greatest-ever player.

If Peter had a vulnerability it was to cross-shots, when on occasion his positional sense deserted him. There was certainly no question that his height (five feet ten inches) was ever an issue.

Still, with his bravery in coming for high balls, Catty was open to being roughed up by a burly opponent. Injury was a feature of his incredible performance in the 1970 Cup Final replay at Old Trafford. Mick Jones had 'done' the Chelsea keeper in a challenge and capitalized himself soon after with the opening goal. The Cat lay on the pitch receiving treatment for several minutes surrounded by anxious teammates. A pain-killing injection allowed him to see out the match and, of course, we ran out 2–1 winners through Osgood and Webb. Crucially, if Catty hadn't recovered, Webby would have been his stand-in...

Apart from that famous night, Peter also figured in the League Cup victory of 1965 (Gordon Banks playing for Leicester), the Wembley defeat at the hands of Spurs in 1967, and the Cup Winners' Cup final, 1971, when he recovered from injury during the earlier rounds to supersede long-suffering understudy John Phillips. In the replay at the Karaiskaki Stadium, he earned his win bonus with the save of the season from Zoco's goal-bound close-range header in the dying moments.

Strange to think his Chelsea career was only just over half-completed, though the major honours were history. Even when he was allowed to leave for the NASL in 1975 a recall was soon in the offing, and he stuck around between the sticks for another four years, grizzled but still agile.

Over twenty years Peter was challenged by successors but never outperformed until the arrival of an eccentric Yugoslavian of the same initials, Petar Borota in 1979. In total he made a record 729 appearances between the sticks. His 600 League games was an English goalkeeping record for one club until surpassed by Portsmouth's Alan Knight during the 1996/97 season.

On his retirement Peter opened a guest house and post office on the island of Mull, where the occasional Chelsea supporter would pop in to see him. Subsequently, Peter returned to Chelsea briefly as English football's first specialist goalkeeping coach. A few years earlier he'd vowed, 'I enjoy coaching, but it will be with some schoolboy or amateur team.'

It was a role he would perform for the English national set-up for some time until Glenn Hoddle brought in Ray Clemence.

The fantastic Catty remains the yardstick by which any Chelsea keeper has to be measured. They either 'don't come out for crosses like he did', 'lack his reflexes' or 'don't have his brilliant throwing ability'.

In February 1998, sitting watching Pegguy Arphexad of

Leicester scramble and claim every cross no matter where, in a match we should have won, we were suddenly struck by a resemblance in approach. 'It's a black Bonetti,' someone proffered at last. At that moment Arphexad, having collected a Chelsea cross on his penalty spot at full stretch, booted the ball low and feebly, about twenty yards short of the halfway line. 'It IS Bonetti!' we all chorused.

He was the best, though. Don't let them go on about Germany at Mexico in 1970. Tell them about Old Trafford, the Karaiskaki Stadium and untold arenas where his impossible saves left opposing fans shaking their heads and wishing he was theirs.

TOM BOYD

1991's £800,000 signing from Motherwell had all the makings of a classic Chelsea buy: Scottish, an international, and an attacking left-back. It was intended that he would replace, nay surpass, the departed Tony Dorigo. It didn't work out like that.

'You don't join a club that's going to be beaten every week,' he ventured, adding: 'I'm sure we'll be pushing the front-runners this season.' Pushing, yes. Shoving and fouling even. But not competing with them – we finished fourteenth behind Wimbledon, QPR and Crystal Palace in 1991/92. Tommy, lightweight and lacking confidence appeared overawed when faced with the power and skill of English First Division strikers. He was a thoroughbred without suss. Though he obviously had qualities on the ball and sound technique, he was unable to apply that on the pitch, especially under Ian Porterfield's management. Newly-wed, he found it hard to settle in London. After twenty-two starts and one sub appearance he was gone.

The vacant slot was filled in turns by Andy Myers, Frank Sinclair and even David Lee, and it became a troublesome position until the return of Graeme Le Saux and the arrival of Celestine Babayaro.

After leaving for Celtic, where he turned to following his disillusioning spell in SW6, Tommy became a local and international hero, playing for his country at Euro 96 and France 98, where he unfortunately scored an own goal to hand Brazil victory. Ah well.

JOHNNY BOYLE

Likeable Scot Johnny, now a trades union official in the security industry, strolled into the club on the off-chance of employment as a fifteen-year-old on holiday.

Showing such initiative, he was made skipper of the youth team and became a vital auxiliary in the first-team squad from 1965 until 1972. Like his contemporary Ron Harris, Motherwell's rock-hard son was a beneficiary of his manager's policy of giving youth (especially the flower of Scotland) a chance.

Boylers joined a squad given typical Doc financial incentives – crowd bonuses and three-year contracts – to encourage entertainment and loyalty. Only three of the thirty pros were over twenty-three when the short-legged left-half took the field in the two-leg League Cup Final victory a year later. When Tommy Docherty tried him out in his habitual testing ground, the earlier stages of the League Cup, Boylers proved himself with a twenty-five-yard winner against Aston Villa in the first leg of the semi-final. He also figured in the 1967 FA Cup Final defeat by Spurs and the European triumph over Real Madrid four years on – in different positions.

Johnny Boyle made 266 appearances in his ten years at the club, scoring just twelve times – a record Steve Clarke might like to ponder.

Boylers was what you might call a defender in a midfielder's shirt, picking up the loose ends or surging forward to stretch the opposition. His defensive attributes were much prized by Dave Sexton, whose instinct was a firm foundation.

The hustling, uncompromising style suggested a temper that was liable to flare and did – in 1966 he fought manfully with Brighton's Wally Gould during the fourth round FA Cup tie and missed the subsequent match in the competition versus Sheffield Wednesday.

Johnny missed out on FA Cup glory in 1970, but shared in our European triumph the following season, playing at right-back and helping to create the opening for Ossie to score in the first match of the final.

Brought in to the midfield before he bulked out, he relaunched himself as a right-back (before losing his place to Paddy Mulligan) and more often than not carried it off with aplomb (and bloody shins). Few who saw him will forget his occasional overlapping forays and tigerish endeavour.

Boylers was born on Christmas Day 1946, and a devotion to making merry was a feature of his off-field life; when he was transfer-listed in 1973 he looked a lot older than his twenty-six years, it has to be said. He eventually moved to Brighton and then Orient.

PETER BRABROOK

Peter was a quality player but what is now unkindly called a 'luxury' one in that his inability to earn the regular return that might have been expected of such talent had him dubbed inconsistent. That possibly explains just three England caps, earned in the build-up to the 1958 World Cup. His disenchantment with Chelsea (a team as maddeningly flighty as he) was indicated by his understandable willingness to jump from the sinking ship after relegation in 1962. After that he carved out a career at West Ham, where he was a prototype Brooking and the Hammers like that languid, stylish sort of player. He now scouts for West Ham and is occasionally seen in that professional capacity at Chelsea reserve games.

BILLY BRAWN

One of David Calderhead's 'open cheque book' emergency buys in 1907, the Aston Villa and England right-winger replaced the injured and diminutive Martin Moran. It didn't take him long to establish a rapport. On his debut, he worked an opening and slipped the ball through for George Hilsdon to score. We won 4–1 and moved off the bottom. Huzzah!

BARRY BRIDGES

Although he scaled the heights and played for England on several occasions as the 1966 World Cup loomed, Barry was all about pace and very little else. He mishit more passes than anyone until Ian Britton and Dennis Rofe came along and eventually lost his place to the young Peter Osgood. Interestingly, when England manager Alf Ramsey set up a match between England and Chelsea, he elected to 'borrow' Ossie, not Barry, announcing that he wanted Chelsea 'to have their strongest side'. Barry scored and, as if by magic, was reinstated in the Chelsea first team instead of Ossie.

In the longer term, though, manager Docherty knew who the better player was. Following the Blackpool Incident, Barry was hastily singled out along with several others and shipped out. The inexorable law of the ex struck as you'd expect: in 1969, playing for Birmingham, he contributed the goal that put Chelsea out of the FA Cup in the sixth round. In later years Barry ran a newsagent's and figured in the press a few years ago when he was badly injured in a robbery on his shop. Thankfully he has made a full recovery.

BILL BRIDGEMAN

A short and nippy winger from Bromley who played and made goals for others over thirteen consecutive seasons at the Bridge between 1906 and 1919, having travelled across London from West Ham. He moved from 'east' to 'west' on the pitch too, beginning his Chelsea career at inside-right, and finishing it at outside-left.

JOHN BUMSTEAD

The John Hollins of his generation, veteran teammate Holly having converted to full-back. Between 1978, when he made his debut days short of his twentieth birthday, and 1991, when he was passed on to Charlton, 'Johnny B' was a hard-running, tough-tackling midfielder with defensive qualities and willingness to do the dog job so that others like Pat Nevin and Mickey Hazard might flaunt their less prosaic skills. For a while, too, he was our dead-ball expert (partly because, at five feet seven inches, he was no threat in the air), and earned a Second Division

AMAZING DEBUTS

Albert Tennant signed professional terms with Chelsea in November 1934 but did not make his League debut until May 1947. (Maybe he couldn't find the ground.) Most of his Blues career was spent in the reserves or playing wartime football. His eight official first-team games included all six FA Cup matches in 1945/46. There was no official League programme that year and the Cup was played over two legs.

    Craig Burley's first appearance was as a sub for Kerry Dixon in the 0–7 defeat at Forest in April 1991. His full debut came at home to Swindon in the Full Members' Cup in October 1991 – but he wasn't expecting it. He had downed a pint in the players' bar when he was called on to replace **Andy Townsend**, who'd injured himself in the warm-up.

    Keeper **Bill Robertson**'s first four games for Chelsea were the last four league matches of 1950/51, when Chelsea, virtually certain to be relegated, survived by 0.0044 of a goal after winning winners' medal for promotion in 1983/84. Injury robbed him of more regular starts.

CRAIG BURLEY

So when did 'nephew of Ipswich manager George' become 'uncle of Scottish international Craig'? Certainly not on his debut. Craig, you see, had the misfortune to make his bow in the 0–7 debacle at Nottingham Forest in 1991.

Although it didn't seem to affect him directly, that match appeared to set some invisible limit on Craig's career at the Bridge, and he consistently suffered bouts of self-doubt, thankfully overcome for the most part by an agitated determination to prove himself.

their last four games. Robertson let in just two goals in a team that hadn't won in fourteen and had let in twenty-eight in those games. He went on to win a League Championship medal.

Colin Court's debut was Chelsea's first-ever European match – a Fairs Cup tie at Frem of Copenhagen on 20 September 1958. It was his only appearance too.

Frank Sinclair debuted in the left-back slot at home to Luton in April 1991, and Chelsea were 3–0 down in twenty minutes. A stirring comeback made the final score 3–3. **Andy Myers** also made his debut, as a sub, in this match.

George Hilsdon scored five goals on his debut for Chelsea in a 9–2 win over Glossop North End in September 1906.

Welsh international goalkeeper **John Phillips** played his first game for the Blues at Blackpool on 24 October, 1970, thanks to injury ruling out **Peter Bonetti**. He promptly let three goals in to a team lying twenty-first in Division One (Chelsea were fifth). However, Chelsea scored four in the last twenty minutes, the clincher an own goal from Hatton in injury time, to cap an astounding comeback.

Craig was a quiet, amusing and pleasant bloke, but he maybe bottled too much up. Amongst his teammates he was known as 'Mr Angry', always annoyed about something. If he'd channelled more of that into his play on the pitch, his five years at Chelsea might have been very different.

Craig alternated between the wing-back role favoured by managers Hoddle and Gullit, and which was his usual Scottish international position, and the midfield slot, particularly at centre, that he coveted.

Fans will remember, however, that the inspirational performance in the FA Cup quarter-final of 1996 against Wimbledon in that berth was countered by the pass back at Villa Park in the semi that sealed Manchester United's undeserved victory. He'd been superb again up to that point, but all anyone will remember is that aberrant volley...

Craig should have scored many more goals than he did, blessed with such a good shot in both feet. His goal at Liverpool in 1994 was a sensational twenty-five-yard strike that could and should have been replicated. At six feet one inch he really should have been more dominant with his head in what was, until the advent of Rudi, a notably diminutive squad.

There were prolonged injuries too, including cartilage operations in both knees.

In 1997, having fought his way back into contention for a starting place in the FA Cup final, Craig made the mistake of expressing publicly his desire to move away from Chelsea. As a direct result, Ruud selected Andy Myers for the bench instead.

Craig moved on to Celtic in summer 1997 and, to no-one's particular surprise at his old club, won the Celts' player of the season award, scoring fifteen goals, many from distance. He also figured strongly in Scotland's France 98 campaign.

DAVID CALDERHEAD

Following promotion to the big time – the First League – in 1907, a full-time manager was sought. David, a great centre-half for Lincoln in the 1890s who had become the same club's manager, was brought south, where he stayed for twenty-six years, cementing the Scottish influence that has been so strong an element in Chelsea's history. Sphinx-like and generous, David assembled a team in the now recognized flavour: they didn't win much, but they were always good to watch.

David's legacy to Chelsea history though may be less appreciated. His tenure seemed to coincide with an explosion of material for the music hall comedians. None more comical than the match at Blackpool in the winter of the 1932/33 season, when in a snow storm and freezing conditions evidently much like the recent European match at Tromso, no less than five Chelsea players sloped off to the dressing room before the conclusion of the match, suffering from 'cold and exhaustion'. Poor dears.

The game was lost 4–0. No greater disservice could have been done to a squad already tagged as reluctant trainers who preferred the comforts of a cosy hostelry in proximity to the bright lights than the 'midweek winter night up north' of football doctrine. The enshrining forever of Stamford Bridge as the capital of the 'Soft South' was complete. And within a few months David Calderhead retired.

PAUL CANOVILLE

Impetuous and inconsistent he may have been, but when Canners was on song, he was very very good. Basically a winger,

Paul broke into the Chelsea side in 1981 at a time when racism on the terraces was at its height. He became the first black player to overturn the bigots and 'earn' his own song, albeit the uninspired '*Canoville, Canoville, Canovi-ille...*'

The clinching factor in his achievement was his part in the brilliant comeback from 0–3 down in the League Cup at Hillsborough in January 1985.

With his first touch as a half-time sub Paul pulled one back. With Pat Nevin turning it on, Paul's stately dribbling runs ripped Wednesday apart. He scored again, with Mickey Thomas and David Speedie adding the other two, to set up a famous victory. Unfortunately Doug Rougvie saw fit to concede a needless penalty in the closing minutes and the match finished 4–4.

Paul's appearances decreased after that, troubled as he was by injury. In 1986 he moved on to Reading. Sadly, in 1998 it emerged that Paul was undergoing treatment for cancer. Hopefully he'll overcome this new hurdle too.

TONY CASCARINO

Cas, derided as the 'Irish ice cream salesman', was one of the great Chelsea characters during his brief stay at the Bridge. The lanky, experienced twenty-nine-year-old Irish international arrived as ballast in the deal that took unsettled Tom Boyd to Celtic in February 1992 and instantly allayed fears about his star quality by scoring on his debut against Palace, albeit with a typically freaky goal. More emphatic was his memorable hat-trick in the 4–0 demolition of Spurs on their home soil in the Makita Tournament of summer 1993.

Stories about Cas abounded the instant he arrived (he's that type of bloke – the butt and the raconteur of many jokes). Chelsea members' magazine *Onside* interviewed his wife Sarah on his signing, asking her what career her husband would have settled into had football not turned up. 'He'd be a male model,' she proclaimed, loyally, and with a straight face.

The immensely popular striker was involved in several Chelsea dressing-room classics, one involving his own 'secret' thirtieth birthday, arranged by Sarah behind his back with military precision. The party was to be at the family home, and all the players were going to turn up to surprise him. That is until Frank Sinclair asked him, 'Cas, how do I get to your place tonight?' Luckily, as with one or two crosses in his time, Cas didn't latch on.

The arrival of similar-styled Mick Harford under Ian Porterfield limited Tony's appearances in his second season, but Dave Webb's arrival resurrected a career that was drifting. Glenn Hoddle got the best out of Cas, his aerial strength contributing in no small measure to many victories, including the semi-final victory over Luton Town at Wembley in 1994, but he was always expendable.

Cas's two league goals in two games at the end of the 1993/94 season (his first since September) proved to be his swansong and he was allowed to leave for Wimbledon in 1994 on the back of a World Cup appearance the same year. In a final twist, Cas proceeded to become a prolific, goal-scoring cult hero in France.

PIERLUIGI CASIRAGHI

A long-rumoured target of Gianluca Vialli's before his signing in June 1998. The six-foot Italian international centre-forward arrived, often cited as the physical type of striker well suited to the English game. An azzurri Mark Hughes, if you like, who had played thirty-four internationals and scored the play-off goal against Russia that sealed qualification for the 1998 World Cup before missing the cut for Cesare Maldini's Italian squad for France. With a nickname like 'Little Bison', and suggestions that he may have been a lawyer had the professional football boots not fitted, he arrived with the promise of two great assets: strength and slyness. The twenty-nine-year-old was signed from Lazio, having previously starred for Juventus and Monza, his home town club. At £5.4m he was a new Chelsea record signing, surpassing the £4.9m paid for another cult hero from the Rome club, Roberto Di Matteo.

STEVE CLARKE

Arriving at his prime in better times, Steve Clarke would undoubtedly have figured in many fans' list of all-time greats. It was his misfortune to begin his Chelsea career during a period when uncertainties on and off the field and a ruinous lack of confidence draped around Stamford Bridge like sackcloth.

£400,000 brought him south from St Mirren in January 1987, but he joined a side on the slide from the all too short John Neal era of Dixon–Speedie–Nevin.

Clarkey nipped in front of Darren Wood in the right-back slot, his adventurousness down the flank quickly noted and appreciated. But if fans thought that would convert into goals, they were sadly mistaken – the ridiculously under-capped Scottish international has scored fewer times than one of Cleopatra's eunuchs.

Happily, the memory of his superb finish against Spurs in the 4–1 win at White Hart Lane in 1989 remains to prove he was capable. Others of that rare crop spring to mind.

Everton away, November 1989, a delightful run down the right wing, cut inside and stroke past Southall with a degree of proficiency. That only goal of the game put Chelsea top of the League – until we came down with the Christmas decorations.

QPR at home, April 1992. Clarkey burst into the area and attempted a shot. The ball rebounded and he was able to loop a header from just inside the box. Helped Chelsea to one of only three wins in the last fifteen League games.

And how about the classic punt at home to Liverpool in the 4–1 demolition of April 1998? Better late than never...

Managerial instability contributed to a period when he had to vie for his place in the side. The club's PFA rep wouldn't let it

TOP APPEARANCE MAKERS

Steve Clarke's third major medal-winning match for Chelsea, the Cup Winners' Cup final defeat of Stuttgart in Stockholm, took his to 421 appearances – and into a clear fourth place in the all-time appearance list, one ahead of Kerry Dixon.

However, saving bizarre circumstances, he's unlikely to overtake any of the three players still above him. The list of '400-clubbers' reads as followed:

1 **Ron Harris** (1961–1980) – 795
2 **Peter Bonetti** (1959–1980) – 729
3 **John Hollins** (1963–1975 & 1983-1984) – 592
4 **Steve Clarke** (1987–present) – 421
5 **Kerry Dixon** (1983–1992) – 420
6 **Eddie McCreadie** (1962–1974) – 410
7 **John Bumstead** (1978–1992) – 409
8 **Ken Armstrong** (1946–1957) – 402

During 1997/98, **Dennis Wise** became the twenty-sixth player to reach the 300 first team games mark with the Blues.

go, though. Routinely, this consummate pro worked hard on his defensive technique and eventually, rightly, saw off all comers, including the sometimes favoured Gareth Hall.

Under Glenn Hoddle, Clarkey showed just what experience and dedication he had added to his game. His reading of play, anticipation and coolness on the ball offered a number of new options in the centre of defence as well as in the more demanding wing-back role.

He suffered a bout of hepatitis as a child and that robbed him of his speed for two years. 'I think it made me a better player,' he said years later. 'I used to rely on my speed all the time but when I came back after the illness at thirteen everyone kept telling me how slow I was. It meant I had to build on other aspects of my game.'

Steve was there for the 1994 Cup Final (having almost scored on a run into the box at the semi-final to cap a superbly assured performance against Luton), and he was there again when it all came good in the three-cup, twelve-month spree of 1997 and 1998, perhaps recognizing more than most what that first 2–0 victory over Middlesbrough, and the first silverware in twenty-six years, meant to the fans.

JACK COCK

After the First World War, in which he had won the military medal, Brentford-born 'Cockney Jack' soon found himself a casualty of Huddersfield's cost-cutting. He and his wife caught the train up from London and were met by representatives of the Yorkshire club at the station. 'Chelsea want you,' he was told. 'The train to London leaves in five minutes on the other platform.' No doubt bemused by the independence of the modern footballer, Jack duly signed for Chelsea for £2,500 in October 1919. He'd started his career at Kingstonian so he must have felt reasonably at home. The fans certainly took to him during the four seasons he was at Chelsea. No doubt twenty-one goals in his first twenty-five games helped. But there was more to it. Jack was the complete character. Long black hair beloved of cartoonists, powerful net-finders in either foot, great with his head, and a great singing voice. Oh yes? Oh yes – his fine tenor voice habitually accompanied the players' march from dressing room to pitch. At the end of his career he even became a film star, playing lead in the 1930s drama about football, *The Great Game*.

If he was an actor, he must have been from the method school, because training to him was addictive. He had sometimes to be forcibly restrained from exercising by trainer Jack Whitley. No wonder the crowd sensed this well-built striker's passion for the game and took him to their hearts. At the end of his stay at

THE LAD'S A BIT GOOD ON HIS DEBUT

The following seventy-five players have scored on their debuts for Chelsea

James Robertson, Francis O'Hara, Frank Pearson, George Hilsdon, James Frost, Ben Whitehouse, Arthur Wileman, James Bradshaw, George Dodd, John Brown, George Hunter, Harold Halse, Andy Walker, Bobby McNeil, Harry Wilding, Jack Cock, Buchanan Sharp, James Ferris, Dr John Bell, William Haywood, James Armstrong, Andy Wilson, William Brown, Bob Turnbull, Jimmy Thompson, William Jackson, Sidney Elliot, John Meredith, Reg Weaver, Wilf Chitty, James Copeland, Harry Burgess, Sidney Bidewell, Tommy Lawton, Alex Machin, John McInnes, Jimmy Bowie, Bobby Campbell, Jack Allister, Jim Lewis, Frank Blunstone, Seamus O'Connell, Ron Tindall, Jimmy Greaves, Barry Bridges, Bobby Tambling, John Brooks, George Graham, Peter Osgood, John Boyle, Tommy Baldwin, Ian Hamilton, Alan Birchenall, Peter Feely, Tommy Ord, Duncan McKenzie, Chris Hutchings, Bryan Robson, David Speedie, Kerry Dixon, Nigel Spackman, Gordon Davies, Duncan Shearer, Colin West, David Lee, Graham Stuart, Paul Elliott, Joe Allon, Tony Cascarino, Eddie Newton, Mick Harford, Gavin Peacock, Paul Furlong, Paul Hughes, Tore Andre Flo

the Bridge he moved to Everton, then Millwall, where for a time he became manager.

CHARLIE COOKE

Charlie was the schemer all dreamers adored. A stunningly gifted ball-player who'd learned his art kicking cans around his

PLAYERS OF THE YEAR

Since the official Player of the Year award – Joe Mears Memorial Trophy as it was then – was first presented to **Peter Bonetti** in 1967 (and not including season 1997/98), only five players have won it twice – **Charlie Cooke** (1968 and 1975), **Dave Webb** (1969 and 1972), **John Hollins** (1970 and 1971), **Ray Wilkins** (1976 and 1977) and **Pat Nevin** (1984 and 1987). The supporters' honour has been won by a different individual each year since Pat's last triumph. It has been awarded twelve times to defenders, nine to midfielders, seven to forwards and just three times to goalkeepers (**Bonetti**, 1967; **Borota**, 1981; **Niedzwiecki**, 1986). The first black player to win the award was **Ken Monkou** in 1990, who was also the first overseas player to do so – he, **Erland Johnsen** (1995) and **Ruud Gullit** (1996) remain the only three overseas Players of the Year. In 1996 Rudi was also runner-up in the Football Writers' Footballer of the Year poll, and made the PFA Premier League XI (the first Chelsea player since **Andy Townsend** in 1991). When **Gianfranco Zola** was named Footballer of the Year in 1997, he became the first Chelsea player to be honoured in that way.

native Fife (it was said), he is a cultured and deeply likeable man but one who was only fitfully certain of his own talents. The strengths he often publicly admired in others were those perceived to be lacking from his own repertoire: commitment and consistency. He would always cite the grafters as his type of player. 'That "darling of the terraces" bit never meant much to me,' he confessed, 'because I could always see qualities in other players that I wished I had.'

The fans brazenly ignored his observations. From the moment Tommy Docherty brought him south from Dundee for

£72,000 in 1966, ostensibly to replace Terry Venables, the Chelsea crowd took him to their hearts. Charlie was indeed everyone's darling.

Cookie left school with three 'A'- levels, in Maths, English, and Art. By the age of seventeen he was painting pretty patterns around the pitch for Aberdeen's first team. Then in 1964 he replaced the Spurs-bound striker Alan Gilzean at Dundee. The two would face each other as opponents in the first all-London FA Cup Final of 1967. Dundee's performances in Europe, with Charlie instrumental, convinced Chelsea boss Tommy Doc that a swift offer was required in May 1966. On the evening of the Dundee supporters' Player of the Year dinner, the deal was cut. Embarrassingly, both Cookie and Doc, guests at the function, were required to keep quiet until the presentations were over, and Charlie, to compound matters, won the fans' award. When the announcement of his impending departure was made there were no lynchings, but plenty of civilized uproar.

The twenty-three-year-old immediately linked up with his new colleagues after a flight to Barcelona for the play-off match of the Inter-City Fairs Cup semi-final. There was an introduction, full of apprehension for Terry Venables, in the dressing room at the Nou Camp. Charlie wore Terry's shirt that evening. Bridges and McCreadie were also absent. Chelsea lost 5–0.

Cookie settled well, though. A winger who successfully converted to a modern midfield role, in no time he had the charmed crowd chanting his name. In that 1967 final, one dazzling run took him past Mackay, twice, and ended with a shot that Jennings brilliantly turned over the bar.

He was the best player on the pitch in the 1967/68 England–Scotland clash, his full-tilt dribbling contrasting with the foot-on-the-ball 'snake charmer' technique of others, including the more recent maestroes Gullit and Zola. Like Pat Nevin, Charlie was just as fast running with the ball as without it.

In the early days, he sometimes appeared to want to beat

the whole opposition team once (a feat he was infinitely capable of), then go back and beat them again. New manager Dave Sexton – who initially agreed a transfer for Cookie the player rejected – coached that out of him. Charlie had excellent acceleration. The manager schooled him to use it more regularly. Understandably, Tommy Doc tried to take him to Villa Park for £100,000. No way.

He did leave Chelsea, for Palace in September 1972, but knew where his heart was and returned sixteen months later to play some of his most consistent football and pass on his experience to a young side.

Cookie, often a carouser along with the rest of the King's Road crew, was apt to acts of seriousness. The FA Cup Final replay had prompted one such display. From the Saturday to the Tuesday before the game he took no food or water. A tailor had to take in the trousers of his Cup Final suit. But 'with less weight I was running farther and faster,' he commented. The first match at Wembley, on a rutted, alien landscape of a pitch, had been no place for his exalted trickery. Old Trafford would be different. In fact, it proved his stage: the sharp shift of gear and midfield run with twenty minutes to go that ended with the exquisite lob for Ossie's equalizing goal was Charlie at his best, the kind of uncommon skill that was vital to the successes in that period at Old Trafford and in Greece for the Cup Winners' Cup final.

In May 1972 Real recognized the influence of Cookie on Chelsea's creative play. 'If we stop Cooke, we will win,' suggested their great Spanish international striker Amancio. But in the second match, revelling in the deeper role normally adopted by Johnny Hollins, Cookie probed and battled non-stop. And he took the superb corner that led to Demps's opening goal.

It wasn't always easy deploying such skills. Charlie was always a thinker. Perhaps sensitivity was part of the problem. 'Professional footballers are like babies,' he once observed. 'We go abroad and they count us on and off the bus, on and off the plane. They take our passports, look after our baggage, pay our bills, order our food. They don't stick labels round our necks, but that's about all.'

Charlie's form was badly affected by a divorce – something you don't often hear about in football. He once talked about the 'degradation of being paid to take your trousers down in front of 50,000 people, for giving them licence to praise you or tear lumps out of you as they think fit.' That sense of football's absurdity was shared by a later Scot in Charlie's image, Pat Nevin. They even used to eat out at the same café, separated by decades rather than tables, on Fulham Broadway.

'I'm one of the most selfish bastards alive,' Cooke said, 'but when I'm out there I'm not doing it for personal glory. I'm not doing it for money to keep the wolf from the door. I'm not doing it for a 50,000 crowd. I'm doing it so that the handful of people I really respect can hold their head high in a pub when they say, "Yes, I know Charlie Cooke".'

On his second departure from the Bridge in 1978, Charlie tried his luck in the Stateside football league.

America suited Cookie and he settled in Seattle, becoming a vaunted representative of the Coerver Coaching scheme, respected now for his coaching as well as his heroic playing career.

Charlie received a spine-tingling welcome when he finally returned to Stamford Bridge as a half-time guest in 1995. Afterwards, in Drake's Bar, he looked as fit as ever, tanned and dapper like a retired gunslinger, except he'd been teetotal for a decade and a half.

DAVIE COPELAND

Born in Ayrshire in 1877, the former Walsall and Spurs favourite was vastly experienced even before he joined the 'Buns' (fans had still to settle on a decent nickname in 1906). In 1901 he was part of the Tottenham team that brought the FA Cup to London for the first time since Clapham Rovers in 1880. (His later Chelsea colleague, Sheffield United keeper Willie Foulke, was on the receiving end.) The fit, hard-working inside-left and Chelsea skipper formed a formidable wing partnership with another ex-Spur, outside-left Jack Kirwan, and was no shirker when it came to scoring goals himself. He was also keen to help defensively. Davie's biggest drawback was having the look of Dracula about him at a time when movies were first making the bloodsucking count's visage widely known.

JASON CUNDY

Briefly hailed as the best defensive YTS discovery of the 1990s, the fast, bullish young Wimbledonian acquitted himself well as an unadorned, athletic and occasionally impetuous centre-back. It was a surprise, then, that after barely one promising season he was sold to London rivals Tottenham in March 1992 for just under a million pounds. It was the source of some regret amongst Chelsea fans (and some graffiti outside the Bridge) but the defender proved more fallible in a side that he had not grown up with, and was sidelined for long periods, his notable contribution being a wind-assisted goal scored from the halfway line against Ipswich Town, the team he was to move on to in November 1996. Having recovered from testicular cancer, Jason featured in *Hello!* Magazine, perhaps the first English ex-Chelsea player to do so.

ED DE GOEY

Chelsea's second most successful goalkeeper of all time was signed from Feyenoord following a chance meeting with Blues boss and former Holland teammate Ruud Gullit on a plane back from South Africa. Both players had been invited to a match for Nelson Mandela and happened to be sitting next to each other. It transpired that the giant Dutch international was available. Rudi wanted a new goalie. The deal was soon done and at six feet six inches he became our tallest ever player.

There was something clumsy and almost lumpen about him to begin with. Finding the game in England more physical and pre-season training more demanding, he started slowly, conceding three on his debut at Coventry, and too casually allowing Saints' Kevin Davies to charge in and prod the ball off his feet into the goal.

Some were concerned about his agility. When he kicked a post in Tromso during that unrewarding Cup Winners' Cup trip within the Arctic Circle, a load of snow landed on top of his head. It seemed to sum up those early days.

But not all of the goals he conceded were his fault as defensive errors left him exposed. And quietly the clean sheets began to stack up – eleven before Christmas 1997.

It gradually became clear that his understated no-nonsense style was disguising the fact that it took a very good shot to beat him.

The thirty-one-year-old's experience was vital to the successful Cup Winners' Cup campaign too as he added a command of his box, unusual for European keepers, to his formidable armoury. In Betis he was quite brilliant, snuffing out the Spaniards' waves of attacks with the minimum of fuss, never allowing them to build up a head of steam.

In the next round against Vicenza, he almost single-handedly kept the score to a narrow 1–0 defeat in northern Italy. In the return leg he was to make one of the all-time great saves by a Chelsea goalkeeper, using his full length to guide a perilous cross-shot out of reach of the onrushing Luiso to maintain the 3–1 lead.

And those games came on the back of two stellar performances, home and away, against Arsenal in the Coca-Cola Cup semi-final. Without Ed's outstanding saves, the away leg might have been a 1–7 drubbing, the home leg a formality. By now he'd acquired the nickname Lan (as in 'Land ahoy!') and fondness was growing.

The corollary to this was that Chelsea had changed managers between the two ties. Out was the man who'd hired Ed, Ruud Gullit. In was Luca Vialli. One of the Italian's first proclamations in the matchday magazine was that he would alternate Dmitri Kharine and Ed in the starting line-up for the last eighteen or so games. It was Ed for the Cups, Dimmi for the League. Loyal Hitchy would remain supersub on the bench.

In the event, a poor performance by the Russian at Elland Road broke the pattern, and Ed also figured in the last League game of the season against Bolton. In the Coca-Cola Cup final the tall Netherlander was called upon only a few times and always looked comfortable as Chelsea cruised to a 2–0 victory after extra time.

The Cup Winners' Cup final was a different matter. A tight game required 100 per cent concentration for ninety minutes, and after twenty minutes Balakov was put away by Bobic, and drove to Ed's right, the keeper diving low superbly and putting the ball round the post. A mark of his growing confidence was his frequent back-up of the defence, killing off attacks and bringing the ball back into play. The newspapers had been full of 'want-away De Goey' stories. During the extended celebrations at the end the normally laconic loner was transformed into a beaming, touchy-feely type, a deserved double winner. Like Tore Andre Flo, though, he might be forgiven for thinking Chelsea is always like this. Someone had better tell them!

JOHN DEMPSEY

Furrow-browed Demps was signed from Fulham in 1969 and for two years was a formidable centre-half – one of the four 'assassins', as Ossie had it: Webb, Harris, Dempsey and McCreadie. His role, like that of Harris's was purely and simply man-marking, acting as an individual stewarded by his skipper, Chopper. Tall and commanding with his head, with his wispy hair flailing in the air, his reading of play and unpretentious distribution brought him Irish international recognition, and he is overlooked as a tower of strength in the team during the two years that brought the FA and Cup Winners' Cups.

His experience in the latter final oddly replicated Webby's in the former. In the first match, Ossie put us 1–0 ahead. Seconds remained, indeed the trophy, adorned with the blue ribbons of the 'winners', was on its way down to the field of play, and the band was assembling pitchside, when Real played the ball despairingly into the Chelsea box. Demps stretched for it, deflecting it into the path of Zoco, who lashed it past Peter Bonetti.

'Out of the corner of my eye,' said the villain of the piece, 'I saw a linesman's flag go up as I went to clear, but I miskicked and put the ball straight to Zoco. He couldn't miss. I could have cried.'

Before the second match, at the Karaiskaki Stadium two nights later, John was treated by physio Harry Medhurst. Good job too – following on from a decent shout for a penalty for Chopper's unsubtle stifling of the troublesome Amancio's run, goalie Borja conceded a corner from Webby's header. Demps drove another header from Cookie's cross that the Spanish sticks man could only feebly fist out. Demps was lurking inside the box. 'When Borja punched out my header,' he said, 'Keith Weller was shaping up for a shot but as the ball was coming straight back to me I shouted for him to leave it and I whacked it on the volley. It went like a rocket. After giving away Real's equalizer in the first game, I was delighted to see this one go in.'

It soared just under the crossbar. Brilliant finishing from a player who would only find the net on six other occasions in 207 matches. We won 2–1, Ossie scoring the second.

There was more for Demps to be content about than just victory. His season had started uncertainly with Dave Sexton's new 'zonal marking' system, where defenders were required to mark 'space' rather than players. Demps appeared to struggle to kick the old player-hugging habit and was replaced in September 1970 by the less tigerish Marvin Hinton until Chelsea went out of the FA Cup to Manchester City. By then, Demps had mastered his brief.

As the gargantuan Micky Droy began to make his mark in the first team in 1972/73, Demps had fewer appearances. In 1978 he was sold to Philadelphia Furies, but football was never going to dominate his life forever. John's life took a rewarding turn into the caring profession. He now works with children with learning difficulties in Harrow. One of the last charitable acts of Matthew Harding was to donate a minibus for the double Cup-winning legend's work.

MARCEL DESAILLY

The tall, muscular midfielder-cum-centre-back is one of the most distinguished Chelsea signings in history. Born in Ghana, he began his career as a teenager with Nantes in France as a central defender, and eventually made his debut in his adopted country in that position in August 1993. A move to Marseille in 1992 brought him to wider attention as the southern French side won the Championship and the European Cup, with Marcel outstanding throughout. The beaten finalists in Munich, AC Milan, bought him in November 1993 and, restyled by coach Fabio Capello as a dominating, rampaging midfielder Marcel 'doubled up' again, winning Serie A's Scudetto and the European Cup again in 1993/94. He is the first player to achieve this remarkable feat for two different teams consecutively. It was with his awesome display in the 4–0 annihilation of Barcelona in Athens that Marcel first came to the attention of many Chelsea fans. How many that night wished he would come and bolster our team, so soon after our identical scoreline at Wembley in the FA Cup Final? And how many ever believed Chelsea would sign him, aged twenty-nine and still effective? Once it was evident Milan, after a disappointing season for the club, were prepared to let Marcel go, Luca Vialli and Colin Hutchinson didn't mess around. 'All I keep hearing from Milan is "Chelsea, Chelsea",' the Frenchman was said to have complained. It will have served as a neat apprenticeship for his first hearing of the Bridge's rendition of Blue Day! On Tuesday 9 June 1998, the day before the start of France 98, and in the French World Cup centre, one of the greatest players in the world joined Chelsea for £4.6m a very happy man, setting his target – as usual – on the Champions' League. Marcel, player of the tournament, starred in France's Final victory, despite being sent off.

ROBERTO DI MATTEO

'42 seconds. Di Matteo' – the shirt for all seasons. When Robbie Di Matteo signed for Chelsea in the summer of 1996, the distraught, uncomprehending fans of Lazio hounded his car out of the club's Rome HQ and bombarded the board with protests. In England the Swiss-born Italian international's transfer forced a sceptical press finally to take Chelsea seriously again, and upped the ante in the import stakes. At twenty-six, he was the first current Italian international to arrive in England. With his dashing good looks, silken playing style, spontaneous celebrations and impulsive shooting –

CUP KINGS

A number of players have the bizarre distinction of only ever playing for Chelsea in cup competitions.

Joe Goodwin played only in the cup ties against Southend and Palace in 1905/06.

Colin Court made just one appearance, against Frem of Copenhagen in the Fairs Cup in September 1958.

John O'Rourke made his solo bow in a League Cup tie at Swindon in September 1963 – Chelsea lost 0–3.

James Toomer and **Frank Wolff** both managed their only games for Chelsea in the 1–7 defeat by Crystal Palace in the 1905/06 FA Cup – Chelsea had to field a weakened team because a League match had been scheduled for the same day.

Michael Gilke's moment of glory whilst on loan from Reading came in the ZDS Cup southern final second leg, a 1–3 home defeat by Southampton on 29 January 1992.

To the end of the 1997/98 season, **Stevie Hampshire**'s single appearance was in the Coca-Cola Cup tie at home to Blackburn in October 1997.

a talent that was never illuminated among the many evident in his play back home – Robbie overcame initial criticism in some quarters and over-expectation in others to become an essential element in Chelsea's fluent counter-attacking style.

Robbie was Chelsea's record transfer when Ruud Gullit paid £4.9m for him after Euro 96. In fact, as would happen throughout his early Chelsea career, his importance in that tournament to the Italian squad was more poignantly evident in a game he missed. Robbie was one of the 'famous five' rested for the crucial Czech republic game the Azzurri lost.

Too often Chelsea fans were blind to the many intangible

contributions he made to the game – a quick foot in, neat one-touch pass to get the attack moving. Sure he could eat up ground in the middle, hold off opponents and put others in, but didn't he 'disappear' during some games?

Luckily, he's the sort of player who writes his own head-lines too. The outstanding strikes, beginning with Chelsea's first goal of the season at home to Middlesbrough, a twenty yarder that put the lie to his inability to score in Serie A for Lazio, was just the start. There were unbelievable thunderbolts in his first two seasons against Tottenham and Leicester on the way to the 1997 FA Cup Final, Arsenal in the Coca-Cola semi-final and many others.

But the goal for which he will always be joyously remembered is the astonishing, spine-chilling forty-two second strike at Wembley in May 1997. Only Steve Clarke and Dennis Wise had touched the ball for Chelsea before Robbie picked the ball up in midfield, strode purposely forward, watched Hughesie make a decoy run to the right that opened up Boro's centre, then struck a shot from thirty-five yards that looped over their extended keeper, skimmed the underside of the bar and settled in the centre of the net.

Everyone was taken aback. All Alan Greene on Radio 5 Live could offer was, 'Well, how about this!' It was faster than Jackie Milburn's. The fastest ever. There was something satisfying about a 'fancy foreigner' virtually sealing Middlesbrough's fate while the nation was still setting its collective video recorder. How great was that?

Robbie shattered his own assassin's cool with a celebration that was not one of his best choreographed jobs. In fact up to that point he'd shown himself to be Chelsea's most imaginative goal celebrant, the 'Roman banquet' winning particular approval and helping win over fans of all clubs to our glam appeal.

It's fair to say that Robbie's second campaign wasn't as stunning as his first – how could it be? The main news to report was that he switched from looking like one Thunderbird to another; from Parker to the Hood in one shave of the head.

His experience in our successful European Cup Winners' and Coca-Cola Cup campaigns was vital. The Swiss-born star punished Bratislava (at the risk of making him sound like a Mafia hitman) in both legs, and his combative midfield link work, such a feature of our excellent League form too, was vital in overcoming the last obstacle, Arsenal, on our way to further Wembley glory. His stinging drive past Gunners' keeper Manninger was worthy of winning any match; that it was his friend Luca Vialli's first match as player-manager made it all the more piquant.

He graced both finals that season, scoring, as was now his habit, against the unfortunate Boro in the Coca-Cola after Frank Sinclair's extra-time opener.

He was far quieter in the Stockholm final. Afterwards, though, Robbie Di Matteo decided not to travel back with the rest of the team and could be found out on the town celebrating with some of the Chelsea followers in town that night.

And in two years in a London he'd come to adore, he'd won three medals, his first medals since the early days with Schaffhausen in the land of the cuckoo clock. It's terrific when stars sign to win things at your club and your club sees them right.

KERRY DIXON

In 1987 you could join the Kerry Dixon Fan Club. £5 membership got you: newsletter ('Kerry missed a sitter etc, etc'), autograph, colour pictures, badge, special offers.

The soul boy Kerry, born in Luton in 1961, arrived at Chelsea in August 1983 as a £175,000 buy for John Neal and Ian McNeill's management team. Tall and powerful, his reputation was made in the lower divisions with Reading, but the transition to top-flight football came relatively easily. In his first year with

TOP GOALSCORERS

One of the most agonizing features of recent Chelsea history was watching a fading **Kerry Dixon** inch his way painfully towards the club goalscoring record – only to miss overhauling **Bobby Tambling**'s mark by just ten strokes. Nevertheless, in these days of more cautious football and dwindling one-club loyalty, Kerry's strike rate was impressive and he remains a Chelsea legend. Chelsea's top scorers are as follows:

1 **Bobby Tambling** (1958–1969) – 202 in 370 appearances
2 **Kerry Dixon** (1983–1992) – 193 in 420 appearances
3 **Roy Bentley** (1947–1956) – 150 in 367 appearances
4 **Peter Osgood** (1964–1974 and 1978–79), 150 in 380 appearances
5 **Jimmy Greaves** (1957–1961) – 132 in 169 appearances
6 **George Mills** (1929–1938) – 123 in 239 appearances
7 **George Hilsdon** (1906–1911) – 107 in 164 appearances
8 **Barry Bridges** (1958–1965) – 93 in 205 appearances
9 **Tommy Baldwin** (1966–1974) – 92 in 238 appearances
10 **Hughie Gallacher** (1930–1934) – 81 in 144 appearances

Chelsea he grabbed twenty-eight goals, including a pair on his debut against Derby (always Kerry's fall guys) to power us to promotion. In his second campaign he managed twenty-four. The four successive divisional top scores he accrued in successive years set a new league record.

Not the most technically-styled player in the world, Kerry's main assets were his ability to hustle defences and acute knowledge of where the goal was. He top scored for Chelsea in six of his first eight seasons. Unsurprisingly, he is the club's second top scorer of all time, behind Bobby Tambling. Such consistency was enough to allay concerns about his genuine quality at international level and ensure his place in England's 1986 World Cup squad.

It was as part of the diverse attacking trio that included Pat Nevin and David Speedie that 'Mary' is best remembered, his strength and intuition perfectly complementing Pat's skills and Speedo's feistiness. Once the partnership was broken up between 1986 and 1987, Kerry was exposed by the lack of quality provision from midfield and a consistent partner.

With the arrival of Gordon Durie and, latterly, Kevin Wilson his scoring touch returned in 1989's Division Two promotion season (twenty-five goals from thirty-nine games, including four against Barnsley) and carried on into our fifth-placed campaign in the First Division (twenty from thirty-eight, with a hat-trick against Millwall).

His fortunes with the boot were a barometer of our seasons. Bobby Campbell's comment that, 'Kerry's the man to get us out of jail' summed up the too often negative perspective of the club at the time.

Needing just thirteen goals to overhaul Bobby Tambing's 202-goal haul at the start of the 1991/92 season, the thirty-year-old Kerry suffered a crisis of confidence and closed the season, and an era, short of the record and a Southampton player.

The next time Chelsea noticed him he was playing for Luton in the FA Cup semi-final at Wembley. In one of the most moving Chelsea moments, Blues fans brought a lump to his throat with a final, heartfelt rendition of 'There's only one Kerry Dixon'. Secretly, no-one was happier for the club's first Cup final for twenty-three years than our great servant.

Blue blood still coursed through Kerry's veins. A personal favourite of chairman Bates, despite the personal messes he sometimes found himself in, Kerry was granted a testimonial match in 1995. It was a time for reflection on a great dressing-room joker, a great player and a thoroughly nice fellow.

TOMMY DOCHERTY

As a player he was a slow, hard defender. As player-coach he played just four games, one of them a 6–1 victory that was the record away win in the top-flight right up until the 6–0 thrashing of Barnsley on their home patch one week into the 1997/98 season.

Before his arrival at Chelsea Tommy's reasonably distinguished career had taken him from Celtic in 1948 to Arsenal in 1958 with a nine-year stint at Preston North-End sandwiched in between. He played 25 times for Scotland, often as skipper (and was later to manage his national side).

As manager he was unpredictable, hard and a genius. Tommy assumed the manager's role from Ted Drake in September 1961 when the team was already virtually consigned to relegation from the First Division. The squad needed rebuilding and the training regimen resurrecting. Young players coming through the ranks noted that some of the older staff seemed barely to train and a laissez-faire attitude had taken hold.

The Grahams, Harmers, Hintons and McCreadies amongst Tommy's purchases were astute ones, though those that weren't – Moore, Kevan, Hateley – were prominent failures.

He also made the most of a youth-team set-up that won the prestigious FA Youth Cup two seasons running, in 1960 and 1961, unafraid to give the likes of Ron Harris, John Hollins, Peter Osgood and other teenagers their first team bow.

The force of the Doc's maverick personality and gift for public relations shaped the Chelsea side of the mid-1960s. His ideas went. In 1964, at Bentalls in Kingston Christmas was brightened by coaching clinics involving a different Chelsea star each day, whether Terry Venables, Barry Bridges, Bobby Tambling, Peter Bonetti or Ron Harris. He'd also invite his young charges to drinks parties where he would play the fool hilariously.

Another stunt was his decision to accept an invitation to play the German national side, thus aiding them in their prepa-

MANAGERS' ROLL CALL

John Tait Robertson 1905–1906	**Ken Shellito** 1977–1978
David Calderhead 1907–1933	**Danny Blanchflower** 1978–1979
Leslie Knighton 1933–1939	**Geoff Hurst** 1979–1981
William Birrell 1939–1952	**John Neal** 1981–1985
Ted Drake 1952–1961	**John Hollins** 1985–1988
Tommy Docherty 1962–1967	**Bobby Campbell** 1988–1992
Dave Sexton 1967–1974	**Ian Porterfield** 1992–1993
Ron Suart 1974–1975	**Glenn Hoddle** 1993–1996
Eddie McCreadie 1975–1977	**Ruud Gullit** 1996–1998
	Gianluca Vialli 1998–

rations for the 1966 World Cup. It was all-for-one with Doc's young side, despite his often temperamental behaviour.

They were 'Docherty's Diamonds' and they shone with their compelling teamwork and individual flair. For all that, Doc's sole silverware in his six-year stay was the 1965 League Cup.

They were perhaps the most consistent Chelsea side not to win a major trophy, though they reached three successive FA Cup semi-finals, and the final at the third attempt in 1967, when they lost 2–1 to Tottenham and genuinely challenged for the Championship between 1964 and 1966, finishing fifth, third and fifth successively – the club's best top-flight spell.

Doc also shepherded his boys to the semi-finals of Europe's Fairs Cup in 1965/66. His team beat Roma, Milan and Munich, but lost out in a play-off game at the penultimate stage to Barcelona.

A hallmark of the period was the passing and movement going forward, with McCreadie and Shellito overlapping down the flanks and skipper Terry Venables directing play like a traffic cop. As Venners' influence over his peers grew Doc perceived him as a threat and the Blackpool Incident in spring 1965 handed the manager the excuse he needed to rid him of his midfield general, as well as many of his 'co-conspirators'.

Ask any of the players of that era about the period and they'll shake their heads at Doc's impatience. Always liable to intemperate outbursts after vital losses, the manager decided to break up his brilliant young side, inadvertently building the basis for his successor, Dave Sexton, firstly by hiring the man himself as assistant, then by bringing in Charlie Cooke and Johnny Boyle, stalwarts-to-be of the late-1960s and early 1970s.

The brilliant Tommy Doc's reign came to an end in typically reckless fashion. During a summer tour match in Bermuda the Chelsea manager directed disgraceful remarks at the local referee. The report reached the Football League and he was suspended, banned from the club's training ground for the beginning of the 1967/68 season. The board found the situation intolerable and Bill Pratt reluctantly gave the popular, wise-cracking boss his cards. The week after his departure, we lost 0–7.

Tommy's subsequent management career was notable for his spell with Manchester United, which also ended in disgrace, this time after an affair with the club physio's wife.

The outspoken Scotsman is still a lively commentator on contemporary football, but nothing pleases him more than to recall the glorious exploits of his favourite Diamonds: Bonetti, Osgood, Hollins, McCreadie, Chopper and the rest.

MAL DONAGHY

The experienced former Luton and Northern Ireland defender, signed from Manchester United for £150,000 in summer 1992 to play alongside the soon-to-be injured Paul Elliott at centre back, was already thirty-four before he kicked a ball for Chelsea. Immensely fit for his years, with an economy of passing and reading of the game that compensated for a lack of pace and physical presence, the likeable 'old gent' in the Chelsea camp adapted to a system which placed him at left-back or even, later, midfield to the extent that he did something he hadn't done at Old Trafford for five years – scored goals. Having struck to earn Chelsea a point away to Leeds, the slim, grey-haired Irishman grabbed the opener in a 4–0 thrashing of Middlesbrough in his next match. His unbridled joy was almost as thrilling as the goals themselves. The word 'Shoot!' was never far away from any fan's lips after that.

Under Glenn Hoddle Mal's chances were restricted and he was often subbed, though at thirty-seven he still managed a place on the Blues bench for the semi-final and was in the squad for the final in the 1993/94 FA Cup campaign.

At the end of his contract in summer 1995 he was released and drifted out of football.

TONY DORIGO

Think of Tony Dorigo and two things come to mind: the banana shot in the Zenith Data Systems trophy final of 1990 against Manchester City and the declaration the same year that he wanted to leave Chelsea in order to win something proper – he went to Leeds the following season.

In many ways the Aussie-born left-back represented the type of quality Chelsea needed to hold onto in order to contest the major honours. He had pace, attacking ingenuity, a decent tackle and impressive recovery if passed. His interceptions of opponents' passes frequently led to goals. And he was professional, for the most part utterly focused on the job at hand. He was a true heir of Eddie McCreadie's left-back slot, joining from Aston Villa for £475,000, aged twenty-three. Tony's England career took off in 1989 during Chelsea's unstoppable surge to promotion from Division Two, in which he played a sizeable part with his overlapping runs and powerful shot. He scored six times

---

THE LAD'S A BIT GEOGRAPHICAL

Alfred **BOWER**   Craig **FORREST**

Robert **BUSH**   George **LAKE**

George **DALE**   Graham **MOORE**

Charles **DYKE**   George **STONE**

Harry **FORD**   Darren **WOOD**

Sidney **FOSS**   Wilson **MARSH**

---

in 1989/90 including the superb winner against Manchester City at Maine Road in March. Another memorable contribution was the cut in and shot that led to Chelsea's second 3–2 defeat of Manchester United in his last season, 1990/91.

There's little doubt that towards the end Tony lost heart playing in a side that just wasn't good enough. And there was no point in maintaining his half-baked presence. The £1.3m secured in May 1991 helped underpin the purchase of Paul Elliott and (whisper it) Tommy Boyd.

TED DRAKE

Chelsea's first manager to steward the team to the First Division title was a breath of fresh air at the club when he joined in 1952. He announced on his arrival that the root-and-branch changes to Chelsea FC would take three years to bear fruit. Three years later the Championship was won. How did he succeed where others had failed?

To begin with, the former Arsenal striker developed a more technical and professional approach to the running of the club at every level. One of his first acts was to appoint John Battersby secretary. He would handle the press and administrative elements of the manager's role, freeing up Ted to work purely on the football.

An ebullient and magnetic character, Ted worked strongly on the psychological side of the game, ditching the old 'Pensioner' nickname in favour of the more modern 'Blues' and urging greater partisanship from the Stamford Bridge faithful. The old crest was also removed too, replaced by the more belligerent lion-and-crozier.

So much for the trimmings. His playing staff were transformed, if not in body (and there were several changes to be made in personnel), then in mind. He set about creating a team of grafters in his own never-say-die image, lurching away from the pretty-pretty underachievers towards the 'different Chelsea' he had promised. The new manager preferred plucky amateurs like Lewis, Saunders and O'Connell to more skilled, less diligent senior pros.

His psychology worked on another level though. Eric 'Rabbit' Parsons was given stick by some sections of the Stamford Bridge crowd. When he'd recovered from a cartilage problem, it was the attentive Drake who nursed him back to confidence on the park.

The training regime was drastically overhauled in 1952 and the effects were huge. Ted suffered from back trouble – no surprise given his fearless physical approach as a player – but wanted to lead by example. So when the double session of fitness work was introduced he partook too. If it meant that he had to lie prostrate afterwards, being massaged back to a tolerable level of pain, well, that was the price he had to pay.

In a few years Chelsea became not simply the fittest team in the League but also, with some of the players Ted introduced, one of the most solidly consistent. It was a Chelsea team unlike almost any other, except in defence, where in 1954 Seamus O'Connell could score a hat-trick on his debut and still finish on the losing side 5–6 to Manchester United.

Chelsea's Golden Jubilee year proved a unique one in the history of the club. After they had beaten a disinterested

Sheffield Wednesday on the penultimate Saturday of the season, the score from Cardiff was read out. 1–1. Chelsea's only challengers Portsmouth had faltered. The title was won and there were wild scenes all over the pitch.

Hastily, players and officials rose in the stand to make their speeches. Chairman Mears, Ted himself (reminding jubilant fans of his three-year prediction) and skipper Roy Bentley (who sportingly introduced the man he'd deposed, John Harris). Then the crowd called for the man they wanted, and it must have touched Ted Drake to hear them yelling for 'Rabbit! Rabbit!', the man whose career he'd turned around.

That year Chelsea also won the Combination, South-East Counties and Metropolitan leagues. Unfortunately, Ted was unable to follow up his single success. The defence of the Championship foundered as the opposition sussed out how to stop the team playing. And by the end of the 1950s the team was ageing and lacked direction. Ted himself seemed to have lost his hunger.

Peter Sillett used to tell the story of how he was a passenger once in Ted's car when he pulled up at some traffic lights. The lights turned green, then red again, then green. A passing policeman tapped on the window to see if Ted was all right. 'Do you know what, Peter,' Ted said, once he'd reassured the copper. 'I thought you were driving.'

The manager who will always occupy a special place in Chelsea hearts left in September 1961, to be replaced by Tommy Docherty. He dabbled with bookmaking for a while, then fleetingly became assistant manager at Barcelona in 1970, then chief scout at Fulham.

'At Chelsea I could always count on receiving 100 per cent from my players,' he related in 1991, 'and in 1955 they carried that right through to win the League. I was proud to manage a title-winning team, but I'm not one to get carried away by records.'

Ted passed away in 1995.

MICKY DROY

The six-foot four-inch nineteen-year-old amateur from Slough Town made his debut in a testing match at Molineux in February 1971 when Wolves' striker Derek Dougan was at his most deadly. Soon after, he figured in the Cup Winners' Cup semi-final against Manchester City. It was clear that the defender, a ringer for 'Jaws' from the James Bond movies or (with beard) Bluto from the old Popeye cartoons, was unfazed by the heat of battle. Obviously dominant in the air, his mighty head and thick neck appeared atop goal area melées reassuringly frequently. He could also surprise people with his deftness on the ground, particularly with his left foot. How the messages from his brain ever got down to his toes as quickly as they did is a mystery to this day.

Unhappily for Micky, his star was in its ascendancy while most of those 1970s champs around him were fading for one reason or another, and he survived at the Bridge through thick and wafer thin for fifteen years. For a dozen of those he was a superb, if limited, performer. From 1974 onwards he was partnered by a succession of inexperienced and often incomplete footballers. Perhaps the most effective accomplice at the back was Steve Wicks between 1975 and 1978, though Micky was still around to bolster the likes of Colin Pates in the early 1980s.

Moving to Palace on a free in 1985, he had already established a thriving car business. Indeed his firm would service all Chelsea's company vehicles.

MICHAEL DUBERRY

'Doobs' was the find of Glenn Hoddle's career as Chelsea manager. And it was quite by accident. A centre-half crisis in November 1995 meant an urgent recall from loan at Bournemouth and a first-team start alongside recalled sweeper David Lee and behind Dan Petrescu making his debut. It all seemed to click, even if the result was 1–0 to Leeds.

His debut had come about more than a year earlier in the Coventry game just before the 1994 FA Cup final. He'd shown none of the same promise in that 2–1 defeat. Perhaps we should thank Bournemouth for his progress. No wonder they wanted to buy him before his emergency call-up.

For the rest of that season the Enfield-born youngster did well enough to warrant third place in the Player of the Year poll, behind Rudi, of course. His finest moments were defensive, such as his shepherding of Cantona et al at Old Trafford, and in the semi-final at Old Trafford (during which, owing to injuries to Clarke and Petrescu, he ended up scaring the hell out of United with his runs down the right flank).

His offensive play was improving too. He headed down for Rudi's goal in the FA Cup win over Newcastle and thundered in a crucial header from Spencer's clever chip against Wimbledon in the quarter-final. Most importantly, he'd bucked the trend of Chelsea centre-backs and was proving consistent and focused.

By the end of the season he'd gone from squad surplus to England Under-21. Although the clamour for a full England cap subsided a little in subsequent seasons as injury struck and form wavered a little, Doobs proved that some talent and a lot of application goes a long way.

He was still learning in his third full season. The switch to four at the back presented a new technical challenge as he'd only ever played as part of a central three throughout his Chelsea career. But his attitude towards new challenges is spot on.

KEITH DUBLIN

The confident, fast and able young defender debuted impressively at home to Barnsley in Division Two towards the close of the 1983/84 season. Despite some promising performances, a youngster like Keith needs breathing space and must be allowed to make mistakes without vilification. His fledgling self-assurance was rapidly tested and found wanting in a poor side with

THE LAD'S A BIT EASY TO PLACE

Keith **DUBLIN**

Steve **HAMPSHIRE**

James **ASHFORD**

Samuel **DUDLEY**

Ian 'Chico' **HAMILTON**

Colin **HAMPTON**

Jack **HARROW**

Stewart **HOUSTON**

Michael **PINNER**

Alex **STEPNEY**

Ian **BRITTON**

Frank **LYON**

Steve **SHERWOOD**

Benjamin **WHITEHOUSE**

William **WHITTON**

Peter **PICKERING**

little defensive cover. One of Keith's problems was that he was really a centre-back, not a full-back. Another was that he is black, and a certain section of the Stamford Bridge crowd hounded him mercilessly if not solely for that reason (his performance level fell off and, given little time to recover in the reserves, he became too accident-prone to justify his selection), then more vehemently for it. The usual support groups for victims of Stamford Bridge boo-boys stepped in: Brighton, Charlton, and more recently Southend provided Keith with a decent career at a good level. But you wonder how different things might have been. In 1996/97, he was Player of the Year at Roots Hall.

JOHN DUNN

Not the most decisive of keepers in the late-1950s, and in the face of a young incumbent, Peter Bonetti, who claimed anything within his own personal fifteen-yard exclusion zone, never likely to have the best of times at the Bridge.

GORDON DURIE

Is that Jukebox, or Judas? There were times when the strong, pacy, aggressive Scotsman looked the answer to some of Chelsea's prayers when he signed in 1986 for £380,000 from Hibs. And in his first full season the six-footer impressed enough to earn his first Scottish call-up. (He was still in the national team eleven years later at France 98.) He could trouble defences and score goals with foot or head.

For three seasons, when uninjured and fully motivated, he struck up an effective partnership with Kerry Dixon, often matching the Sheddites' favourite goal for goal, brace for brace. In February 1989 he surpassed himself with a sensational five-goal performance, even if it was against lowly Walsall in the Second Division.

But there was always the whiff of the whingeing journey-man about him, and the sense that he was never committed to Chelsea except as a stepping stone to greater things (or Glasgow Rangers, via Spurs in 1991, as it turned out). He didn't seem that bothered by our defeats and was evidently never the most popular player in the dressing room – or physiotherapist's room, to which he was a frequent visitor. Good luck to him, though. He carved a career at Ibrox and won enough caps to show he was a decent player.

PAUL ELLIOTT

Celtic's and the Scottish Premier's Player of the Year was a magnificent catch in July 1991. At £1.4m, he'd been convinced of Chelsea's ambition and arrived at the age of twenty-seven in his prime. A tall, dominant figure in the heart of the defence, 'Jamaica' (so named because of his regular conversation about the island of his forefathers) scored on his debut, a 2–2 draw with Wimbledon in which fellow debutant Joe Allon also registered his first goal.

Although there were problems with the partnership between he and Player of the Year Kenny Monkou – they found themselves duplicating the same moves and runs – his leadership qualities and talismanic presence buoyed up a team that had lacked such a player since the departure of Graham Roberts in 1990. 1991/92 wasn't a great season, but it would have been a hell of a lot more disappointing without the England 'B' international's powerful, fist-shaking performances.

Injury disrupted the end of that first season but worse was to come soon into his second.

A slow start without a win in four games turned into a more promising couple of wins over QPR and Aston Villa. Then disaster struck at Anfield. Jamaica had missed the previous year's historic victory. This match would be remembered for being his last ever. A 60:40 ball in his favour was enthusiastically contested by Liverpool's Dean Saunders. The two collided and Paul lay prone, his cruciate ligament ruptured beyond repair, despite a brave, extended comeback and the extraordinary outpouring of goodwill from Chelsea fans. A court case to claim damages from the

Liverpool player failed, and Saunders has been *persona non grata* with Blues fans ever since.

Paul enjoyed a testimonial at the Bridge, became club captain under Glenn Hoddle – who did as much as he could to aid the centre-half's recovery – and still retains fond memories of his brief but inspiring spell.

Paul is now a pundit for Channel 4's *Football Italia*, having spent the middle part of his career with Pisa.

ALL ABOARD

The **Mears** family, led by 'Father of the Club' H.A., known as Gus, were responsible for establishing Chelsea (rejecting alternative names such as London or Kensington FC) at Stamford Bridge in 1905. The Mears 'dynasty' dominated the club's boardroom until 1982.

Claude Kirby was Chelsea's first chairman, serving until his death in 1935.

Joe Mears, nephew of Gus, was chairman when the club won its first league title in 1955, and was also elected chair of the Football League in September 1963.

Brian Mears, who in his early Seventies heyday drove around in a Jaguar with the registration plate 'CFC II', was chairman from the death of his father Joe in 1966 until 1982, and therefore presided over our two cup successes in 1970 and 1971.

Ken Bates, in charge since buying the club for a nominal £1 in 1982, is Chelsea's most successful chairman. Chelsea have won the FA Cup (1997), Coca-Cola Cup and Cup Winners' Cup (both 1998) during his historic term of office.

JOE FASCIONE

The bow-legged bloke everyone sings 'Who the ****ing hell are you?!' to when he comes onto the pitch with Roy Bentley, Frank Blunstone *et al* at Stamford Bridge. He was nippy, but not an exceptional talent. The endearing thing about Joe was that he looked like Bernie Winters (ask your grandfather). Unfortunately he played more like Schnorbitz (ditto), waiting wide on the wing for someone to throw the stick, and then off he'd bomb to fetch it. One of those who survived his part in the Blackpool boozing incident, but had no great impact in the first team.

ALBERT FERRER

Chelsea fans got their first view of the short, stocky Spanish international right-back Colin Hutchinson had bought for £2.25m at France 98 – in his first game he faced Celestine Babayaro of Nigeria. Albert, nicknamed 'Chapi' for some reason (A likeness to Charlie Chaplin??), has won everything with Barcelona, from the Spanish Primera title and Cup to the European Cup Winners' Cup (beating Paris St Germain) in 1997.

MIKE FILLERY

From 1978 to 1983, and mostly on the less exacting battlefields of the Second Division, YTS graduate midfielder Micky Fillery demonstrated much of the style and swagger of players from the 'golden age', 1965–71, without the consistency and often the heart to make either worthwhile attributes.

A skilled player on the ball, with cultured feet and a decent shot, his ability reliably to impose himself on a match in the way fans had occasionally seen him do was compounded by the loss of his nearest equivalent, Ray Wilkins, in 1980. Naturally languid, he became a target for abuse elements in the crowd. Disillusioned, he moved on to QPR for £200,000, still only twenty-two.

STEVE FINNIESTON

'Jock' might have been a goalscoring legend had he sustained the impact he made on graduating from the youth scheme. In his first full season, the Second Division promotion campaign of 1976/77, Steve top-scored with twenty-four goals. Unfortunately injury marred his subsequent Chelsea days and he moved on to Sheffield United in 1978. Further physical damage put an end to his football career.

ROBERT FLECK

Flecky, nice fellow though he is, was living proof of the folly of buying those who score great goals against you.

When he was at Norwich every run took him past two Chelsea players, every pass split our defence, every shot hit our net.

So he was a popular selection when bought in 1992 for £2.1m. As a goalscorer. Sadly, he never really was – except against us. And he wasn't about to become one at the age of twenty-seven.

Though there weren't many goals, his approach and link play was astute and fruitful enough in partnership with Mick Harford that Chelsea claimed fourth place in the First Division at Christmas. But Mick Harford succumbed to injury and suddenly, with two goals to show for the best part of a season, the hard-working Glaswegian suddenly looked very exposed. Chelsea finished eleventh. Nevertheless, his popularity was confirmed by the appearance on the terraces of a surreal version of the Beatles' song 'Yellow Submarine', with the chorus 'We all live in a Robert

Fleck world' and a verse along the lines of: 'Number one was Robert Fleck, number two was Robert Fleck . . .'

From that point on though Flecky seemed to settle for a well-paid reserve team status and Cascarino, Shipperley, Stein and others took their chances. On the odd occasion when he was recalled to the starting line-up like some long-lost ancestor summoned by a shaman, or an old cow fattened and washed for sale, he was very unconvincing. In the Shed End at one such evening match a well-connected supporter was overheard fixing up his plans for a late-night bender after the game. 'It's gonna be great – Flecky's promised he's coming out for a skinful too.' Lord knows why, but it instilled in those who heard it an even deeper sense of depression about the bloke and, in 1996, a correspondingly greater relief at his return to carrot-crunching at Carrow Road.

TORE ANDRE FLO

Look, just don't call him 'good with his head', okay? The six-foot three-inch Norwegian, one of five footballing brothers, took almost four months into his debut season 1997/98 to score a Premiership goal with his feet, lovingly completing his hat-trick against, of all people, Tottenham, in a dazzling, hilarious 6–1 victory.

Tore Andre was modest enough to accept that despite his much-heralded arrival, following a pay-off to accelerate his post-Bosman free transfer, Ruud Gullit's squad rotation was likely to limit his starts. Still, he enjoyed his maiden hat-trick.

'It's an incredible feeling,' he said afterwards. 'I cannot believe I am playing in the Premiership and to have scored a hat-trick really is incredible for me. It's a dream come true. I only found out two hours before the game that I was going to play. I was surprised when Ruud told me as the squad was preparing for the match, that I was in the team.'

At twenty-four he occasionally showed he had something to learn when he appeared to run out of ideas and wasn't getting the service he needed. He likes the ball to feet, where his lanky legs can wave like wands, skilfully manipulating the ball before passing bewildered defenders, or turning instantly to catch an opponent unawares with a mobility that is exceptional for a man of his size.

His finest moments came just like that. In Real Betis, his startling footwork, turn and direct running and finishing had Chelsea 2–0 up and cruising before the first half of the first leg was over.

His brilliant performance for Norway against Brazil at France 98 confirmed what many delighted Chelsea fans already knew. The best is yet to come from this brilliant young international.

DICK FOSS

Dick was one of only three registered Chelsea players to turn out in the 1944 League South Cup Final, having turned out an 'invisible' 200 times during wartime, when stats didn't count. A forward who converted to the more defensive wing-half slot with aplomb and composure, his major contribution to Chelsea Football Club was not to be as a player, but as a major figurehead for years in the Chelsea youth training scheme established by manager Billy Birrell. He joined this on his retirement as a player in 1952 at the age of forty. Nurturer of so many fantastic talents in the late-1950s and 1960s, Dick Foss sadly died in 1995.

WILLIE FOULKE

Variously known as 'Fatty', 'Little Willie' or 'Baby', the most celebrated English keeper until Gordon Banks came along moved south from Sheffield United to join the new Chelsea set-up and win over the hearts of the 'footerin' Cockney', as he put it. His motto? 'I don't care what they call me as long as they don't call me late for dinner.' He was a huge six-foot two-inch, twenty-two-stone Yorkshireman with a comic strip personality.

SEEING DOUBLE

Chelsea have achieved 225 "doubles" (beating a team home and away in the league) since being formed in 1905. The Blues have beaten the eventual League champions twice on two occasions: Wolves in 1958/59 and Manchester United in 1993/94.

We have doubled:
Wolves 9 times
Blackpool, Fulham, Stoke 8
Birmingham 7
Arsenal, Coventry, Derby, Everton, Huddersfield, Manchester United, Newcastle, Sunderland 6
Barnsley, Hull, Ipswich, Manchester Cty, Tottenham, WBA 5
Aston Villa, Blackburn, Bolton, Leicester, Leyton Orient, Luton, Middlesbrough, Nottingham Forest, Preston, Sheffield United 4
Bradford City, Cambridge, Cardiff, Charlton, Grimsby, Leeds, Notts County, Oldham, Portsmouth, Sheffield Wednesday, Southampton 3
Bradford PA, Brighton, Burnley, Crystal Palace, Glossop, Lincoln, QPR, Swansea 2
Brentford, Burton United, Carlisle, Derby County, Gainsborough, Leeds City, Liverpool, Millwall, Northampton, Plymouth, Port Vale, Rotherham, Shrewsbury, Stockport, Swindon, Walsall, Watford, West Ham 1

The stories are legion. One suggests that during one hotel stay, Willie woke early and couldn't get back to sleep, and became the first man down for breakfast, already promptly laid out. When the rest of the team stirred half an hour later, they ventured into the dining room to discover that Willie had polished off all the breakfasts, not just his own.

His reputation for intimidating players and fans alike was well established by the time he arrived at the Bridge for the club's debut season, 1905/06. He hated his team conceding free-kicks or penalties and would argue fervently with the referee. Not that spot-kicks were much of a problem when you virtually filled the goal. He saved the first spot-kick Chelsea ever conceded. Unfortunately his parry achieved such power that it rebounded off his hapless defender McEwan and crossed the line anyway.

His third match for Chelsea was against West Brom. Their fledgling forward Haycock, unaccustomed to Willies as big as this one, muttered to his manager at half-time, knees knocking, that 'when he (Foulke) came forward to meet me and stretched out his big arms it was as though darkness had come over the area.'

A Burton United forward, having seen his second penalty saved by Little Willie, was quietly reprimanded by his skipper. 'Put it out of his reach?!' replied the frustrated spot-kicker. 'All bloody well to talk! He's got arms as long as a blooming gorilla and there ain't more than a yard between his hands and the posts on either side.'

Yet another moaned that Willie filled the goal to such an extent 'there is nothing left to aim at.' His solution to the 'problem' was never implemented. The striker wanted the outline of an average-sized keeper sketched onto Foulke's frame, so that any ball hitting outside that line counted as a goal.

To emphasize his enormity, Chelsea would place two small boys behind the goal, the germ of today's fetch-and-carry ball boys. Another trick was to enter the field of play accompanied by tiny teammate Martin Moran – always a tickler with the Chelsea crowd.

Off the field the skipper would mark out his superiority to his teammates with a silk scarf fastened by a gold pin, in contrast to the others' typically loud check caps and woollen mufflers.

One of his massive hands could pick up a heavy football and hurl it like a cricket ball. Posterity has it that some people would come to watch his mighty arcing throws and punchouts alone, oohing and aahing as if at some firework display as the missile hit the halfway line. Showbiz, it seems, was always in his heart. When he quit Chelsea for Bradford City after just one season in 1906 – having ballooned another four stones in weight – he fell on hard times. In the final years before his death from pneumonia in 1916, he could often be found touring with a fairground as one of its attractions: charging a few coppers to all-comers in a penalty prize competition.

ROGER FREESTONE

One of the best goalies never to make it at Chelsea. He signed in 1987, played six games in his first season but, despite his safe handling and dominant presence, didn't get the breaks after that. Moving on, he became a penalty-taker, scoring three for Swansea in 1995 and 1996.

PAUL FURLONG

At £2.3m Furs (Sidney Poitier to his team-mates) cost £200,000 more than previous record signing Robert Fleck, left the same time as his fellow striker, and had only marginally more impact.

The former Watford striker had a good left foot (two of them in fact) when Chelsea needed balance in a patchwork side. It may also have had something to do with the fact that assistant coach Peter Shreeves always liked left-footers like himself.

Athletic, agile but often careless and lightweight, Paul could dribble at pace past three players and beat the keeper at the near post in the manner you'd expect of an Ian Wright or Tore Andre Flo. But then he could slice the ball wide from six yards out or fail to win a single header for an entire match.

Ironically, while in the League opposing goalies could file their nails in his presence, in Europe-1994/95, Furs top-scored with three goals, including an outstanding slide-in during the spirited overturning of FC Bruges' 1–0 home lead at the Bridge.

THE LAD'S A BIT EASY TO MEASURE

Paul **FURLONG**

James **GALLON**

Alex **CHEYNE**

George **STONE**

Peter **PROUDFOOT**

David **STRIDE**

He began the move himself on the edge of the Chelsea box, ran the length of the field full-tilt and was first to Mark Stein's precipitous cross from the right.

For the most part Paul's first-team chances came when the preferred Mark Hughes was suspended or injured. It was therefore no surprise when after two seasons he was flogged off to Birmingham at a cut-price £1.5m.

HUGHIE GALLACHER

'I was almost a stranger when I moved to London, and Chelsea Football Club. I had never been too happy about the South and wondered whether I could settle down.' So, Mr Gallacher, feeling good about the move, then?

Chelsea wasn't all wine and roses for Hughie. At one stage he went on a 'milk diet', which may or may not have included the odd stout. He would also skip training when he fancied it.

Happily Hughie settled in on the pitch. One of the smallest professionals in the history of the game, Hughie's armoury of skills was big enough for Goliath. Chief sorcerer of Scotland's 1928 'Wembley Wizards' 5–1 victory, the Lanarkshire player signed two years later and set Stamford Bridge alight for just over four seasons.

He was, as someone put it 'the butt and the bane' of opposing centre-halves, no matter their physical supremacy. He possessed bewildering ball skills and the balance and control of his body produced amazing twisting, feinting runs with the ball tied to his feet. He was also a great exponent of the short pass-and-return game, and preferred to beat or place the ball past the keeper than waste energy on powering in his shots. One strike though, at Upton Park, stood out.

West Ham's big burly Barrett, who dwarfed Chelsea's diminutive striker, jostled to defend a corner and rose for the ball. Cleverly, Hughie quickly backed off him, and as Barrett's header dropped handily for him inside the area he leaned back and flashed a volley emphatically home. Sheer brilliance.

He became one of the most famous stars in the Stamford

QUICK OFF THE MARK

The fastest Chelsea goal ever recorded was scored by **Ben Whitehouse** – he notched after thirteen seconds against Blackburn Rovers in Division Two on 2 December 1907.

Of course, the one remembered with most affection was **Roberto Di Matteo**'s thunderbolt after forty-two seconds of the FA Cup final on 17 May 1997.

Not forgetting, of course, **Paul Canoville**, just on as a sub, scoring within eleven seconds of the second half kicking off at Hillsborough during the famous 4–4 draw with Sheffield Wednesday, a Milk Cup quarter-final replay. Chelsea were 0–3 down at half-time – Paul's goal inspired the most famous comeback.

Gianfranco Zola's winning goal in the 1998 European Cup Winners' Cup final against Stuttgart in Stockholm was officially timed as coming seventeen seconds after he replaced **Tore**

Bridge constellation. His return to Tyneside with Chelsea after a few months produced a biggest ever midweek crowd of more than 68,000. But the Blues team of sometimes nine internationals – 'paper conquerors' they were called – lacked a system. Still, there was always the entertainment. The last day of the 1933/34 season, when Gracie Fields entertained a Highbury crowd before handing over to the brilliant strikers of either side, was typical. Top Gunner Alex James and wee Hughie starred in a dazzling 3–3 draw with over 50,000 star-struck fans inside.

Within six months Hughie was on his way to Derby, where he enjoyed a further two good seasons before drifting into lower division football as war loomed. The fragments of Hughie's personality showed after the war, though. Back on Tyneside in 1957, he committed suicide by throwing himself in front of an express train. He was 54.

CHRIS GARLAND

The Bristolian striker, always battling for a starting place between 1971 and 1975 – the years of decline – was bought for £100,000 from Bristol City. Like others drafted by Dave Sexton into the troubled side of the time – Weller, Smethurst, Kember, Garner – with the intention of adding consistency, the blond glamour boy ultimately disappointed even though he did manage thirty-one goals in eleven matches, including two glorious finishes in the 4–0 drubbing of Leeds on the opening day of the 1972/73 season.

A subtle player who divided opinion on the terraces, Chris moved on to Leicester City for five grand less than Chelsea paid for him in February 1975.

BILL GARNER

September 1972 saw the arrival from Southend United of a Chelsea striker who in different times may have become a legend. While he wasn't blessed with the flair and technique of an Osgood (and not many are), the striker, built like a caveman with a temper to match, was most dangerous in the box, nodding in crosses or shielding the ball to bring others into play. Scorer of a memorable goal at Old Trafford September 1977, and of thirty-seven goals in 119 appearances lasting from the twilight of the Sexton era to play alongside Eddie McCreadie's young braves in 1977/78, Bill's career is summed up by one statistic. From the twenty-eight League goals he scored for Chelsea, in only twelve instances did the Blues go on to win the match.

TONY GODDEN

The West Bromwich Albion goalie was taken on loan following serious injury to the incumbent Eddie Niedzwiecki in March

1986 and two performances by the Welshman's understudy Steve Francis that saw ten goals fly into the Chelsea net. At the age of thirty, he proved a reliable handler, bold shot-stopper and all-action custodian. The signing was made permanent in the summer, and he vied with Eddie Neddie and Roger Freestone for top slot during the following season before Birmingham's speculative offer for him was accepted in July 1987.

LEN GOULDEN

In his thirties and past his best when he arrived in 1946, Len was one of the finest inside-forwards of his generation, and there was still more than a glimmer of the magic seen at the Bridge over four fitful seasons for the club.

With his cultured left foot, Len was a direct and expeditious dribbler, swaying and body-swerving in the manner of the day to throw backing off defenders into turmoil and make space for others. Playing just behind the main strikers, he would spray the ball around with slide-rule passes to feet and create openings for others to do the scoring he seemed less capable of – nineteen goals from 111 starts was not a great record.

On his retirement from playing, Len briefly became coach before moving on to manage Watford in 1952 when Ted Drake succeeded Billy Birrell as manager and engaged Albert Tennant in his stead. It was no secret that managing Chelsea had been his ambition.

DARIO GRADI

Milan-born Dario was Dave Sexton's assistant coach from January 1971 until 1974. Best known nowadays for the production line of brilliant young talent he has nurtured at Crewe over the years since then – Rob Jones, David Platt amongst them – Dario was eminently talented but apparently not considered a leader of men, hence his misfortune not to have been given a stab at the first team when Sexton and Suart moved on.

GEORGE GRAHAM

'The Stroller', a victim of The Doc's revenge for the Blackpool Incident, opened one of the epic chapters in English football by travelling across town to Arsenal (the team he would later manage) in exchange for Tommy Baldwin in September 1966, after two great seasons.

In Chelsea circles he's best remembered for his rocket header versus Milan in the Fairs Cup, the terrific volley at Crystal Palace which won Goal of the Month on BBC, and his looping header from an impossible angle in the Cup against Shrewsbury. Smooth and subtle and intelligent with it, he struck an eighty-goal partnership with pacy Barry Bridges in his fleeting stay.

Rejected publicly and explicitly by the Chelsea terraces in 1996 as a successor to Glenn Hoddle, George now manages Leeds United. Though he admits enormous respect for the likes of Franco Zola and Robbie Di Matteo, it doesn't stop him asking his players to get stuck in. In 1997, at the 'battle of Stamford Bridge', two Leeds players were sent off in the first half.

JIMMY GREAVES

29 April 1961. Greavesie's last match of the season against Nottingham Forest ended with the legendary goalscorer grabbing all four in a 4–3 pummelling and saying farewell to a distressed Stamford Bridge. He was on his way to Milan for the moolah.

He was probably Chelsea's greatest forward. English football felt the loss equally. 'We lose him to Italy with bitter regret,' wrote one wistful journalist. 'What Chelsea are going to do without him does not bear contemplation.'

Too right. As Jimmy himself observed, Drake's Ducklings, the 'all the best' team, were 'boys doing men's work'. No matter how many goals he scored at one end, the defence was sure to be proportionally generous at the other. Despite the energy and impetus of Drake's successor Tommy Doc and the ascension of tenderfoot centre-forward Bobby Tambling, relegation was inevitable within one season. But when we were struggling for survival, Jimmy was the magnet that attracted the crowds.

His speed of movement and deed was incredible from the moment he debuted at White Hart Lane, where he would later also star. With his sudden acceleration and slick, swaying runs, he would weave through defences like a snake through grass, usually to add to his own extraordinary tally of goals.

He also had uncanny anticipation. He seemed to know just where the loose ball in a penalty area would land, or where a defender would slice it, and where best to be to take the greatest advantage. There were thirty- and forty-yarders amongst his haul.

Off the back of an English club's record haul at youth level of 114 goals, his debut senior season returned thirty-two strikes, then the most ever in a Chelsea shirt.

His final campaign in 1960/61, by which time he was the tightest marked player in the game, saw forty-one scored. He also scored thirteen goals in eight England games while at the Bridge.

A sociable soul, Jimmy's best friends at Chelsea were the hard-drinking Sillett brothers. Jimmy found it hard to keep up with Peter, but had fun in trying until he later confessed to alcoholism. Still, the tightly knit squad had camaraderie.

Before he left the Bridge Jimmy was wry about his impending 'Italian job'. 'I shout out "ciao" when I enter the dressing room every morning,' he commented in 1960. 'When the team goes into a restaurant for a meal I always order spaghetti. And I've swapped my Ford for a Fiat.'

Fans joked that there were so many player-hungry Italian agents around English stadiums that you wouldn't get into the ground if they caught you with a 'Neapolitan' ice lolly.

The move turned sour swiftly. 'These English players are bandits,' moaned one Milanese club owner. 'All they're

HAT-TRICKERY

To the end of the 1997/98 season, 123 hat-tricks had been scored in first team games by fifty-seven different Chelsea players. The first was hit by **James Robertson** against Stockport County at Stamford Bridge on 30 December 1905 – revenge for defeat in the Blues' first-ever game. The most recent was **Tore Andre Flo**'s at Tottenham on 6 December 1997.

Not surprisingly, **Jimmy Greaves** remains the Stamford Bridge hat-trick king, scoring an incredible thirteen in his four years, including three five-goal hauls and three four-goal returns. **George Hilsdon**, who is the only player to have hit six in a Blues shirt, notched ten hat-tricks, including one five-goal and one four-goal triumph. **Kerry Dixon** hit eight (including four goals on three occasions), **Bobby Tambling** seven (one five-goal game, four lots of four goals) and **Peter Osgood** five (with one five-goal spree and one four-goal game).

Of the rest, **Jimmy Windridge** and **Joe Bambrick** got four hat-tricks each, whilst **Bob Whittingham**, **Bob Turnbull**, one-eyed **Bob Thomson**, **Dick Spence** and **George Mills** notched three. Another nine players have scored two hat-tricks each, and 33 more just one.

---

interested in is money.' Today, Jimmy freely admits that plunder, not professional advancement was the primary motive for his move. Ironically, as the lucrative bonus packages dissolved in a hail of fines for 'indiscipline' (things like playing for his country), so English football took the mammoth step of abolishing the £20 maximum wage. Jimmy calculated that, one season on, he would have been better off if he'd stayed with Chelsea, always one of the top payers.

When he became available, contrary to contemporary reports that Jimmy refused the Blues' offer, Chelsea dispatched secretary

The 1960/61 season saw the most hat-tricks in one season – six, all scored by **Greaves**. **Hilsdon** scored five in 1907/08.

There has been just the one six-goal return, seven five-goal hauls (**Greaves** three times, **Tambling**, **Osgood**, **Hilsdon** and **Gordon Durie** once each) and nineteen four-goal sprees, the most recent by **Luca Vialli** at Barnsley in August 1997.

Only one game has seen hat-tricks by two different Chelsea players – the 1971 European Cup Winners' Cup match against Jeunesse Hautcharage at the Bridge, which ended 13–0. **Osgood** and **Tommy Baldwin** were the deadly duo.

David Speedie reserved his only hat-trick for Chelsea for the 1986 Full Members' Cup Final against Manchester City – the first Wembley trio since **Geoff Hurst** twenty years before. **Luca Vialli** scored the Blues' third European hat-trick against Tromsø in November 1997.

Three players have scored hat-tricks for Chelsea and been on the losing side: **Hilsdon** against Bury in December 1907 (lost 3–4); **Joe Bambrick** against Stoke in September 1935 (3–5); and **Seamus O'Connell** in the famous 5–6 defeat by Manchester United, October 1954. **Jimmy Argue** scored three in a 5–5 draw with Bolton in October 1937.

John Battersby under instructions to underbid Spurs' Billy Nicholson. The Cockerels brought him back for a pound under £100,000, ten grand more than we got from AC Milan for him.

Jimmy's Spurs and West Ham career included beating his first club in the 1967 FA Cup Final against us, though he only scored four times against us in ten years. (He never fancied facing Chopper Harris.) Still, he became England's third top scorer with forty-four goals from fifty-seven appearances.

Never forget that he was a Chelsea player at his peak. Never forget that perhaps the all-time great English goalscorer learned his trade with and starred for Chelsea FC. Jimmy doesn't.

'Those swerves,' a writer of the day eulogized, 'those sudden bursts, those side-steps, that sleight of foot in front of goal, those chances made and taken when none would exist for anyone but him; above all, that transcendent, impish confidence. Where are we to find a player like him?'

Chelsea never really have.

RON GREENWOOD

Ron is one of an impressive number of former Chelsea players to enjoy the most coveted of managerial honours for an Englishman – managing his national side. For such a thoughtful and respected individual within the game, the amiable Lancastrian had a mixed career with the Blues.

He first arrived to play wartime football, rubbing shoulders with nearby-billeted guests at Stamford Bridge including later Mancunian legends, Matt Busby and Joe Mercer. Another guest, Wolves' international defender John Harris became the expensive signing (£35,000 in August 1945) and future captain who barred Ron's route to a place in the Chelsea team.

So, once demobbed, the cultured centre-half settled for a career at Bradford Park Avenue where his services were more regularly to be employed than at Chelsea. A few years later, an impressive spell at Brentford rekindled a neighbourly interest and Ted Drake swooped to add experience to his increasingly able squad, nabbing back the League veteran, by then just a matter of weeks short of his thirty-first birthday, in the autumn of 1952.

Ron still had to fight for a starting place – the most appearances he made were thirty-three in the season before the Championship was won. And in that triumphant 1954/45 campaign Ron found himself moving on again while the country was still in the grip of winter. In February 1955 Ron left for Fulham, a well-worn route over the years.

ENGLAND MANAGERS WHO PLAYED FOR CHELSEA

Walter Winterbottom 1946–62
Joe Mercer (caretaker) 1974
Ron Greenwood 1977–82
Terry Venables (coach) 1994–1996
Glenn Hoddle 1996–

In the 1970s Ron's agile football brain was applied to putting the England team back on track after the upheaval of the Revie years. And, curiously, it was Ron who in 1978 introduced Chelsea's next England manager to the Lancaster Gate set-up as an Under-21 coach: Terry Venables.

FRODE GRODAS

'Growbag' to his detractors, the six-foot two-inch Robin Williams doppelganger from Norway arrived as a temp but quickly wrote his name into the pantheon of Chelsea heroes in the Stamford Bridge boardroom.

It seemed a distant prospect on the night of his competitive debut between the Stamford Bridge sticks in the Coca-Cola Cup, when he was beaten from distance by a wicked shot as Blackpool upset the odds and ran out 3–1 winners. Indeed, the easy-going Scandinavian, number one choice for his country for the past two years, and captain too, was supposed to be 'just passing through' on his way to Sturm Graz from Lillestrom. The deal with the Austrians would come to fruition at the end of the year, but goal-keeping coach Eddie Niedzwiecki saw enough in a Lillestrom performance in September 1996 to make him work hard to convince the thirty-one-year-old that the Kings Road was the place to while away the autumn.

The catalyst for the move was the injury to Dmitri Kharine. When, shortly after the Blackpool game, the next incumbent, Kevin Hitchcock, damaged an elbow, Frode was thrown in at the deep end. His rapid acclimatization to the physical pressures of the Premiership underscored a permanent contract and an FA Cup run. And it was in the Cup competition that Frode truly showed his quality.

The semi-final against Wimbledon at Highbury was always likely to be the greatest test. Frode's new-found confidence, domination of the box, all-round sureness and determination not to be intimidated formed the foundation of one of Chelsea's smoothest Cup final arrivals.

It was only right that a man so highly rated on the international stage should also help raise the silverware in the most cosmopolitan of Wembley finals.

His brave – and crucial – rush out to close down the encroaching Boro forward Vickers ensured a stress-free conclusion to a glorious day. Frode wore a fan's Viking helmet with pride as the celebrations stretched on at Wembley and indulged enthusiastically in the first of the three link-handed run and slides that have become a Chelsea trademark.

The arrival of another top-grade keeper in Ed de Goey and the recovery of his Russian rival restricted Frode to virtually no football in Rudi's last season, and he was allowed to go to Tottenham for a small fee, still Norway's number one.

RUUD GULLIT

Can you remember what your first thoughts were when you heard Rudi was coming to Stamford Bridge? Ecstasy? Trepidation? Disbelief? And how about when he first shook his locks on the pitch, then sprayed the ball around and toyed with it 'like a man amongst children' as his manager put it?

The Dutchman, born Rudi Dil in Amsterdam, 1962, whose career took in Haarlem, Feyenoord, PSV Eindhoven, Milan and

SQUAD SIZE

As the list below shows, it is almost – almost – a rule of thumb that Chelsea do best when not employing large numbers of players in a season. That may all have changed over the past couple of years with the greater use of substitutes being sanctioned. Hence, our most successful seasons before 1996 all saw twenty players or less used.

However, the two seasons 1996–98 have arguably been the club's most successful ever, with Chelsea holding three trophies for three glorious days (until Arsenal won the 1998 FA Cup) and recording the first trophy double in our history – making the most of a sizeable squad.

Fewest players used

1969/70	19 (won FA Cup, third in league)
1926/27	20 (fourth in Division Two, sixth round of FA Cup)
1954/55	20 (League Champions)
1968/69	20 (fifth in League, sixth round of FA Cup)
1970/71	20 (won European Cup Winners' Cup, sixth in league)
1976/77	20 (second in Division Two)
1983/84	20 (Division Two Champions)
1989/90	20 (fifth in League, won ZDS Cup)

Most players used

1909/10	34 (nineteenth in league and relegated)
1992/93	32 (eleventh in league, quarter-final League Cup)
1978/79	31 (bottom of Division One)
1996/97	31 (FA Cup winners, sixth in Premiership)
1997/98	30 (European Cup Winners' Cup winners, League Cup winners, fourth in Premiership)

Sampdoria (from whom Chelsea hired him on a free transfer), had been there, done that before he arrived for his latest challenge at a crumbly Stamford Bridge. He made his debut as an 18-year-old sweeper in the Dutch international side in 1981, coming on for his great friend Frank Rijkaard, and went on to become perhaps the best player of his generation. He starred in Feyenoord's League and Cup 'double' in 1984, graced the European stage with Eindhoven and, now converted to attack where his pace and guile were most lethal, moved to Milan for a record £6m in 1987, winning both European and World Footballer of the Year titles that year. As the famous trio of Gullit, Van Basten and Rijkaard began to revolutionize Italian football, he played a large part in Milan's Scudetto victory of 1988 and Holland's barnstorming of the European Championship the same year.

The pinnacle of Milan club success was reached in 1989 when two-goal Rudi shone in the 4–0 European Cup Final demolition of 1989 against Dan Petrescu and Steaua Bucharest, a performance often described as among the most complete in football history. A knee injury curtailed his later career at the San Siro, but still the World Club Championship and Super Cup brought him medals in 1990.

Now using his fame and status to expound his views on race, apartheid and other matters, Rudi had become more than just a footballer when he moved to Sampdoria in 1993. By the time he arrived in SW6 he was a living legend. It was an extraordinary Chelsea signing. Perhaps the shrewdest ever.

And yet, when for the first time in living memory the name Chelsea was news the world over for signing the charismatic, controversial Netherlander, the insider's tip was, 'His legs have gone, haven't they. All those knee injuries and operations. Where will he be on a cold winter's night on Tyneside with those creaking joints?' We laughed at such suggestions during that first season, especially when he scored from close range and ran the show at St James' Park in the FA Cup match third round replay of January 1996, the one dramatically concluded by Eddie Newton's penalty shootout winner. Rudi had fitness problems that first season, but nothing like people predicted.

His impact swiftly overturned the pre-season rumours. His genuinely dazzling skills on the ball – those teasing cat-and-mouse games he played with the likes of Dicks and Perry, the ghosting runs into space, the sheer dread he induced in opposing fans and players when he bore down on defences in full flow, his locks swaying, legs eating up ground, was unparalleled.

Lest we forget, Rudi gave us a psychological edge by his awesome presence whenever he appeared on the pitch in those first two seasons. Managers like Ferguson and Redknapp, O'Neill and Graham were almost lavish in their praise of 'Big Bird', citing his absence or presence on the team sheet as factors in their feeelings about how the game would go. He was that influential.

His shock departure was a messy business. The negotiations... the wage demands... the lack of communication... conspiracy... aloofness... tactical errors... take your pick.

After Hoddle's persistence with 3–5–2, Rudi produced a new rigid tactical dogma: 4–4–2. Even if the personnel weren't available, 4–4–2 it was. Towards the end of his tenure, and especially in the pivotal games against Leeds United, West Ham United and Arsenal in the winter of 1997/98, this inflexibility appeared to cost his team points, as it had his predecessor.

At the same time the much-vaunted squad rotation system – really only applied to the attack – appeared to militate against the kind of bonding between regular partners that occurs as a season progresses. Form players like Flo and Vialli would not always book their next place with a goalscoring performance.

And Rudi would never explain his team selections to anyone else.

His successor was obvious and swiftly appointed. The first

act of Gianluca Vialli, brunt of some of Ruud's tough team selections, was to overturn the deficit inflicted by Arsenal in the Coca-Cola semi-final first leg when Rudi miscalculated badly and played his worst-ever game for Chelsea. Victory was fought for and won 3–1 on a night high on emotion and adrenalin.

He was perhaps the greatest player ever to wear a Chelsea shirt and, potentially, one of our finest managers. Whatever the rights and wrongs of his dismissal, you don't lose a man of his stature without missing him.

GARETH HALL

'G', to the players, kept right-back rival Clarke out of the Chelsea starting line-up. A combative defender who could pass a bit but was too often found wanting in his decision-making and pace, his finest moment came in the February 1990 scrap at home to Manchester United. Gareth grabbed the sole goal – a rarity – and our victory came close to ending Reds manager Ferguson's tenure at Old Trafford.

In his time G earned nine Welsh caps, a 1989 Second Division Promotion medal and a ZDS Full Members' Cup winner's medal the following year.

Moody, with a nice line in wry humour, when asked by the Chelsea matchday magazine what song Chelsea should run out to, he cheekily suggested: 'Road To Nowhere, by Talking Heads'. Typically, he was furious when it was printed.

A great pal of David Lee and Jason Cundy, the U2-loving golfer moved on to Sunderland in 1996. Hopefully the Mackems knew how to prepare his favourite pre-match meal: cheese omelette.

MICK HARFORD

The 'dirtiest ever player' according to one who marked him: Michael Duberry. With his wine bar in Luton, Mick arrived as a stop-gap in 1992 and scored nine league goals in twenty-eight games before injury curtailed his towering presence in our attack.

TOMMY HARMER

Perhaps our skinniest-ever player. Often decribed as an under-achiever, Tommy played his last league game in a thirteen-year career against the team that gave him his first break, and at the same ground too. And in that match in 1964 at White Hart Lane he created two goals for Bobby Tambling, strolled around and gestured 'like a tiny, mobile signal box', as Brian Glanville observed, chipped, ghosted and generally ran the show. Just the reasons the skilful midfielder had been hired in the first place.

He was all left. Having scored 'off his hickory' at Sunderland in that vital promotion-chasing game at the end of the 1962/63 season, he starred in the decisive 7–0 thrashing of Portsmouth that ushered in one of the most successful spells in the top flight. Playing for Pompey that day was a young Bobby Campbell, later to manage Chelsea. Asked whether he marked his opposite number during the game years later, Bobby laughed: 'Well, I was *out* there!'

ALLAN HARRIS

Allan, least celebrated of all the Chelsea Harrises, was the most successful in management, following his old Chelsea spar Terry Venables from club to club as assistant as far as Barcelona. His playing career was less substantial. Sold to QPR, he was brought back in time for the 1967 Cup Final defeat by Spurs. Venners, of course, played for the winning side just behind Greavesie.

JOHN HARRIS

Sterling servant John made nearly 500 appearances (if you include his wartime turnouts) and was skipper for a considerable number of those games. Though his lack of great height some-times made him fallible in the air, and put paid to a lengthy inter-national service, he was well-built and athletic with plenty of defensive nous whether at centre-half or right-back. He was an accurate short-range passer, sharp tidy tackler with good anticipation that made up for a lack of genuine pace. Such was his contribution leading up to our title win in 1955 he was awarded a Championship winner's medal as '12th' man (there were no subs in those days).

RON HARRIS

Where quantity is concerned, 'Chopper' was the most successful Chelsea skipper of all time until Dennis Wise enjoyed his spell beginning in 1997. (Roy Bentley must be counted as top man in terms of quality, since he's the only Chelsea skipper to have lifted the Championship to date.) The Hackney boy lifted the then little-regarded League Cup in 1965, the FA Cup in 1970 and the Cup Winners' Cup a year later.

Ron served the Blues in more games than any other player, turning professional in November 1961. He made his League debut within three months, and captained England Youth to victory in the 'Little World Cup' final eighteen months later.

Given the reputation he has in posterity, it is unthinkable that he might have performed the same feat at senior international level. For Ron is, and always will be 'Chopper' Harris, in and out of trouble like a dog at a fair. Like his World War Two namesake 'Bomber', the commander who scorched and flattened Dresden and elsewhere, Chopper will always be known for the effectiveness of his talent for destruction rather than the fact that he led Chelsea to two Cup victories and a third place in 1970. It's hard now to picture him as the England schoolboy cricketer he was!

Like some android programmed to defend and destroy, he appeared entirely without sentiment in regard to his craft. Before the 1972 League Cup Final tussle with Stoke City and their ageing maestro George Eastham, manager Dave Sexton sought out his skipper. 'Ronnie,' he said, 'could you kick an old man?' 'Yes,' asserted Chopper, promptly. 'Course I can.' What he couldn't do was stop him running the show, and Stoke ran out

BLUES BROTHERS

Three sets of brothers have played for Chelsea: **Peter** and **John Sillett**; **Ron** and **Allan Harris**; and **Ray** and **Graham Wilkins**. Both **Les Allen** and his son **Clive** have pulled on the blue shirt, and **David Calderhead jnr.** spent three seasons under the management of his father, **David** in the 1930s.

One-time Chelsea goalkeeper **Harry Medhurst** became head trainer in 1960 and physio in 1973; he was succeeded in both of the latter duties by his son **Norman**, who was also associated with the England set-up.

2–1 winners. Perhaps there was the lingering memory of a previous encounter with a vintage Stoke favourite, Stanley Matthews. Ron marked Sir Stan, then an incredible *half century* old, at Stamford Bridge in one of his final games in the mid-1960s, and for once the sympathies of the home crowd were not with his combine-harvesting approach. In fact, whenever Ron got close to the 'King Of Football', boos and hisses of admonition could be heard on the terraces. He may have been happy to kick an old man but his fans weren't prepared to let him.

The training matches played in the car park space at the Bridge were another matter. Chopper's 'welcome' challenges were legendary. Whacking a new boy was his way of establishing seniority. Keith Weller apparently wound Ronnie up with some comments about his wife, which was inadvisable, and Ron wasn't too concerned if his victim missed a few days' training as a result of injuries inflicted. Ron played at Chelsea for eighteen years, appearing in more games – 655 – than any other Blue, though towards the end of his career his inadequacies in the areas of creativity and pace were exposed when he was asked to play full-back.

'I like to think that apart from being a bit of a butcher I've something else to offer,' he once said. Well, yes, he was a decent organizer. A reasonable passer over fifteen yards too. And, despite not being the tallest centre-back, he could put a striker off in any challenge. No doubt about it, there were fewer more effective in 'one-on-ones'. When the 1963/64 FA Cup third round replay finished 2–0 to Chelsea he'd managed a shut-out against the prolific Jimmy Greaves in five consecutive games – surely some sort of record.

Apart from the famous exception of George Best – witness the footage of Chopper having two 'goes' at Best on the way to one of his best-ever goals – it's hard to think of any forward who regularly got the better of Ron. And most were simply scared of him.

Three tosses of the coin in Europe determined the greater part of his early captaincy. In the 1965/66 Fairs Cup campaign, Chelsea faced the mighty AC Milan in the third round; 1–2 away, 2–1 at home brought deadlock. A toss of the coin decided where the play-off would be, and the Italian skipper won. The game and extra-time concluded with both sides locked at 1–1, so the tie went to the toss of a coin. Ron called 'heads', and won. It wasn't exactly a hat-trick, but just as effective.

Then three seasons later in the same competition DWS of Amsterdam completed a two-leg shutout, gambling on the fifty-fifty outcome of a toss-up. Ron called wrongly, allowing the Netherlanders to progress. The coin, disconcertingly, was a Dutch guilder.

Coins were never much of a problem after that for Ron. He quit Chelsea to go on a free transfer to Brentford in 1980 and then became general manager of Aldershot four years later. Chopper invested his money wisely in a run-down golf club and became a millionaire through its subsequent sale. Championship winner Roy Bentley does his book-keeping, but close contact with the club in the 1980s was never likely after a series of hatchet jobs on successive squads in the tabloids. Nevertheless, Ron has returned every now and then, and travelled with Chelsea fans to see Gianfranco Zola end twenty-seven years of lucrative dinner party speeches with the goal that meant Chelsea had won the European Cup Winners' Cup for a second time.

Today, Chopper sees a lot of himself in Frank Sinclair. Except, he's fond of saying, when Frank makes a tackle the victim normally gets up, whereas 'when I did it, they never.' Nice.

MIKE HARRISON

Powerfully built left-flanker who played sixty-one games for Chelsea with a return of eight goals, and who quit us after relegation in 1962. A good winger, direct and skilful, his best days came after becoming part of the free-scoring Blackburn side of 1962–64, averaging a goal every four games. Why didn't he do it for us?

TONY HATELEY

Useless feet, but a brilliant head. His finest moment came in scoring the winner in the FA Cup semi-final of 1967 at Villa Park against Leeds. But nine goals in thirty-two matches wasn't enough and Tommy Doc wanted to get rid of him.

Bill Shankly is often credited with responding to The Doc's announcement that '£100,000 wouldn't buy Tony Hateley' with the statement, 'Aye, Tom, and I'm one of the hundred thousand!'. However, Shanks did fork out £95,000.

It took Tony (father of Mark) three months to score for Liverpool after his move there in July 1967, but at the other end he managed one of the all-time great own goals after a matter of weeks.

DAVID HAY

Could have been a contender. David, Celtic's skipper and inspiration, arrived for a record fee (£225,000) on the back of the reputation he had established in the 1974 World Cup with Scotland.

But he took time to settle into a very young and inexperienced side and had a body that he could injure in his sleep. In the promotion year, 1976/77, David and his central defensive partner Steve Wicks were simply outstanding. There was also one delicious moment when he nearly scored a seventy-yard goal, picking the ball up in his own half, whacking it into space and chasing onto it with a pack of opposition haring after him. Injuries curtailed his Chelsea career drastically and robbed us of an inspirational figure. Quite simply he was hardly ever there after that promotion season. And in 1978, following surgeons' advice that he had a detached retina in one eye, he had to retire from playing. David was always highly rated as a bloke, too. He was manager of Celtic when they met Nottingham Forest in the European Cup in 1980. Before the game he knocked on the opposition dressing-room door and asked to come in, simply to seek out and shake the hand of an old Chelsea teammate, Kenny Swain.

MICKEY HAZARD

The best player of his generation in Europe – according to himself. He was patenter of the 'Newton' swivel turn while Eddie was still in our kids' team, and despite a passion that burned in his breast for chips, was always wiry and impressive in cross-countries. Like Duncan McKenzie before him, he was self-evidently the best player in the team, popular with the fans, but unable to apply that prowess for ninety minutes. His last game was against QPR under Bobby Campbell. He was subbed at half-time following a dismal team display lacking in heart. More famously, this was the moment when 'The Meat' (as Campbell was known) threw one of his regular rages during the interval, kicked out, hitting a table and nearly breaking his leg. It was all his players could do to stifle the giggles. Mickey was the last in a spate of ex-Spurs players arriving at the Bridge, beginning with Mark Falco and ending with Graham Roberts. He moved on to several clubs, notably Swindon.

THE LAD'S A BIT TOUGH

James **ARGUE**

William **BRAWN**

Augustus **HARDING**

Tommy **HARMER**

Mickey **HAZARD**

Joe **PAYNE**

Fred **ROUSE**

Buchanan **SHARP**

James **SHARP**

Craig **BURLEY**

James **SMART**

GEORGE HILSDON

That weather-vane atop the East Stand – you *do* know who it represents, don't you? 'Gatling-Gun George', that's who. Manager Jackie Robertson went to watch a colleague of George's in the West Ham reserves and, deciding he wasn't worth 'a handfu' o' bawbees', turned his attention to the 'finest young inside-left I've seen for years. I'll tell ye what,' he added, positively, 'he's our centre-forward next season.' Jackie's words were his deed and George was signed in May 1906.

A rare Cockney boy in a side (and a League in fact) dominated by the Caledonian connection, the legendary striker assumed the number nine shirt from the prolific Frank Pearson during the 1906/07 season – to some degree of consternation on the terraces before his debut, it's said. Any doubts about the unassuming twenty-year-old East Ender were soon allayed. His record debut haul – no less than five – still stands as an all-comers record. 9–2 was the final score in the Division Two 'clash' with Glossop on that scorching hot day, 1 September 1906, and George even had a hand in all the ones he didn't get himself.

Within two months he was representing the English League in its first international match against their Irish counterparts, and grabbed a hat-trick as well as winning plaudits for the sharpness and brilliance of his play. His style was in the mould that would last in England for decades: a strong, mobile, fleet-footed target man with a shrewd sense of when to bring his wingers into play and where to run for the 'killer' forward pass.

Less commonplace was his skill in 'drifting' away from markers to find space for himself. But the main virtue, recorded for posterity in his nickname, was an ability to fire in thunderous shots from either foot with a range-finder that regularly extended beyond thirty yards. From the spot he was just as ferocious. His biggest haul was six goals in a thrashing of Worksop.

His international career was crammed into 1907 and 1908 against the likes of Austria, Hungary and Belgium and by 1912 he'd burned himself out for Chelsea (on and off the pitch, it seems), crossing town to West Ham for a fresh challenge and a new set of nightspots. He was the first Chelsea player to top 100 goals, but, in the words of Chelsea officials, 'didn't husband vitality and strength'. In other words, he drank to excess and stayed out late. But his reputation was built at Stamford Bridge even if his popularity extended way beyond SW6.

In that respect, like Greaves, Osgood and Dixon to follow, he was a centre-forward 'Made In Chelsea' that other fans learned to respect, even to cherish. The Great War intervened as it did in so many careers, though, and George – although held back till the final 'great push' – was gassed at Arras. He barely recovered from the effects of the noxious mustard gas, racked by terrible pain in his legs. His football career was over, and he died in 1941 at the age of fifty-six.

The story of the vane is also rather melancholy. The one that creaks in the wind above the East Stand is a replica. The weather-beaten original was sent to a specialist ironworks in the Midlands for expensive repairs some time in the late 1960s or early 1970s. Seemingly the work was never done, or the bill never paid, for when Chelsea officials next stumbled across it, poor George was rusting in the now bankrupt yard's scrap piles. Using the irreparable vane as a guide, a new vane was made, still in the mould of old 'Gatling Gun'.

MARVIN HINTON

Manager Tommy Doc loved him. He was our first-ever sweeper, though not in the Beckenbauer mould. He was more of a 'last man' than a thrusting forward-moving *libero*, making his bow as understudy for the injured centre-back John Mortimore in September 1963. It was such sturdiness that also allowed him to be equally at home as right full-back. Some rated him the best passer in the Chelsea side of the mid-1960s with those precision side-footers over thirty yards. Only the form of Everton's Brian Labone and Jack Charlton of Leeds kept him out of Alf Ramsey's final 1966 World Cup squad; he made the early forty.

Marvin epitomized cool. Once, during a crucial European tie, he came off the bench and strolled on still wearing a watch. Ossie alerted him to the fact and noted 'he fancied it didn't he!'

In the early years, at either centre- or right-back, he showed plenty of power to go with the polish and was ear-marked as a future international. Indirectly, he was responsible for the departure of Chelsea's mid-1960s skipper Terry Venables too. The incident occurred in the tumultuous Fairs Cup decider against Roma in 1966. Chelsea were defending a 4–1 home advantage, and Tommy Docherty decided to preserve the successful flat four from that leg. Terry and the team had other ideas, however, and he encouraged Marvin to ignore the manager and play sweeper when he saw fit. Chelsea drew 0–0 in appallingly intimidating crowd circumstances, progressed to the semi, and drew the wrath of the Doc, who was still furious about the Blackpool Incident. It wasn't principally directed at the laid-back Marvin, who was once bewildered to be given a friendly love-bite by the high-spirited manager and told, 'Explain that to your wife', but at Venners, who was soon off.

Marvin never really established his first-choice status, and although he figured in great finals like the 1970 FA Cup and 1971 Cup Winners' Cup wins as a sub, was probably not enough of a grafter to please Dave Sexton.

During Eddie McCreadie's rule in 1976, with 344 games in thirteen years behind him, Marv moved to Barnet, eventually drifting out of football, leaving the impression that a pushier personality may well have exploited his natural talent more. He went into mini-cabbing and was unfortunately involved in a serious car accident, the after-effects of which still debilitate him.

KEVIN HITCHCOCK

In the 1990s, a period of great renovation, few of the old fixtures and fittings at Stamford Bridge survived. Thankfully, one long-suffering stalwart remained loyal despite frequent knock-backs in the shape of injury and non-selection and, given the recent trouble in that area, it was lucky he was a goalkeeper.

Hitchy is one of those players every club loves to have: not simply an adept performer in his own right, but a patient understudy.

Hitchy, who could be forgiven for mulling over the qualification as an electrician at various stages of his Chelsea career, is the kind of player who is at his best when he has something to prove. Once established, the edge can sometimes go out of his play, and he did have a worrying habit of crocking his own players at one stage, including the fracture Eddie Newton suffered in the collision during the West Ham match, and his kicking was surprisingly poor for someone of his professionalism. Still, by 1998 the thirty-five-year-old had been a Chelsea professional for ten years and had rarely let anyone down.

It might have been so much longer too: as a young East London schoolboy he was rejected from the Bridge before trainee stage and only returned via Barking, Forest and Mansfield as manager Bobby Campbell's first signing.

It was £250,000 well spent, as the six-footer stepped straight into the first team as a replacement for the sadly retired Eddie Niedzwiecki. Unfortunately, the first of a series of injuries the following term prompted the purchase of the first of several rivals Hitchy has seen come and go, Dave Beasant.

A brilliant shot-stopper, regular penalty shootout hero and morale-boosting dressing-room presence, Hitchy won his 1997 FA Cup winners' medal, inevitably occupying the bench for the duration, and joined in the celebrations at the end with the 100-percent involvement he always felt. Likewise the Coca-Cola and Cup Winners' Cup finals the following year, when towards the end of the season he was in the bizarre position of being understudy to Ed de Goey in the knockout competitions and old spar Dmitri Kharine in the League.

When he does eventually quit the Bridge to spend more time with his beloved golf clubs, he'll leave a hole that'll be hard to plug.

GLENN HODDLE

The appointment of Chelsea's first player-manager since Jackie Robinson, marked the beginning of a new era. No Bridge boss since Ted Drake arrived with the same reputation as a been-there-done-that player. Neither, since the early 1950s, was anyone able to embark on such a modernization of the club's footballing side. Yet, whereas the hallmarks of Drake's Ducklings would be hard graft and commitment, Glenn's ethos was all about style and professionalism. The same time the ex-Spur brought the club kicking and screaming into the late-twentieth century with radical new ideas on diet, lifestyle, training, physiotherapy and media management.

His transformation of the club in three years was so convincing that he was chosen as Terry Venables' successor as England manager.

Glenn arrived from Swindon with most of his managerial

THE LAD'S A BIT OF A WRITER

Gianfranco 'Emile' **ZOLA**

Alan 'Charles' **DICKENS**

John 'Robert' **BROWNING**

Ronald 'Walter' **GREENWOOD**

Harold 'Arthur' **MILLER**

Marshall 'Ian' **MCEWAN**

John 'JB' **PRIESTLEY**

Colin 'George Bernard' **SHAW**

Alexander 'Edmund' **WHITE**

Reginald 'Tennessee' **WILLIAMS**

Frank 'Virginia' **WOLFF**

John 'Colin' **MCINNES**

James 'EP' **THOMPSON**

David 'Margaret' **MITCHELL**

ideas fully formed. Some of them, particularly his credo to play the beautiful game at all cost, even when you're in the bottom three at your first Christmas, were sorely tested. Most, though, have remained intact since the transition to international gaffer.

With his former Tottenham boss Peter Shreeves arriving as assistant (John Gorman wouldn't leave Swindon), training changed from hard physical effort to work on touch and technique, combined with warm-downs and massage. The Harlington training ground metamorphosed from Edwardian school gym to a decent locker room with state-of-the-art treatment machines. Diet was strictly moderated – previously players had picked up fast food or sarnies on the way home.

'Everything became very professional after Glenn's arrival,' says veteran keeper Kevin Hitchcock. 'From training kit right the way through to the type of balls we would use to prepare for a match. If he found out Liverpool, say, used Tango balls then that is what we would use all week before we played them. It all changed from the time he took over and it has carried on since then.'

And on the pitch Glenn's mantra – master the ball or the ball masters you – was translated into possession football. Glenn led by example, slipping in sublimely as sweeper in a back three, pinging fantastic fifty-yard balls to his forwards' feet.

While some of his purchases were poor, others, such as his signing of Mark Hughes and Dan Petrescu, were visionary.

Avoiding momentary brushes with relegation, Glenn managed to take a reasonable side to the FA Cup Final in his first year and the semi-final of the Cup Winners' Cup in his second. 'To tell you the truth, I didn't really enjoy the football of the first two seasons, apart from, of course, the cup runs,' he said later. 'The third year for me was the one. We began to play football you haven't seen at Chelsea for many a year, since before I came.'

Home-grown players fared variably under Glenn. John Spencer looks back now on his rejection of the roles Glenn designated for him as churlish, since he later recognizes that the manager was right. Dennis Wise, one of the few players to contradict the boss's approach when relegation threatened, said as soon as the FA confirmed Glenn's appointment as England manager that he'd won his last international cap. Others, like cultured sweeper David Lee, who saw first Glenn, then Rudi, then Frank Leboeuf standing in the way of a first-team place, might have expected to benefit more from the Hoddle regime than he did.

The catalyst for that quantum leap was the arrival of Ruud Gullit, personally convinced of the challenge awaiting him at Stamford Bridge by Glenn himself. It was a magical move, and although once again the season ended in FA Cup semi-final sorrow, at the hands of Manchester United, the platform for long-term success was beginning to be built on at last.

Hod was obstinate in his aims. When the chairman's plans involved a reduction of pitch size to accommodate a larger development, the manager put his foot down, arguing successfully for a retention of the larger playing surface that would allow his team's fluent football to expand. And at the peak of our European campaign, when an extensive injury list reduced his options beyond acceptability, he urged the club to free up some money to invest in players.

At the same time, through Hod's stewardship Chelsea was beginning to acquire a national and international reputation for brilliant attacking football and sound husbandry. These were the elements that enabled Ruud Gullit to sign Gianfranco Zola, Robbie Di Matteo, Luca Vialli, Frank Leboeuf, Tore Andre Flo, Celestine Babayaro and the returning Graeme Le Saux, and Luca in turn to hire Brian Laudrup, Marcel Desailly and Pierluigi Casiraghi.

Glenn came and went like some guardian angel. He was careful to leave on good terms, stating for the record that 'there is no other job I would have left Chelsea for' – even managing Spurs. Glenn made mistakes in tactics, dogmatically attached to the 3–5–2 formation that he also imposed on England. He also made some bad buys – Andy Dow, Paul Furlong, Anthony Barness – and he never managed to defeat Coventry in any game!

As it is, the Chelsea fans had already decided on a successor – and it wasn't the rumoured old boy George Graham. And in the last match of the campaign, another defeat by Blackburn, we anointed the chosen one, Ruud Gullit.

JOHN HOLLINS

How did this cherub-faced midfielder not win more England caps? In October 1964 the latest in a long line of 'new Duncan Edwardses' became youngest ever League captain at eighteen years and three months, playing fifty-two games in his second season. The same year he broke into the England Under-23 side, impressing enough against the Austrians to challenge for the senior slot of Mullery, Peters and Stiles. No mean feat for a teenager.

'This was Tommy Docherty's Chelsea, packed with players convinced that the future was theirs, and Hollins was playing a major role in securing converts to that conviction,' reminisced the anonymous contributor to 1974's *Book Of Football*.

Doc loved Holly. He had skill, of course, but he was a

THE LAD'S A BIT CONSISTENT

Long-time servant **John Hollins** still holds the record for the most consecutive appearances in the Chelsea first team. He played 167 times in a row between 14 August 1971 and 25 September 1974. He was thus ever-present for over three years in 135 league matches, ten FA Cup games, eighteen League Cup ties and four European Cup Winners' Cup matches.

---

grafter, and Doc liked that in a player. He had urgency too. The bursts from midfield and conversions of defence to attack were hallmarks of his play, not to mention the blistering shots and saving tackles.

The first time he was made skipper for Chelsea was against his goalie brother Dave (who incidentally played for Wales, not England) of Newcastle. Both were given the honour that day.

Once he'd beefed up a little and avoided the tendency to flag late in a game Holly was formidable.

It was under Dave Sexton that Holly's star was really ascendant though. His leather-lunged enthusiasm fired Chelsea through many a game when others weren't up for it. And he'll always be remembered for that incredible 'goal of the decade' in 1970 when, gathering up a ball on the edge of the Arsenal box he fired a looping shot over keeper Bob Wilson, reacted quickest to the rebound off the bar, and drove in from just inside the area. Sensational. He was there for all the major trophies won and lost, and survived longer than most of his 1960s colleagues when turmoil set in around 1973. Holly needed a fresh challenge, however, and quit in 1975.

Even into his dotage Holly was a useful squad member on and off the pitch. In 1983/84, following spells at QPR and Arsenal he returned as player-coach under John Neal and could still keep out younger players like Nutton and push Joey Jones over to the left flank.

When the manager's health took a dive, Ken Bates offered the job to Holly, who took Ernie Walley as his assistant. Surprisingly it was an unmitigated disaster. As beloved stars like Pat Nevin were sidelined and Walley's sometimes unfathomable 'invisible ball' coaching techniques went down like all-too notice-able lead balloons, the crowd turned against their former hero. The days of flare-propelled fifth-place finishes were long gone and the press stirred up ill-feeling.

At one stage some elements in the Shed began a cruel chant of 'Johnny Hollins – UB40'. In spring 1988 a plodding Chelsea side went four months without a win and by March Johnny was out on his ear, an embittered man.

Batesy always maintained that if Holly's wife had picked the team for him he'd have stayed as manager a lot longer than he did. (Maybe she fancied Pat Nevin whereas Holly clearly didn't.)

Holly returned to QPR, occupying various coaching and scouting roles ever since.

PETER HOUSEMAN

'Chelsea's chess expert', according to a report in 1974. The sur-prise was that he ever found a partner among that carefree squad.

A left-sided striker and sometime left-back or midfielder whose early brilliance at youth and Under-23 level for England, and consistency as a supplier to goalscorers like Tambling, Ossie, Hutch,was only partially recognized by Chelsea fans. For ten years between 1964 and 1974/75 he was the boo boy. In part it was because of his languid style and propensity to slice a seven iron cross behind the goal from an advantageous position. In part it was because of the rumours as to who wanted to come and play for Chelsea in that position, George Best for example.

And in part it was down to his Tudor hairstyle and anachronistic dress sense. He didn't look like a Chelsea swinger, he looked like a pet shop owner. Whatever, the barrage of abuse from his own fans could be alarming. He got his revenge one night though. The match at the Bridge was the slaughter of Jeunesse Hautcharage. Harangued as usual, he suddenly provided a great cross for Ossie to convert, turned triumphantly to his tormentors in the West Stand and stuck two fingers up. Huddy, in a symbolic gesture of support, ran over and cuddled him as if to say, 'I'm on his side.'

Some of the crowd called him Bingo (as in 'housey-housey'), but the players dubbed him Nobby, though no-one seems to know why. It led to confusion during a game against Manchester United when Peter was involved in a petty fracas of his own making with the combative midfielder Stiles. Webby ran over to calm things down and advised his team-mate, 'Drop it Nobby'. Stiles, overhearing a remark he thought was directed at him, turned on Webby, spouted 'It weren't me it were him!' through that toothless mouth and the whole thing kicked off again. Peter won FA and Cup Winners' Cup medals with Chelsea before moving to hometown club Oxford United. In March 1977 he was tragically killed, along with wife Sally, in a car crash. Their three young sons were orphaned and a benefit, attended by 17,000, was staged at the Bridge.

STEWART HOUSTON

Broke into the squad in 1968, broke his leg badly, recovered and moved to Manchester United via Brentford in 1973. It worked, as they were soon relegated.

BEN HOWARD BAKER

This lanky goalkeeper arrived in 1921 with something of an athletic reputation – at one stage he had been world-record holder at the high jump. Like so many Chelsea custodians, the amateur

THE LAD'S A BIT OF A WORKER

Benjamin Howard **BAKER**

Owen **MARSHALL**

Duncan **SHEARER**

Charlie **COOKE**

Reginald and Sam **WEAVER**

George **BARBER**

George **HUNTER**

Peter **HOUSEMAN**

William **PORTER**

Fred **TAYLOR**

Andrew **BOWMAN**

William **BRIDGEMAN**

Sid **BISHOP**

Dennis and Geoff **BUTLER**

Harold and Thomas **MILLER**

Phil **DRIVER**

James **BARRON**

England international was something of an eccentric during his five-season stay. He enjoyed nothing better than to join in with the game outside his box as some sort of auxiliary back. His specialities beyond that were his leaps (obviously, though it's unlikely he Fosbury flopped the bar during games) and his powerful goal kicks.

The other thing Ben enjoyed was taking penalties. That is until his opposite number in the Arsenal goal saved one of them. In consternation, recognising the potential danger, Ben hared back, not turning back until he reached the safety of his own area. And yet the laughter in the crowd said it all: the Gunners' goalie had actually palmed the ball away for a corner, and Ben's flight had been surplus to requirements. Funny, fans thought, he never usually liked his own box...

ALAN HUDSON

Perhaps the most talented all-round player Chelsea had between Lawton and Gullit. But didn't he know it. (Try reading his illuminating but narcissistic autobiography *Working Men's Ballet*.) The picture taken on the tarmac at Salonika in front of the

Olympic Airways jet that had taken the squad there is remarkable. Ron Harris looks like a boxer in civvies; Paddy Mulligan like a bookmaker at a posh do; Charlie Cooke like a professional Vegas gambler; Keith Weller looks the lary lad, as do Hutch and Ossie; but Huddy, he's holding a duty free bag (probably with some swanky men's cologne inside). He's looking sideways, hand on hip to reveal the fancy floral shirt and kipper tie in their full glory. Huddy is one of our most local old boys, born 400 yards from Stamford Bridge in 1951. He honed his skills in the backstreets of Fulham and overcame a bone disorder – Osgood–Schlatter disease – in his second trainee year to star in and skipper Chelsea's FA Youth Cup-winning side. He made his debut at seventeen in February 1969. 'He isn't in on sentiment,' insisted manager Sexton, 'but because he is a fine young player. The way he organizes things in midfield is first-class.'

He knitted play together with his meandering runs and slick passing. Strong and authoritative too, he dominated midfield like few Chelsea players since. As his manager said, Huddy liked to organize. Long before Ruud Gullit would stand over the ball, orchestrating his teammates into the positions he wanted, Huddy pointed, cajoled and instructed players sometimes nearly twice his age.

He made other things happen. His goal that never was against Ipswich, for example: a shot that brushed the outside of side-netting, hit a stanchion and sprang out. The referee thought the ball had gone in and awarded it to the incredulity of the Suffolk players and hilarity of the Stamford Bridge faithful. It was the winning goal.

But his was another career marred by injury. As Sexton acknowledged, given his form in every round on the way to it, it's unlikely we would have struggled so much against Leeds in the 1970 Final had Huddy not been out with a ligament problem.

The manager argued that Huddy's contribution deserved a winner's medal. The FA's rules stated that only twelve medals could be handed out, but a year later, they sent him an FA Cup winner's medal with the FA emblem erased. Nice touch.

A hairline fracture was discovered in 1970/71, but Huddy was able finally to star in a Cup final for the Blues in 1971 and the Cup Winners' Cup victory over Real. He also picked up a loser's medal in the League Cup final a year later.

His bravado was both an asset and a worry. He was fond of taking off his shin pads and rolling down his socks, almost as some tacit dare to the Bremners, Storeys and Stileses of the time to try and get near him. The problem was that they did. And after a severe injury to his left foot his two-footedness began to desert him in favour of preference to deftness with the outside of his right. More pertinently his attitude, built on self-confidence, collided with that of his manager, Dave Sexton. Mutual respect was the casualty, and once Sexton had convinced himself that Alan was an irredeemable member of the drinkers' club there was probably no way back. During the 1972/73 season Huddy had evidently lost his appetite for playing in royal blue. Neither man was prepared to back down and tragically Huddy felt no remorse about quitting Chelsea for Stoke City in the New Year of 1974.

Tony Waddington was rated by the midfielder as the best boss he served under, not Don Revie, the dour former Leeds boss, and for a short, misguided period of England's manager. Huddy maintained that Revie always threw him into impossible situations. And Sir Alf Ramsey, in contrast, rated Huddy so highly he once commented: 'There is no limit to what this boy can achieve.' Sir Alf picked him amongst the forty for Mexico but Alan missed the final cut for the World Cup finals.

Like other internationals of that Chelsea period – Scotland's Cookie, Ossie, Holly and Harris of England – Huddy can be described as an underachiever at the top level.

He returned to Chelsea in 1983 unfit but with experience invaluable to a young squad. Illness and injury conspired against him and he drifted back to Stoke again. Following a series of lurid tabloid stories alleging his involvement in a Stoke 'hostess' ring, Huddy eventually settled down and became a sports reporter for Radio Stoke.

In 1995 Chelsea recruited him as post-match host in Drake's at the Bridge. Not for the first time, Huddy was splashed all over the back pages following a bust-up involving Terry McDermott and Kevin Keegan in the tunnel area after a Newcastle game. Too headstrong for his own good, and perhaps frustrated that he couldn't then get a publisher for his autobiography, Huddy was 'banned' from the press room and didn't come back.

Tragedy followed just before Christmas 1997 when he was knocked down by a car and severely injured. Written off, happily he pulled through after some four months but will take a long time to record a full recovery. Huddy's a great bloke to have a drink with. It's not just the stories, it's his joyously cavalier reinterpretations of the past and pithy commentaries on the present that are so wonderful.

Although he respects the likes of Gullit and Zola, Huddy quite clearly believes that he would be one of the 1970s vets to cope easily with the superior pace and technique on offer today. He's probably right.

MARK HUGHES

Hysterically dubbed 'an old warlord' by Derby's matchday programme in 1998, Hughes is more like a timelord. After the 1994 FA Cup final, when Sparky helped Manchester United sink Chelsea with one of the four goals that day, few would have placed money on him returning for his post-war record fourth winner's medal with the defeated opponents three years later.

Glenn Hoddle bought the veteran Welsh international, thirty-one at the time, for £1.5m in July 1995, taking advantage of his uncertain future following the arrival of pricey centre-forward Andy Cole.

It might have been a difficult conversion for both player and

THE LAD'S SURNAME IS A BIT COMMON

1 Smith	6		4= Harris	4
2= Jones	5		4= Robertson	4
2= Hughes	5		4= Williams	4
4= Brown	4			

The following Chelsea players' surnames have cropped up three times: Ferguson, Jackson, Lee, Mitchell, McKenzie, Nicholas, Saunders, Thomson (unusually, all without the 'p'), Walker, Wilson

fans, since the level of professionalism at Old Trafford was higher than at the Bridge when Sparky arrived and he had previously been one of Chelsea supporters' least favourite opponents.

The changes wrought by Glenn Hoddle on and off the pitch assisted his settling in, especially after Zola and Vialli replaced Furlong and Stein as his partners. And the striker's performances soon won over any doubters. It helped, too, that the month before he signed Mark had been interviewed for a Manchester United video mag and had revealed that as a kid in Wrexham he'd supported the Chelsea side of Osgood and Hudson and owned a Peter Bonetti goalie's jersey.

Never the most prolific of goalscorers, Sparky's contribution was in leading the line, holding the ball up and the occasional vital, match-turning goal.

With thighs as thick as most footballers' waists, his sheer physical presence was something the Bridge hadn't witnessed for decades. He was frequently caught offside, though, and too often booked.

In his second season, with Ruud Gullit as manager, Sparky's slow start alongside Luca was transformed by the

Italian's injury and replacement by Gianfranco Zola, a different type of player with whom he built an irresistible partnership based on intuition and awareness of each others' strengths.

Sparky was still coming to terms with the Dutch manager's squad system, and was on the bench for the first half of the now almost mythical FA Cup match at the Bridge versus Liverpool. With his team 0–2 down and struggling, Rudi withdrew Franco to midfield and put Hughesie on as a target man. Within minutes he swivelled just in front of the previously impervious 'Pool defence and lashed in the first Chelsea goal that injected adrenalin into a formidable comeback to win 4–2. (It was the first time Liverpool had lost from a 2–0 lead for more than thirty years.)

On the way to the FA Cup triumph of 1997 he top-scored with five goals, including a stunning volley at Portsmouth and a brilliant brace against Wimbledon.

He commented after the 2–0 demolition of Boro that his fourth FA triumph was perhaps the sweetest. 'The more times you get there, you enjoy it more because you notice everything,' he told Chelsea's official web site. 'The fans have amazed me. We all appreciated how they were feeling and I think that's why the players didn't want to leave the pitch because you could see the fans were enjoying themselves so much. It's the best experience I've had with that.'

Sparky's third season in blue required even more tolerance of Rudi's squad rotation. He barely played in Europe, watching as Luca Vialli established himself as Euro conqueror, but maintained his standard in the League, and simply got better as the season progressed. It was in the Cups that this was most marked.

In a virtual re-enactment of his Liverpool stinger, Hughesie was brought on with thirty minutes to go at Highbury in the first leg of the Coca-Cola Cup semi-final, and almost immediately collected the ball on the edge of the Arsenal box, turned and powered a right-foot shot past Manninger. The match finished 1–2 but that goal was the crucial platform for the 3–1 storming of the

Gunners in the second leg, and Sparky scored in that match too.

Yet he saved his best for nearly last: the Cup Winners' Cup semi-final second leg at home to the Italians of Vicenza, who were leading 1–0 from the first leg. Again coming off the bench as a sub on seventy minutes, with his first touch the Welshman flicked a header past his challenger and with the second powered a left-footed drive on the left of the box across the keeper and into the far side of the goal.

Sparky's winners' medals for the Coca-Cola and Cup Winners' Cups, coupled with an OBE awarded during his third year at the Bridge and the FA Cup in his second, were ripe reward for one of Chelsea's best buys and most effective players of the 1990s.

As rumours abounded of a move in response to the arrival of Laudrup and Casiraghi in June 1998, Sparky mused about his long-term future: 'I've been thinking along the lines of management a lot more in the last couple of years. I've played under a lot of the top people in the game and I've got experience in winning things and losing things. So I think I could have something to offer. Where it's going to be I don't know.' In June 1998, the warhorse moved on to Southampton for £650,000.

TOMMY HUGHES

A Bonetti understudy. The season Chelsea first won the Cup, 1969/70, he stood in against Leeds, when his mistakes could be excused because of 'flu (2–5), and Everton (2–5). Hence the contemporary joke: 'What's the time?' 'Five past Hughes.'

Bonetti wasn't threatened. Tommy switched to Villa in 1971 for £12,500.

SIR GEOFF HURST

England's 1966 World Cup hero was appointed manager in succession to the lamentable Danny Blanchflower in September 1979.

This was the Chelsea board's dismal fling at projecting

some glamour and, let's face it, interest, onto the fading Chelsea edifice. Bobby Gould came with him, like the free carton of conditioner you sometimes get with a tub of shampoo.

Some of the players felt that Geoff had orchestrated the former Spurs legend's resignation, having been appointed his assistant six weeks earlier. But Danny needed replacing. We were in our worst ever League position – eighteenth in the Second Division.

Hurst's inspiration and attacking formation were effective but fleeting. A run of five consecutive wins almost helped secure promotion that first campaign, and the new season began equally promisingly, but the quality of some of those selected for the side – including Dennis Rofe and Phil 'Learner' Driver – had to be questioned. A sequence of six games without a point, then nine without a goal followed. The next step might have been relegation, and perhaps forty-two games without a *ground* the following season.

With a year and a half of their contracts still to run, the Hurst–Gould spacecraft was spun out of Chelsea's orbit. Geoff at first tried to sue for wrongful dismissal but he settled for 'substantial compensation' instead.

Following this disillusioning experience, Geoff quit football, and set up a highly successful car insurance company with former West Ham and England teammate Martin Peters. (Redundancy has its, erm, compensations.)

Geoff remembers his Chelsea days, though. A Chelsea fan, Jamie Crampton, met him at an exhibition recently, and quizzed him about his dismissal. '23 March 1981, 12.30pm,' he immediately declared. 'Not that he was counting or anything,' said Jamie.

CHRIS HUTCHINGS

Early 1980s glamour boy who looked more like a beach bum than a full-back (especially when playing football). He scored in one of his first games and repeated the feat in one of his last, but managed very little of note in between. He simply didn't have the pace required for the role, nor the application.

IAN HUTCHINSON

Bigger on bravery and endeavour than trifling matters like skill or technique, except in one area: throw-ins. Dave Sexton, who bought the all-action attacker as cover for £2,500 from Cambridge, set a test at the start of the 1969/70 season to see who had the longest throw in the squad. As Lorimer at Leeds had shown, a weighty lob into the box could be as good as a corner. Hutch, especially once he'd perfected the run-up and windmill arms follow-through, could easily reach the near post, and quite often beyond depending on the width of the pitch. Opposition players protested its illegality, so Hutch refined his methodology, dragging a trailing leg to ensure both feet touched the ground. Leeds used to put a man in front of him as intimidation, but it didn't work, as he so superbly demonstrated at Old Trafford in the FA Cup Final replay, when Hutch's missile was glanced on by Charlton for Webby to bundle home the winner. But there was more to his game than long arms. The big goal for him was obviously the brilliant, brave equalising header in the Wembley 'leg' of that Cup decider. He was always prepared to stick a foot or head in where others didn't dare. Subsequently he suffered an horrendous sequence of injuries, especially cartilage damage and broken legs, which utterly disrupted his career from 1970–74. Oddly, the Under-23 England international had been rejected as a full-back at Forest and had to work his way through from non-League Burton Albion to the top flight.

Life after playing was a struggle for Ian, not least because of the crippling legacy of his many injuries.

In 1976 he assumed a new role at the club as Promotions Executive. It didn't last more than a few seasons unfortunately. Still, his bare, medallioned chest was exposed in the programme on his 'page', so it was fun while it lasted.

When asked who of the old boys he would least trust on a night out with his wife, Ossie had no hesitation in citing Hutch, the dirty dog.

After football Ossie and Hutch set up an ill-fated wine bar project together and Ian got into trouble with the police for handling stolen stamps. Ironically, in the 1970 FA Cup semi-final programme he'd given one of his hobbies as coin collecting.

ERLAND JOHNSEN

Signed from Bayern Munich in 1989, the Norwegian got off to a flying start. Tall and commanding in the air, fast and tough in the tackle, with a good reading of the game, Erland was a revelation. In his second season, the hot pre-season summer of 1990 took its toll and a dehydrated Erland struggled for fitness. Puzzlingly, 'Moon Man' found it hard to break into a first team making the best use of Kenny Monkou and Jason Cundy, and his international career suffered. If it all looked uphill from there on, Erland had his crampons ready. Don Howe, Chelsea's coach, noted the frozen-out Norseman working out in the gym and wished some of the English boys had that level of commitment. But he still wouldn't push for him to play.

It took manager Dave Webb with his 'all up for grabs' policy of early 1993 to resurrect Erland's career. The centre-back had never given up hope, even though he rated himself better than the incumbents keeping him out, and was ready to step in and shut out the goals superbly.

When Glenn Hoddle arrived, Erland's hat was thankfully back in the ring. Sturdy and solid, aware of his limitations in passing, he was only half the kind of ball-playing defender Glenn liked, but his season ended with an FA Cup runners-up medal (adding to his 1990 ZDS winner's gong), a return to the international scene for USA 94 after four year's absence and his coveted Player of the Year award.

The following campaign earned him the first two chants of his name from the terraces. Bruges were the visitors in a Cup Winners' Cup match, and Erland helped drain away a few moments until our victory was confirmed by clattering into the Belgian goalkeeper. The second occasion was his inestimable earning of a non-existent penalty that settled the FA Cup replay with Leicester in 1997, performing a 'dying swan' under pressure from Matt Elliott. Chelsea won the Cup that year of course. Plenty of supporters still thank Erland for that invaluable contribution.

Erland was given a hero's send-off at the close of the 1996/97 season, as he headed back to Norway.

JOEY JONES

Wiry, tattooed arm, clenched fist. That's Joey Jones, the former Anfield favourite. He never moved from the Wirral following his move to the Bridge in October 1982, an early acquisition for John Neal, but his influence as a leader on the pitch was extensive. Sent off soon into his Chelsea career, mostly at right-back, he was asked to moderate that side of his game and concentrate on passing on his experience to Chelsea's young defenders. This he did until moving on to Wrexham in 1985.

VINNIE JONES

The Hemel hardnut, later to discover classical music under David Mellor's tutelage, discovered culture of a different kind when he arrived at Chelsea in August 1991 from Sheffield United. If a spell under Howard Wilkinson at Leeds had mellowed the Wimbledon Crazy Gangster, the switch to the Bridge brought out his best. His reputation preceded him and, like Wise before him, he took some time to shake off the 'hoofing Womble' tag.

At Leeds he began to receive some credit for his perceptive passing as well as his conspicuous aggression. At Chelsea, he was in a virtually unbroken line of hard men from Upton, through Chopper Harris and Droy to Roberts, who, the crowd would chirrup, 'is gonna get you'. But it was the movement, passing and willingness (if not expertise) to shoot on the volley that surprised. It's fair to say that in a team that tried to play football based around the likes of Townsend, Wise and Stuart, Vinnie began to be fully appreciated for having decent technique. His finest moments? The booking after two seconds against Sheffield United in 1992 maybe. (He got a dead leg doing it.)

The long throw (the only one of these fabled monsters that ever led to a goal) that Kenny Monkou flicked on for Wisey to convert against QPR. And the 'mugging' of Liverpool, our first League victory at Anfield for just over fifty-six years, in February 1992. Before the match, you may recall, the duo who had so rattled the Scousers in the 1988 FA Cup Final, Jones and Wise, scrawled a message on a Post-it note and stuck it over the intimidatory tunnel motto of legend: 'This Is Anfield'. Their note read, 'We're bothered'. It was just the kind of impudence Liverpool hated. Chelsea won 2–1 that day. Vinnie scored with a volley and Wisey grabbed a late winner. Vincenzo (as some of us liked to call him, as overseas players with exotic skills and names drifted over to the Premiership) slipped quietly back to Wimbledon just before his legs went, never likely to figure in our long-term future under Glenn Hoddle. His churlish wind-ups – such as the jibe that Ruud Gullit 'squealed worse than one of my pot-bellied pigs' – mattered less now that there was some genuine quality to counter the cultured brawn he had represented.

KEITH JONES

'Jonah', a clever and industrious central midfielder, was the most gifted player from the Youth Development Scheme under Gwyn Williams. Popular in the early part of his career (in a period when despicable monkey hoots weren't unknown at the Bridge, even directed at our own players – imagine that) he was a clever passer and had good positional sense. His undoing came in a diabolical managerial decision during the 1984/85 season. The game was against Manchester United at home, or more specifically Bryan Robson, because 'Captain Crutches' dominated our young midfield to such an extent that calling them ragged would be an act of kindness. A clear readjustment of tactics was required to counter the surging midfielder. The problem was that Hollins decided to replace Jonah rather than give him a chance to win the second-half battle, and a scapegoat was born. Jonah never managed to recover form or remove the branding he had received that day. In no time he was off. Kerry Dixon rated him highly and in recent years went on record as saying Jonah was the player he was most disappointed didn't make it. Well, Jonah made it, but outside the top flight. He's been a mainstay of the Charlton team for many years and has carved out a decent professional career for himself. Just a shame he never realized the full early potential shown at Chelsea.

Left: Celestine Babayaro turns up the heat on Cup Winners' Cup opponents Tromsø in November 1997.

Below: Roy Bentley goes that extra yard against Manchester City at the Bridge; John McNichol looks for a contact lens.

Above: Suave, sophisti-
cated, except for that
moustache – Charlie
Cooke just before the
1971 League Cup Final.

Above: Peter Bonetti
illustrating his
patented 'can't kick
far, therefore throw
to nearest player'
technique.

Right: Shoot! Goal
hungry Steve Clarke
surges towards the
halfway line against
Nottingham Forest in
August 1996.

Opposite: I think he
wants it away; Ed de
Goey's third clean
sheet of the 1997/98
season, 3–0 at Crystal
Palace.

Above: A white-booted
Roberto Di Matteo, Boro's
nemesis, on the ball at
Wembley in March 1998.

Opposite: Kerry Dixon
fails to strike gold in
the dismal 0–7 defeat
at Nottingham Forest
in April 1991.

Above: It's the way he tells 'em; manager Tommy Docherty makes a hilarious joke about a ball called Zephyr.

Above: Chelsea's greatest ever youth product? Jimmy Greaves, bearing evidence of Ron Harris's challenge in 1966.

Left: Chelsea's greatest ever player? The elegant Ruud Gullit in full flow against Middlesbrough in the 5–0 whipping in February 1995.

Right: Ron Harris leads the team out as usual, followed by Peters Bonetti and Osgood in May 1971.

Above: John Hollins
overcomes the FA Cup
semi-final quagmire
(and Alan Hudson's
toe) as Chelsea
trounce Watford 5–1
in April 1970.

Left: Soon to be Blue;
Denmark's Brian
Laudrup brings home
the bacon against
Saudi Arabia at
France '98.

Opposite: Chelsea and England star Tommy Lawton overcomes his French opponent (with a well placed elbow) in May 1947.

Above: Eddie McCreadie, the thinking person's hard man, in 1971 before his career ended due to injuries.

Above: Chairman Joe Mears, 'Mr Chelsea', in March 1956, still glowing from the Championship win ten months earlier.

Above: Pat Nevin, post-New Romantic hair and heading towards the end of an illustrious Chelsea career in 1987.

Above: Eddie Newton, Chelsea's 'silent force', back in the midfield after injury in 1998.

Right: Peter Osgood, the king of Stamford Bridge, towards the end of his second ill-fated reign in 1978/79.

Left: Super Dan Petrescu playing his fourth game in Chelsea blue, against Manchester United in December 1995.

Right: Another penalty dispatched; Graham Roberts powers Chelsea towards the First Division against Watford in March 1989.

Above: Bert Murray (left) and Marvin Hinton (right) marvel at flying full-back Ken Shellito's blind heading ability against Everton in 1965.

Right: Ken Shellito, the Chelsea boss in 1978.

Above: Terry Venables, already reluctantly on his way out, plays one of his last Chelsea matches against Nottingham Forest in April 1966.

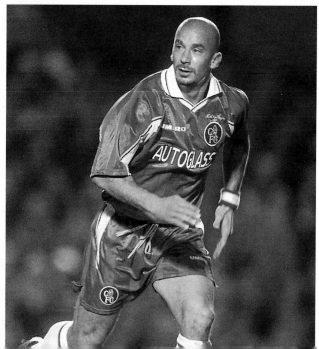

Right: Hat-trick hero Gianluca Vialli eludes Tromsø's defence again in the Cup Winners' Cup in November 1997.

Above: Youth sensation
Clive Walker in his first
big season in 1977/78.

Right: Dave Webb,
Chelsea's self-styled
'Red Adair' manager in
1993.

Above: Sporting the 'caveman' look in August 1970, Dave Webb parades the FA Cup with Alan Hudson and Peter Houseman.

Left: Dennis Wise, Chelsea's most successful skipper, leading Chelsea to a 1–0 win over Newcastle United in 1997.

Above: In a match against Fulham, the athletic Vic Woodley has it covered in front of a massive crowd in February 1936.

Right: Gianfranco Zola celebrates his seventeen second goal in the Cup Winners' Cup Final in 1998.

STEVE KEMBER

A bigger nose than Andy Townsend's, but at least it pointed in the right direction. That wasn't the standout feature of Steve's Chelsea career though; looking back it was littered with doubts and ill omens that seemed to scream 'Don't do it' to all concerned.

In September 1971, he was bought from Palace for a record £170,000 to provide bite and consistency. (Eagles boss Bert Head desperately needed the money to rebuild his struggling side.) The policy of manager Sexton and the Chelsea board at the time was to buy the 'best' players for the first-team squad as and when they became available, a strategy soon to be overtaken by financial events.

There were nineteen other registered players who could count themselves first-teamers at the time of Steve's arrival. 'When I picked up my boots at Selhurst Park, I realized how choked I was,' he commented at the time.

Effectively, the sharp, aggressive twenty-two-year-old midfielder was Alan Hudson's replacement (some hope). Unfortunately Steve didn't have the stomach for the fight, even to break into the team.

'I was joining a team littered with star names like Peter Osgood, Charlie Cooke, Alan Hudson and David Webb,' he recalled in 1996. 'They had all been successful. All that made them a close-knit unit and I found it hard to be accepted. It didn't help either that I was also in and out of the side. I wasn't eligible for the Cup Winners' Cup Chelsea were defending or for the League Cup in which they reached the final against Stoke. It was a difficult season for me. I'd been a big fish at Palace but at Chelsea I was very much a little fish.' Enough said.

It didn't help that he was knocked cold after fifteen minutes by a wildly hacked shot in his first Chelsea match away to Sheffield United.

Bonding in Barbados during the 1972 close season was countered by the sacking of Sexton. New boss Ron Suart appointed Steve skipper but the battle against relegation was over before Eddie McCreadie succeeded Ron and put his faith in kids. Steve asked for a transfer, withdrew it, but was sold anyway, to Leicester. Steve ran a wine bar for a while but moved into coaching with Palace a few years ago.

DEREK KEVAN

A lumpen centre-forward who made Tony Hateley look good. Signed in 1962 just before transfer deadline day to ensure promotion, he managed his first goal in the 7–0 defeat of Portsmouth, the last game of the season. Then he was out. Cheers Derek!

DMITRI KHARINE

Possibly the unluckiest of the quality keepers over the years between Chelsea sticks. Already recovered from a severe knee ligament problem before his arrival at Chelsea in December 1992, the twenty-four-year-old proved he was worth every penny of the £400,000 paid to CSKA Moscow over the coming years. His agility and athleticism was coupled with a dedication to his craft that suited the Hoddle/Gullit/Vialli era, if not some of the sides that preceded it. Replacing the loveable but inconsistent Dave Beasant and vying with the reliable Kevin Hitchcock, the number one slot was his to claim or to lose.

Proclaiming the pre-eminence of Russian rock music, books and television in garbled English, the eccentric Dimmi was a breath of fresh air. At his best he was world class, capable of handling the mundanities of his art with aplomb, but also to provide those extra stunning saves that make for a successful side.

A great shot-stopper with safe hands who was rarely beaten from outside the box in his first three seasons, the Russian international (and 1994 World Cup skipper) could be hesistant in the area and was liable to brainstorms followed by self-doubt and loss of form.

It didn't help that his new home was burgled within weeks of his arrival. But as his English improved and his family settled into village life he demonstrated his quality. As the last line of defence in our 1993/94 FA Cup run, he was formidable, his name rousingly chorused from the terraces to the tune (somewhat bewilderingly) of *Hava Nagila*. 1994/95 began well. Three successive penalty saves maintained a Chelsea tradition of sorts stretching way back to our first custodian Fatty Foulke.

But none of those matched the magnitude of his spot-kick stop away to Viktoria Zizkov in the Cup Winners' Cup. And the clean sheets were stacking up. However, as the vital FC Bruges away leg approached in February 1995, Dimmi was injured at West Ham. Hitchy took over for all but two of the remaining fixtures, including the semi-final defeat over two legs to Real Zaragoza.

The following season the Russian reclaimed his starting slot and kept the opposition out on no less than 10 occasions up to January 1996, when a dramatic error in clearing an innocuous ball against Newcastle in the FA Cup culminated in an ignominious last-minute equalizer for Les Ferdinand. Up to that point most supporters had given Dimmi the benefit of the doubt. Not now. So it was that his rival Hitchy was still between the sticks when Chelsea hobbled out against Manchester United for the semi-final at Villa Park ten weeks later. United won 2–1.

In August 1996 the Russian was once again preferred, proving his worth with three straight clean sheets. The fifth game, though, ended in disaster. Jumping in a challenge at Hillsborough, he landed awkwardly and immediately called for a substitute. He'd

OVERSEAS STARS

Only four players of foreign extraction (not including the Irish Republic) donned the blue shirt in Chelsea's first fifty years. Since then, and up to the summer of 1998, another twenty-three have come and there will doubtless be more.

South Africa is hanging in there as one of the most common countries of origin for 'our' foreigners, even though one of the four – **Colin Viljoen** – had already played for England by the time he graced our turf. We've now also had four each from Italy and France (**Pierluigi Casiraghi** and **Marcel Desailly** the most recent additions), three from Australia, Holland, Norway, and Denmark (**Brian Laudrup** being the latest). Just two – **Craig Forrest** and **Gustavo Poyet** – have come from the Americas, and surprisingly only one player – **Albert Ferrer** – represents Spain on the list. In 1998 London-born **Frank Sinclair** became the club's first Jamaican international.

The full list is:

Nils Middelboe, Denmark – 1913–21
Willi Steffen, Switzerland – 1946–47
Frank Mitchell, Australia – 1949–52
Ralph Oelofse, South Africa – 1951–53
Tony Potrac, South Africa – 1970–73
Derek Smethurst, South Africa – 1971
Petar Borota, Yugoslavia – 1979–82

ruptured a cruciate ligament again. It was to be a long rehabilitation and in the mean time new manager Ruud Gullit, who'd publicly shown his fury at the Newcastle incident the season before, signed two international goalies. One, Norwegian international Frode Grodas, was a one-season wonder, starring throughout the

Colin Viljoen, South Africa (but qualified for England) – 1980–82

Tony Dorigo, Australia (but qualified for England) – 1987–91

David Mitchell, Australia – 1988–91

Kenny Monkou, Holland – 1989–92

Erland Johnsen, Norway – 1989–97

Frank Sinclair, Jamaica – 1991–

Dmitri Kharine, Russia – 1992–

Jakob Kjeldbjerg, Denmark – 1993–96

Dan Petrescu, Romania – 1995–

Ruud Gullit, Holland – 1995–1998

Gianluca Vialli, Italy – 1996–

Frank Leboeuf, France – 1996–

Roberto Di Matteo, Italy – 1996–

Frode Grodas, Norway – 1996–98

Gianfranco Zola, Italy – 1996–

Craig Forrest, Canada – 1997

Ed de Goey, Holland – 1997–

Tore Andre Flo, Norway – 1997–

Celestine Babayaro, Nigeria – 1997–

Gustavo Poyet, Uruguay – 1997–

Bernard Lambourde, France – 1997–

Laurent Charvet, France – 1998–

Pierluigi Casiraghi, Italy – 1998–

Brian Laudrup, Denmark –1998–

Albert Ferrer, Spain – 1998–

Marcel Desailly, France – 1998–

later stages of our glorious FA Cup campaign of 1996/97. The other, Ed de Goey, brought in during the close season, proved more of a threat to Dimmi's long-term future at the club.

Though in the spring Rudi's replacement Luca Vialli decided to give both his international keepers a chance to prove themselves – Dimmi in the Premier League, Ed in the Cups, with Hitchy the perpetual sub – the pendulum swung in the Dutchman's favour when it was clear the Russian was still far from his old sharpness.

As a result, the chess-playing keeper, approaching his thirtieth birthday and apparently keen to acquire British citizenship, faces an uncertain future.

He should just thank his lucky stars he was not around during the Bonetti years!

JOE KIRKUP

A namby-pamby full-back who left for Southampton in a swap deal with David Webb coming the other way in 1968.

JOHNNIE KIRWAN

Signed, along with his wing partner Davie Copeland, from Spurs before a ball was kicked in Chelsea colours in 1905, the even-tempered Irish international (seventeen caps) was renowned as one of the most consistent performers of his era, particularly for a winger. His skill was in killing a ball passed to his feet stone dead, playing around with it in front of a mesmerized back like 'a playful kitten', feinting until he had his back beaten, stealing a yard down the left and getting a troublesome cross in. It was nationally recognized heroes such as Johnnie who launched the Chelsea colours with such a flying start.

He was something of a character. Waiting, like everyone else, for the fog to clear around Bradford's Valley Parade ground before a match in 1907, the sharp-witted Irishman responded to the inane questioning of a local cub reporter with the straight-faced suggestion that such a meteorological event would never stop a match at the Bridge. 'At Chelsea we always sweep it up and cart it off the field,' he avowed. The fans adored him for the two seasons he spent at Chelsea before he headed north of the border to Clyde in 1908.

TOMMY LANGLEY

Remember the dark old merchandising days of the 'Chelsea Collection'? The Chelsea Independent ran a spoof version of their own called the 'Tommy Langley Collection' which the man himself understandably found hilarious. Tommy was an honest footballer and likeable with it. Leather-lunged, mop-headed, first touch like a Tyrannosaurus Rex, his face went red like that unfit boy in the cross country at school. Mobile forward Tommy's unpredictable, ungainly style troubled even the best defences, though not in any consistent manner. People liked him because of his application, and how his mundane skills were pushed to the limit. Every Sunday footballer could relate to him. The problem was, most went to watch players do things they *couldn't* do themselves. Thus Tommy's worth split terrace opinion.

He had made a senior bow while still a trainee in 1974, aged sixteen years and nine months (and he looked even younger). As his tenuous frame grew, so did his importance in the yo-yo Chelsea team. Somewhere along the line he managed to win an England Under-21 cap.

Tommy had the misfortune to establish himself in a squad of ancients and naifs. Hutchinson, Garner and, latterly, the returning Osgood, didn't work out upfront with him. Young rival to the centre-forward slot Steve 'Jock' Finnieston was too frequently injured; winger Clive Walker too fitful. As passengers boarded for season 1977/78 he was the best hope of surviving the now treacherous waters of the First Division, to the extent that he played as emergency goalie at Upton Park in 1978. The game was lost 3–1, with Garner, the usual relief custodian, getting the

THE LAD'S FIRST NAME'S A BIT COMMON

1 John/Jonathan/Jon	44	6 George	20
2 James	38	7 David	15
3= William	28	8= Peter	14
3= Robert	28	8= Michael	14
5 Thomas/Tommy	22	8= Joseph/Joe	14

These are the commonest names of people who played for Chelsea. Altogether now: "There's only one. . .":

Alfred, Angus, Arnold, Augustus, Buchanan, Celestine, Clifford, Dale, Damian, Desmond, Dmitri, Eamonn, English, Erland, Errol, Evan, Frode, Gareth, Gavin, Gianfranco, Gianluca, Glenn, Gustavo, Henry, Jakob, Jason, Jody, Johnson, Kerry, Kingsley, Laurent, Lee, Marcel, Marshall, Martin, Marvin, Maxwell, Miles, Murdoch, Nigel, Nils, Norman, Percy, Perry, Pierluigi, Roelf, Ruud, Scott, Seth, Simeon, Stewart, Sylvan, Timothy, Tore Andre, Trevor, Victor, Vincent, Vivian, Wilfred, Willi, Wilson.

goal then hobbling off. Tom was outstanding. It was, some people said, his best game in a Chelsea shirt.

In fact, Tommy top-scored that campaign (with eleven), and in 1978/79 earned the golden boot again with fifteen goals, playing centrally and as a type of roving inside-forward. Chelsea went down in twenty-second position that year – no-one else scored more than five! Against scant opposition, he was voted Player of the Year by supporters.

The feeling that he simply wasn't good enough took root and he became a victim of the boo-boys. People in the Shed End referred to him disparagingly as 'The Horse'. He definitely wasn't that bad. And he would have died for Chelsea.

The following season in the Second Division Clive Walker found form and eclipsed Tommy. With new arrival Colin Lee mistaken for a cracking centre-forward (a charade he'd been pulling off at White Hart Lane), the Horse bolted his family stable for QPR in August 1980.

Tommy's subsequent career was still mostly played out in the top flight. In fact, he played two games for crack Greek side AEK Athens. Honestly.

There really was, as some on the terraces had it, only one Tommy Langley.

BRIAN LAUDRUP

One of Colin Hutchinson's swoops of summer 1998. The exceptionally gifted Danish winger, brother of midfielder Michael, Brian's cutting in and shooting provided much of the impetus for Glasgow Rangers' amazing run of title triumphs.

Unsurprisingly, his appearances at France 98 were enjoyed to the full by admiring Chelsea fans. He was a free transfer, at the age of twenty-eight.

TOMMY LAW

In 1926, full-back Tommy's arrival in David Calderhead's 'Tartan Chelsea' side should have reaped more reward than it did. Those rewards being nil. He made his debut alongside six other Scots. The stadium resounded to the north of the border brogue. Small wonder that the Glaswegian felt so at home he spent his entire professional career at Chelsea, earning a paltry two caps for season after season of superbly consistent and cultivated defending. One of those was the renowned 5–1 drubbing of England by the 'Wembley Wizards'. And in that game Tommy is reckoned to have made the best-applauded tackle of all time, a twenty-yard slide on the wet surface in his own area concluding with the ball whipped neatly off the England winger's feet. Tommy was slow of leg but not of thought, and his shrewd positional sense and intelligent interceptions made him a terrace hero. He was a ball player from the back in the golden age of the back-line hoofer. Tommy's fifty-yard passes, much like those of Hoddle, Gullit and Leboeuf a lifetime later, were precision sweeps where the forwards wanted them. Right up until 1937 the grace and intelligence remained in his game. Tommy stuck around in London after his retirement from the game and was a frequent and acclaimed visitor to the Bridge up to his death in 1976.

TOMMY LAWTON

Though he was only passing through our system like a dose of salts and was already past his sell-by date, his best days having been spent at Goodison, this master of the English game is one of the great stars of the Chelsea adventure, whose mastery of the air was almost complete.

In an era when the last refuge of the footballing scoundrel is recognized as the phrase 'good with his head', we're in danger of taking him too lightly. He possessed little of Gallacher's trickery or subtlety. But he was a Charles Atlas of his day, a Colossus in the air, good on the ball and hard to shake off it. When we say 'an old-fashioned English centre-forward', we mean Tommy, the wartime prototype.

A one-and-a-bit-season wonder in the League (but oh what a time: twenty-six goals in thirty-four games) beginning in the immediate post-war period, the Boltonian was supposed to be one of the top-quality Birrell purchases to bring glory to the Bridge. Unfortunately he was soon in dispute with the club and even dropped a couple of divisions to Notts County to get away in 1947. Still he went for a record £20,000.

His most famous hour was undoubtedly the legendary visit of Moscow Dinamo to Stamford Bridge in November 1945. So mythical has the scale of this match become over time that it now appears that an unofficially estimated crowd of two million crammed into the Bridge, every schoolboy within a thirty-mile

WORLD WAR TWO GUESTS

Although individual appearances made during the conflict could not count towards official totals, the huge interest in football meant there was an extremely busy football programme, divided for ease of playing into regional competitions. Short-staffed clubs (according to Jack Rollin's *Soccer At War*, forty-four Chelsea players served the war effort in one way or another) made up the numbers by means of guest players from other clubs, some of whom made many appearances for their 'new' team because they were posted nearby.

The records are not complete, but six players made over 100 appearances for Chelsea during the war: **Dick Foss, Dick Spence, Albert Tennant** (all three played over 150 games), **Joe Payne, Vic Woodley** and **John Harris** (the most regular guest, then of Wolves, who subsequently joined Chelsea properly).

Payne was easily the club's top scorer in the war years, knocking in at least 108, despite lengthy spells with injury, including thirty-nine in 1943/44 and the same again the following season, the latter in just twenty-eight fixtures (Chelsea scored 100 goals in thirty games). He scored just twenty-three in his 'real' Blues career. Dick Spence slotted forty-one and Dick Foss twenty-four. **Tommy Lawton**, who joined Chelsea just after the war ended, but before 'proper' football returned, scored nineteen in 1945/46.

Other notable guests included Middlesbrough's **George Hardwick**, who played in both Chelsea's wartime cup finals at Wembley, West Ham's **Len Goulden** (who joined Chelsea after the war), Manchester United's **Charlie Mitten**, Arsenal's **Eddie Hapgood**, future England managers **Walter Winterbottom** and **Joe Mercer**, and **Matt Busby**, who went on to become a coach or something.

radius of London bunked off school to attend, and the King rudely interrupted the French ambassador mid-sentence and skipped the rest of his appointments to see the two teams thrash out a 9–9 draw. In fact, it was 3–3, around 75,000 watched and the home counties schools were full. But it sounds a cracking game and Lawton was the star, scoring what looked like the winning third goal with his, er, head, until the Russians equalized.

Tommy was a sportsman and a gentleman, always genial and approachable, but it didn't stop him signing for Arsenal and scoring the only goal of Christmas Day 1954 against his old chums.

When he moved into management, Tommy settled in Nottingham. On his retirement, even though he became rather frail late in life, he contributed a sports column to a local newspaper, and enjoyed being kept informed about goings-on at Chelsea.

At the time of his death in 1997 the former Bridge hero was making plans to pay a final pilgrimage to SW6.

GRAEME LE SAUX

Jersey-born 'Bergerac' (the nickname derived from a 1980s TV detective from the Channel Islands) has been something of a prodigal son to Chelsea. Signed from local club St Pauls at nineteen in 1987 he broke into the Chelsea first team at the close of the ensuing season, still not sure whether he was a winger or a full-back. One thing was for sure – he was left-footed, fast and talented.

There followed a period of five years where the *Guardian*-reading footballer struggled to establish himself in the Quixotic plans of Chelsea's managers.

His best friend at the time was Kenny Monkou. The two of them drove around Europe together in the summer of 1991. It led to all sorts of rumours, which the pair found highly amusing.

Graeme was an odd-man-out in the dressing room and

when that combined with uncertainty as to his best position on the pitch, his frustration culminated in outbursts such as the notorious incident at Stamford Bridge where he was substituted one too many times and petulantly threw off his shirt in disgust towards manager Ian Porterfield. The fact that Chelsea didn't get the best from one of the brightest England prospects in the country is beyond doubt. But even if he'd played in his favoured position, it is unlikely he would have stayed at a club so becalmed in mid-table mediocrity.

So when Kenny Dalglish came in for him at the start of Dave Webb's short tenure in 1993, the cut-price deal was simply rubber-stamped. The makeweight in the deal, freckled nightmare Steve Livingstone, made one appearance.

At Blackburn Graeme won a Championship, a bucketload of England caps, and the respect of English football at left-back. But he never played in a Wembley final, and when, on the departure of Scott Minto to Benfica in 1997, the chance came to return to a radically overhauled Chelsea, he jumped at it. It was no mistake.

By the close of a season in which his forward runs and energetic work, whether in midfield or as wing-back, had made a superb contribution to the chase for trophies, he had two medals (though he missed the Cup Winners' Cup final through injury) and the memory of two fine goals to cherish. The first was a twenty-five-yard strike of a loose ball at Palace that flew in. The second was a consolation goal at home to Manchester United when he ran on to a throughball and lobbed the onrushing Schmeichel exquisitely from twenty yards.

Graeme, now a relaxed and urbane twenty-nine-year-old, was the only Chelsea player selected for Glenn Hoddle's France 98 squad.

FRANK LEBOEUF

'When I tell myself that Gullit has chosen me then I am sure I

THE LAD'S A TOP BUY –

Up to summer 1998, Chelsea's most expensive players were as follows:

Pierluigi Casiraghi – £5.4m from Lazio, June 1998. Club record at time

Graeme Le Saux – £5m from Blackburn, August 1997. Club record at time

Roberto Di Matteo – £4.9m from Lazio. July 1996. Club record at time

Marcel Desailly – £4.6m from AC Milan, June 1998

Gianfranco Zola – £4.5m from Parma, November 1996

Frank Leboeuf – £2.5m from Strasbourg, June 1996. Club record at time

Albert Ferrer – £2.5m from Barcelona, June 1998

Paul Furlong – £2.3m from Watford, May 1994. Club record at time

Dan Petrescu – £2.3m from Sheffield Wednesday, November 1995. Equalled club record at time

Celestine Babayaro – £2.25m from Anderlecht, June 1997. Still a club record for a teenager

Ed de Goey – £2.25m from Feyenoord, June 1997. Club record for a goalkeeper

Robert Fleck – £2.1m from Norwich City, August 1992. Club record at time

have reached an acceptable level in football. I was astounded when I first heard that he wanted me. To me, Gullit represented someone from another planet,' said Frank Leboeuf, arriviste from France, invisible member of their Euro 96 squad, and immediate hero with the Chelsea massive. It was a far cry from Strasbourg, the team that sold him for £2.5m. Their coach Gilbert Grese, now the Swiss national manager, once told his

Dennis Wise – £1.6m from Wimbledon, July 1990. Club record at time

Mark Stein – £1.5m from Stoke City, October 1993

Mark Hughes – £1.5m from Manchester United, July 1995

Gavin Peacock – £1.25m from Newcastle United, July 1993

David Rocastle – £1.25m from Manchester City, August 1994

Chelsea first paid a £1,000 fee for **Fred Rouse** from Stoke in October 1907.

The first £10,000 fee paid by the club was for **Hughie Gallacher** from Newcastle in May 1930.

Tony Hateley was the club's first £100,000 signing – he came from Aston Villa in October 1966. **Alan Birchenall, Keith Weller** and **Chris Garland** all followed for £100,000. **Steve Kember** came from Crystal Palace in September 1971 for £170,000, then **Dave Sexton** paid £225,000 for Celtic's **David Hay** in July 1974.

Mickey Hazard was the next record buy – £300,000 from Spurs in September 1985, then in April 1986 **Gordon Durie** arrived from Hibernian for £381,000. **Steve Wicks** returned to the Bridge from QPR in July 1986 for £450,000, **Tony Dorigo** arrived from Aston Villa in May 1987 for £475,000, and **Graham Roberts** travelled south from Rangers in July 1988 for the same figure. Finally, **Dave Beasant** came to bolster Blue promotion hopes in January 1989, £725,000 being paid to Newcastle United.

defender, 'Frank, you are a bastard – you will never win anything.' Charming.

'Well,' commented Frank, 'since I left his club I have played for France at Euro 96 and I have won three major cups with Chelsea.'

After the press conference that confirmed Frank's arrival, Graham Rix confided, 'He's Hansen', meaning Alan of that name, the cultured centre-back in the greatest-ever Liverpool team. There was no secret that 'Beefy', the nickname swiftly corrupted from his translated surname, wasn't the first choice in that position. There were rumours that Laurent Blanc, who largely kept Frank out of France's starting line-up, was the primary target. Still, Monsieur Leboeuf was supremely confident, opening up in his first interview, with the author, that he considered himself a *libero*, was more comfortable on the ball than most English defenders he had seen, and was looking forward to establishing himself amongst the 'international brigade' at the Bridge. He was twenty-eight and he had arrived in the big time. His family settled in a huge house in Richmond.

He struck up friendships with the great and good at the club, dining out at top restaurants with Luca and Rudi, as if some of the success his late-starting career had been starved of would rub off. Ken Bates described him as the 'best piece of business this season' as Chelsea established its reputation as a slicker, tougher outfit and cruised to the Cup Final. 'I am ambitious and that's why I came to Chelsea,' he said. Post-Hoddle Chelsea he might have added. 'The thrill and inspiration of playing in England is definitely much greater than back home in France. In some games I was bored and playing in small empty stadiums without any atmosphere.'

But there were other reasons to welcome Frank. A few years earlier, the awarding of a penalty was more likely to cause embarrassment on the terraces than glee. Yet up to the end of the 1997/98 season he hadn't missed a penalty for five years, including many for us, and had proved himself one of the best strikers of a ball around. (Just ask Arphexad, the Leicester keeper in the game at the Bridge in 1997, who flailed in vain at the third of Frank's astonishing long-distance drives.)

Frank simply oozed class in the early matches of 1996/97, when he wasn't oozing blood. Remember the 'tactile' welcome the Dons gave him at the Bridge, and the lump on his forehead that prompted comments about 'Le Oeuf'?

Frustratingly, his dead-ball skills, in teams already blessed with Zola and Gullit, and with the ambitious Di Matteo, Petrescu and Le Saux vying for a kick, have been underused.

Part of the reason is that in his second season the formation switched to a back four and he converted, not altogether smoothly, from rampant *libero* to conventional centre-back. Despite his coolness and immense technical ability Frank looked less commanding in that role alongside Michael Duberry, and the fans noticed.

The newly mixed public perception was often at odds with the 'official' figures. The Opta Index, for example, gathering player statistics from across the Premiership, consistently had the Frenchman as leading defender scoring more than a thousand points for his successful passes long and short, tackles and other aspects of play. There is no measure of lapses in concentration, though, and that is perhaps the Achilles heel of a man who otherwise borders on genius. This was particularly noticeable should he sustain an injury, real or imagined.

The point is, did the visionary sixty-yard passes like the one for Vialli at Old Trafford in 1996/97 compensate for the occasional back-passes that left his keeper stranded? Did his cool stewardship of the back four against Wimbledon in the 1997 FA Cup semifinal make-up for the steam-rollering he sustained against the same club at home in the League? There were fewer sights more glorious to Blues fans than some of those seering sprays with the outside of his right boot to liberate a wing-back or striker; fewer more disappointing than his struggling to assert his authority in the box under pressure from a less skilled opposition striker.

And the answer, most likely, is yes. Frank, you see, contributed in no small measure to our re-establishment as a club of glamour, class and style. As the children on the terrace chorused, 'He's here, he's there, I'm not allowed to swear, Frank Leboeuf, Frank Leboeuf...'

Frank has always risen to the occasion, perhaps out of a determination to have some silverware from a very good career. He was one of Rudi's heroes in the FA Cup at Wembley in 1997 and the Coca-Cola Cup final twelve months later. Then he performed with imperious precision against Stuttgart in the Cup Winners' Cup final on 13 May 1998. One month later, alongside new Chelsea teammate Marcel Desailly, Frank played and won in the World Cup Final.

COLIN LEE

Spurs' star striker converted to centre-half then right-back at Chelsea 1980–88. In truth he could read a game superbly from that position, and passed with considerable subtlety. In some ways he was living proof that a football brain is more crucial than a football body.

DAVID LEE

Two things in football never to believe: the height they put down in the programme for John Spencer; and the weight declared for David Lee at the start of the season. Rodders, one of the best passers the club had in his day, was outstanding in the middle of defence in the first half of the 1989/90 season in which Chelsea finished fifth in the First Division, and again when he came in from the cold three campaigns later. One of the best technicians the YTS scheme produced, it was the application that proved harder, especially as he had the demotivating factors of three world-class players in succession – Hoddle, Gullit, Leboeuf – arriving with prior claim to his position. Nevertheless he proved himself an able understudy to the injured sweeper Ruud Gullit in 1995/96.

Slow and immobile as a super-tanker, Dave's assets outweighed such deficits in many people's eyes. His ability to strike a ball like an arrow, his playful desire to score for the reserves from the halfway line (and ability to do it!), coupled with his astute taste in indie music made him popular with fans.

SUPER-REGULAR SUBS

A total of 161 players had made substitute appearances for Chelsea up to the end of the 1997/98 season. **David Lee** overtook **Kevin McAllister** when coming on at Blackburn on 18 March 1995, and – with the recent changes to the rules on substitutes – has every chance of making that elusive 50 mark. The full list is as follows:

David Lee 46
Kevin McAllister 39
John Spencer 37
Paul Canoville, Kevin Wilson 36
Clive Walker 33
Craig Burley 32
John Bumstead 30
Paul Furlong 26
Eddie Newton 25
Colin Lee 23
Gareth Hall, David Hopkin 22

Phil Driver, Tore Andre Flo, Graham Stuart, Graeme Le Saux 21
Paul Furlong, Mark Nicholls 20
Gianluca Vialli 19
Peter Houseman, Clive Wilson 18
Glenn Hoddle 17
Marvin Hinton 16
Gavin Peacock 15

Injury, though, and lack of fitness have been the enemies in his Chelsea career. When he suggested, post-Bosman, that he would be going down to the club 'with a wheelbarrow' to collect the cash from his free transfer, it was another unfulfilled promise. The Bosman ruling permitted out-of-contract players to move on for free to a club of their choice. Rodders always ended up extending his Blues career for another year. He was the last of his generation of trainees to remain on the club's books, Jason Cundy, Billy Dodds, Paul Canoville, Damien Matthew, Gareth Hall and Les Fridge all long gone.

RAY LEWINGTON

Ray Lew, as he was universally known, was sidekick and hod-carrier for Ray Wilkins from the moment the two arrived as Chelsea schoolboys. Strong, reliable and mindful of his limitations, from the time of his debut in a struggling side in 1974, through to his departure after one too many injuries five years later, Ray walked stride for stride alongside his more illustrious midfield mate, tackling hard and playing the simple ball to Butch's feet for the young maestro to work his magic. Red haired and combative, he was as underrated as a player at Chelsea (and subsequently Fulham) as he was as assistant manager at Craven Cottage and Crystal Palace, where he briefly teamed up again

CRUCIAL GOALS

With four games to go in 1950/51, Chelsea were bottom of Division One, four points behind Sheffield Wednesday and six behind Everton. In those days only two went down, but things were desperate, despite the fact that Chelsea had three home games left. The first of these was won 1–0 against Liverpool – the Blues' first win in fifteen games. Then Wolves were seen off 2–1 by way of a disputed penalty and a goal by **Ken Armstrong** with just a whiff of handball about it. On the penultimate Saturday, Fulham were narrowly beaten 2–1 at Craven Cottage, leaving Chelsea level on thirty points with Sheffield Wednesday and two behind Everton on thirty-two. With the Toffeemen having to travel to Wednesday for their last game, the great escape was on. With Wednesday doing their utmost, a 6–0 win, Chelsea played their part by despatching Bolton 4–0 at the Bridge. Chelsea escaped relegation by just 0.044 of a goal. The all important goals in that match were shared by **Roy Bentley** and **Bobby Smith**.

After the 'big freeze' of winter 1962/63, Chelsea's Second

with his old spar in 1997, before succumbing to a serious leg injury and infection, then embarking on a slow, painful recuperation in 1998.

JIM LEWIS

The records show that a number of Chelsea players have been presented with an 'illuminated address' over the years, most famously James Greaves. But what on earth is an illuminated address when it's at home? No matter, it is only handed to a select few in recognition of great service to the club. And it was handed over to Jim Lewis, one of the Blues' great amateur servants, in 1959. He was, of course, a Championship winner.

Division promotion push was faltering. Having lost a vital home game 0–1 to rivals Stoke City on 11 May 1963, the Blues badly needed a result at Roker Park against promotion rivals Sunderland to maintain any hopes of reaching the top flight. In a tense game on 18 May, the Blues gained a famous win courtesy of **Tommy Harmer**'s only goal for the club, the ball going in off his wedding tackle (or, as he later put it, 'what you wouldn't show your mother') from Tambling's corner. A 7–0 home win over Portsmouth three days later took the Blues up on goal average, by 0.401 of a goal.

In 1983/83 Chelsea finished just two points clear of the Second Division drop zone. Only a 1–0 win at fellow-strugglers Bolton, courtesy of a seventy-first minute twenty-five-yarder from **Clive Walker**, in the penultimate match of the season, banished fears of playing in Division Three for the very first time. Only the Blues' third away win of the season, and their first win of 1983, that single goal win must go down as one of the most important in the club's history, especially given the glorious promotion campaign the following season.

And, in the grand tradition of that unique side, he was a winger with the fleetness of Mercury. Although he shared duties with the better known Frankie Blunstone, he deserves to be acknowledged for his dash and deft footwork, if not the suave styling of his fashionably Brylcreemed hair. The son of another famous amateur England international, JW Lewis, he also knew where the net was, grabbing an invaluable half dozen during our only triumphant League challenge to date. Hackney-born Jim (who arrived in 1952 from Walthamstow Avenue) scored forty goals in ninety-five appearances – not a bad scoring ratio at all for a flanker – and left the club six years later, shortly before his thirty-first birthday. In an age when players, even those like Jim who are not regular starters, earn fantastic amounts for their artistry, it makes you wonder what someone of his effectiveness would have warranted in the professional market today. Now seventy-one, he runs a pub near Southend.

BARRY LLOYD

A poor man's Ray Wilkins, in his way, Barry was just not good enough as a player, though he played for Fulham in the 1975 FA Cup final. As a fan, he followed Chelsea to Tromso in 1997.

GARY LOCKE

In a better team he could have been what Ken Shellito (his youth, then senior team manager) was: attacking, powerful, direct. Going forward, in fact, he was easily England class. Defending he could be more fallible. Nevertheless Dave Sexton's faith in Gary was such that he was blooded at eighteen in the 1972/73 season and all rivals, including the beloved Paddy Mulligan, were sold off. Born in Park Royal, Gary was an England Youth player but injury at crucial times probably robbed him of greater recognition. In his first full season he dislocated his shoulder in a training five-a-side.

Later on, a series of problems requiring surgery led to comparisons with his TV contemporary, the *Bionic Man*, and he virtually lost the ability with the left foot that had kept his options open on those surging runs.

A huge favourite with the fans in a team that was often bereft without him, he was Player of the Year in the promotion year 1976/77 and might have been for rather more of the eleven seasons he played for Chelsea. Perhaps his solid consistency was taken for granted. In 1983, following further injuries, Gary quit for Palace at the age of twenty-nine. He had scored just four times in 317 Chelsea appearances. Soon, though, he was to return with Palace and score for them from thirty yards.

REG MATTHEWS

A record buy of £20,000 in December 1956, who turned out to be something of a disappointing Christmas present when unwrapped. As many as Jimmy Greaves was scoring at the other end, this reputable keeper was letting them in at his. Although he was erratic, some of the blame has to go to a defence that wasn't up to it. Losing his place to spring chicken Peter Bonetti, he moved on to Derby in 1961.

TEDDY MAYBANK

Chiefly remembered for his bare-faced lie when appearing as a would-be lover on Cilla Black's *Blind Date*. It wasn't the fact that he was already married when he went on the popular singles show, though that was substantial enough as porkies go. No. It was that when he was asked what his job was, he announced, 'I used to be a professional footballer', stretching the credulity of anyone outside of Brighton, where he settled after leaving Chelsea in 1977. There are few memories to savour from his two years – a goal that earned a point at home to Sheffield United in his second League match promised more than he could deliver. Opposition fans teased him for being 'a poof'. Far from it, in fact. The blond bombshell was always more concerned about his image than anything else. As he worked his way through the junior ranks at Chelsea in the early 1970s his team manager observed that the best way to mark him was to hold a mirror up.

ALAN MAYES

One of the over-criticized players of his time. He was a second-rate player, admittedly, but in the fourth-rate teams of the early 1980s. Sold in 1983.

KEVIN MCALLISTER

Macca was one of those mighty midgets Chelsea seemed to specialize in during the 1980s on the back of the successful nurturing of Pat Nevin. He was small and Scottish, therefore a winger, right? Wrong, actually. Kevin, a man with a wicked sense of humour and sharp crack for every occasion (except one-on-one with the keeper – dynamic shooting wasn't his forte), was primarily a front man for a 4–3–3 formation, and not an out-and-out flanker. It was his thankless task to replace the popular Mickey Hazard in Division Two. There were occasions when his dribbling and pace prompted the first rumblings of a 'No, I reckon he might just be good enough for the First Division you know' campaign. But the rumblings, like Kevin's career at the Bridge, didn't last long. He moved on (and on), no doubt livening up the dressing rooms of Scotland with his ready wit as he went.

TONY MCANDREW

Tony arrived in 1982 and was gone in two years. In that time, particularly his second season, he scored vital goals (including two penalties and the decisive strike away at Cambridge), skippered the club, and made a vital contribution to Chelsea's promotion.

He was slow and couldn't pass, so poor Tony became a much villified figure, unfairly in many people's view. But as Ken Bates was keen to point out, a professional like Tony had value to a squad beyond performing on the pitch. Tony's heart was always in the club, where many of the players regarded him as a kind of uncle figure.

Even when his days, as the crowd wished it, were numbered, he spared inordinate time to sign autographs and chat with young fans. Pat Nevin also relates that at the start of his first season, he had just played a reserve match with Tony when news arrived of the first team's result against Stoke City: 5–0, it was. Tony and Pat cheered and thrust their fists in the air. The rest of the 'stiffs' muttered expletives in disappointment. It's a crucial difference in mentality. Tony's type wanted the club to succeed – if they proved themselves they'd be able to share in any of that glory eventually. For others, success closed doors. Tony played twenty-three times as a solid midfielder who exploited his limited talent to its utmost. He quit to return to Boro, then local rivals Darlington and Hartlepool.

'Tony McAndrew left Chelsea,' says Pat, 'and Chelsea died for a while. The team spirit fell apart.'

It's not necessarily the headline grabbers who make a club tick.

JIM MCCALLIOG

Sold as a record-fee (£37,000) teenage forward to Sheffield Wednesday, in 1965, after two seasons in which he was never quite good enough, scoring three goals in twelve appearances (two of them in a six-goal victory). More big money deals followed; some players attract the wad even when it's not deserved. Jim, later a Scottish international, is chiefly remembered subsequently for becoming an expensive flop at Old Trafford. (Though Blues still smart from the goal he scored in the 1966 FA Cup semi-final against Chelsea.)

EDDIE MCCREADIE

As usual there's a Tommy Docherty story attached to the uncovering of this rough diamond of a left-back. The Doc went to look at another player at East Stirling but his gaze fell on the fearless, attack-minded defender. A fee of £5,000 was paid at the close of the 1961/62 relegation season and during the beginning of the ensuing campaign 'Clarence' (so named because of his wonky eyes) became the perfect complement to right full-back Ken

Shellito. With those two haring down the flanks it was overlap, overlap, overlap.

Eddie had his run-ins with the capricious Doc, the routine response to which was a transfer request (not granted). The young Scot enjoyed London with a wide-eyed delight that occasionally turned to disillusionment, especially with the showbiz aspects of a professional footballer's life. That was later, though. To begin with Eddie was a delightful madman, one for crazy pranks and extended drinking sessions.

In 1965 he made his first big impact during the final victory over Leicester City in the League Cup, then on the verge of becoming a serious trophy.

The first leg at the Bridge was remarkable in that injury-hit Chelsea deployed Eddie as a makeshift centre-forward. It was one of the Doc's inspired choices. The Blues' third goal in a 3–2 victory came after Peter Bonetti gathered a Foxes corner and rolled it out to Eddie, who had tracked back and was standing on the edge of his own box with just a few of the Leicester players between him and the goal eighty yards away.

'As the ball came to me,' Eddie explained in 1996, 'I could feel one of their midfield players come in and he was going to give me a tickle – I knew that right enough. So I side-stepped him with the ball and I managed to run onto it. And as I turned, I moved it forward and saw Sjoburg and Cross [Leicester defenders] come towards me, both a bit square. I was a bit quick at the time. I hit it between the both of them on the halfway line and I just ran. I got through, they had a few swipes at my heels, and I ran all the way down.

'I got to just outside the box and I'm stretching and stretching and I hit it just a little ahead of me. I've seen Gordon Banks come off his line and and I threw myself at the ball, got a toe to it just as he came out, on the edge of his eighteen-yard box, and it went past him and kind of bobbled into the net.'

It was, according to veterans of the stadium, the finest goal ever scored at Stamford Bridge. Only just over 20,000 saw the 3–2 win with ten men. Eddie's best mate, skipper Terry Venables, scored a penalty too. The return leg at Filbert Street was played out 0–0 in front of 27,000. The *Daily Mirror* the next day prophesied great things for Docherty's Diamonds: '0–0 Chelsea Grab League Cup: A triumph that came like the dawning of a bright new day.'

In contrast, Eddie was given the runaround by Tottenham's man of the match Robertson in the dreadful 1967 FA Cup Final.

Eddie enjoyed the footballing aspects of his time at Chelsea – playing in European competitions, or against Pele and Santos of Brazil in Jamaica were highlights. Apart from the goal-line mix-up with Ron Harris that allowed Jack Charlton to open the scoring in the 1970 FA Cup final, Eddie's uncompromising tackling and fluid forward play were features of the first FA Cup triumph. But the run of bad luck with injuries that kept him out of contention for Cup-Winners' glory in Athens the following May was to have a debilitating effect not only on his playing career but also on his sense of well-being. Although he was appointed captain in March 1972 and stormed back to his old brilliance the ensuing season Chelsea's most capped player (twenty-three for Scotland) retired from playing in 1974.

He'd already taken his FA coaching badge and assumed that role at the Bridge under new manager Ron Suart. A year on Eddie was then appointed head honcho of the now cash-strapped side himself. In the Second Division he let go some of his old friends, retaining others for an astute blend of youthful exuberance and experience. On top of that he applied his own inspirational pyschology, actually convincing his players to accept a wage cut so they could all be kept together. With the brilliance of Ray Wilkins, the enthusiasm of Ian Britton and the goals of Steve Finnieston he returned his club to the top flight at the second attempt. A dispute with the board over a written contract concluded despairingly with the principled Scot's departure from

Stamford Bridge after fourteen years' superb service.

Utterly disillusioned and depressed, Eddie moved into coaching in the States, where he remains. His fear of flying, ruthlessly exploited for fun by some of his teammates during the golden years, perhaps partly accounts for his absence from the Bridge ever since.

DUNCAN MCKENZIE

Was he bought as a gimmick? Or because he always scored great goals (against us)? Context is important. This was 1978. Chelsea's 'glamour kings' crown had tilted badly with relegation, promotion and inertia the order of recent years. When Johan Cruyff played in a testimonial against the Blues at Stamford Bridge, Chelsea tried to buy him. George Best, on record as fancying a move to Stamford Bridge, couldn't be convinced to sign. If Puskas or Di Stefano, in their fifties, could still hobble, Chelsea may well have been in for them. As it was, he announced his presence in the Chelsea programme of the mid-1970s in a typically unorthodox manner – a series of adverts appeared pronouncing 'I'm Duncan McKenzie and I'd like to introduce Chelsea fans' … to a lager beer he'd discovered in Belgium. Chelsea were so impressed, they bought the player. If it was anything like the attacking midfielder promoting it, the lager was spectacularly capable of hitting the spot just when you needed it, varied in effervescence from mouthful to mouthful, came without bottle, but left a memorable after-taste. Duncan's seven stylish months at the Bridge gave us a glimpse of the quality that the rest of the team lacked, but also thought that there was some worth in yeoman-like grafters. Oh yes, and he used to jump over Mini cars from a standing start. Great bloke, Duncan.

BOB MCROBERTS

Bobby McBobby, as he would be known nowadays, was the solid, unadorned sort of centre-half who often performed simple acts that went unnoticed. (Unlike his waxed moustache.) Bob, though, was well-respected throughout the game for his proficiency and strength of character. A teetotaller, at thirty he became the first footballer to sign for Chelsea in 1905, before a ball was kicked by a toecap. His timing, reading of the game and spotting of danger were excellent assets in a game dominated by wing play and the regular cavalry-charging at full-backs. The game was very different then. His ability in the air was formidable too, even in the physical melées that wingers' high crosses produced. Indeed, he scored Chelsea's first two goals. Well done Bob!

Bob lacked pace against the fiercest rival strikers, whose requirements he knew very well, having himself converted from the centre-forward position on arrival from Small Heath (aka Birmingham).

JOHN MILLAR

One of Pat Nevin's protegés, Millar was an intelligent Scot who, like his 'mentor', saw Chelsea, and London, as an opportunity to expand his mind (he studied at college as Pat had done) and have a good time. Pat always said that John was good at everything he tried, especially sports. He played cricket for the Scotland international side.

Unfortunately the timing of his break into the first team (1985/86) could have been better. John was a midfielder asked to play full-back by the new Hollins-Walley management team. He looked a class act on occasion, but like so many before him was broken, perhaps, by a single incident. His fourth appearance of the 1986/87 season brought Nottingham Forest and lightning winger Franz Carr to the Bridge. John knew that he lacked pace – his assets were his technique, passing and reading of the game. So when Walley told him the way to mark Carr was to 'mark him tight' (the accepted wisdom), the left-back protested that he'd get slaughtered. Walley insisted. John was slaughtered. We lost 6–2 at home. John never played for us again. He was sold to Blackburn where a useful career was carved out in more sympathetic – if less glamorous – surroundings. Ironically, Graeme Le Saux, another of Pat's pals, made the same journey a few years later.

It was never quite explained why his kit was sponsored by 'Slush Puppie'.

SCOTT MINTO

He scored the last goal that the late Matthew Harding ever saw, a beautiful right-footed lob from the edge of the box at Bolton in the League Cup. His long-range strike from a sideways pass from a set-piece against Blackburn in his final season was a fantastic effort. And he was an accomplished left-sided defender, or wing-back, in Glenn Hoddle's 3–5–2 formation. But much-touted Scott, who Chelsea fought off Arsenal to buy from Charlton in 1994, was something of a disappointment because injury marred his career at the Bridge. A free agent, Scott signed with Benfica in 1997.

DAVE MITCHELL

Fleetingly reunited with his old Swindon boss when Glenn Hoddle assumed control of Chelsea in 1993, the Aussie international forward – Chelsea's first beardie since Dave Webb and the odd wisp on Eddie Newton's chin – worked hard without credit. He was never going to be another Ossie, but the globetrotting Socceroo, something of a cult figure in his days with Feyenoord, was able to hold the ball up well and knew how to take a chance with either foot. In 1997/98 Dave became player-coach of Sydney United of the Minor Premiership, back Down Under.

KENNY MONKOU

Graeme Le Saux's big mate was our first black Player of the Year in 1989/90. He was also the first Dutchman of Surinamese extraction to play in the Chelsea blue. The second? Ruud Gullit.

GOALS GALORE

To the end of the 1997/98 season, Chelsea had scored a total of 5,087 league goals in the eighty-two competitive seasons of the club's existence. **Scott Minto** was the unlikely scorer of the club's 5,000th league goal with his piledriver against Blackburn Rovers at the Bridge on 5 March 1997. The most league goals in one season came in 1960/61, when the Blues netted ninety-eight times; the least was thirty-one in 1923/24, when Chelsea troubled the scorers just thirty-one times. The worst defensive record also came in 1960/61, when 100 goals went in at the wrong end. The best record came in 1911/12, when only thirty-four were conceded in thirty-eight games.

Inevitably, **Jimmy Greaves** holds the (unlikely to be beaten) record for most League goals in a season, netting forty-one in – you've guessed it – that goal crazy 1960/61 campaign. He also scored thirty-two in 1958/9. **Bobby Tambling**, who scored thirty-five in the Second Division promotion season of 1962/63, and **Bob Whittingham**, who put away thirty in 1910/11 (Division Two), are the only other two to have scored thirty or more league goals in one season. Others to get into the twenties are **George Hilsdon** (1906/07, 1907/08 and 1908/09), **Bob Whittingham** again (1911/12), **Jack Cock** (1919/20), **Bob Turnbull** (1925/26), **Jimmy Thompson** (1927/28), **Hughie Gallacher** (1931/32), **George Mills** (1936/37), **Tommy Lawton** (1946/47), **Roy Bentley** (1948/49, 1953/54 and 1954/55), Greaves (1957/58 and 1959/60), Tambling (1961/62 and 1966/67), **Barry Bridges** (1964/65), **Peter Osgood** (1969/70), **Steve Finnieston** (1976/77) and **Kerry Dixon** (1983/84, 1984/85, 1988/89 and 1989/90). No-one has managed to match this achievement since then.

The lowest number of goals for a top scorer came in 1923/24, when **Andie Wilson** scored just five (and Chelsea scored just eight away goals).

Ken wasn't in that class, and was capable of lapses of concentration, but he was fast, mobile, tough, good in the air and a real personality. He cost £100,000 from Feyenoord in March 1989 and took just a little time to settle. Pretty soon, though, he was 'Super, Super Ken, Super Kenny Monkou', his aggressive tackling comparing favourably with the departed Joe McLaughlin and critical to a defence that needed strengthening for the challenge of Division One.

Alongside David Lee and influential skipper Graham Roberts he formed the platform for Chelsea's barnstorming of the First Division and a fifth-place finish. When they needed to mix it, they could.

Ian Wright, the Palace and Arsenal striker, always harboured a grudge against Kenny, claiming that behind the smiling exterior was a nasty gobby player.

Off the pitch the former model was playful and, well, different to most of his teammates. He read a lot, practised yoga, had a passion for antiques and always promised himself he'd open a little bric-a-brac shop with bijou cafe when he finished in the game. No, definitely not a pub.

Once when he was unavailable for an away game Kenny travelled up independently and stood amongst the Chelsea fans on the terraces, to the jubilation of Blues followers present.

Kenny proved himself for another two seasons, particularly in partnership with Erland Johnsen. Once Ian Porterfield's big money buy Paul Elliott arrived and the idea had taken root that they were too similar, and didn't complement each other, there was only one outcome. Kenny was sold to Southampton, where he provided years of sterling service. As to the coffee shop... who knows?

JODY MORRIS

At just six weeks past his 17th birthday, local lad Jody, another graduate of Lilleshall, made his debut in the 5–0 destruction of

Middlesbrough in February 1996. Needless to say, he was Young Player of the Year by the end of the season. Cultured on the ball, technically excellent and gifted with it, Jody's similarities to Dennis Wise bely a potential beyond even that standard. Injury and lack of match fitness have affected his progress, and at some stages there might have been a temptation on the part of the management to cash in on the England Under-21 midfielder as his ship appeared to be listing badly.

But in 1997/98 the star of Channel Four's documentary on the junior Blues knuckled down and forced his way back into the first-team reckoning, announcing his return with the match-winning twenty-five-yarder in the Coca-Cola Cup against Southampton. Efficiency rather than flamboyance was his game now. And in April 1998 it paid off as Jody was brought on with twenty minutes to go in the sensational overturning of Vicenza's 1–0 first leg lead in the Cup Winners' Cup semi-final. 'I was buzzing,' he told *Onside*. 'I mean there was a great atmosphere, it was a brilliant game to be involved in, from 0–1 down to 3–1. It was the best feeling I've had in football.' But not for long, perhaps.

JOHN MORTIMORE

There are Chelsea fans and ex-players who still bristle at the memory of the popular John's disallowed goal against Liverpool in the 1965 FA Cup semi-final at Villa Park, the stadium where Chelsea Cup campaigns go to die. Typically, it was a header – he had a forehead like a frying pan. An England amateur international, John turned pro at Chelsea for ten seasons' excellent service in 1955. Curiously, this commanding centre-back was allowed to stew in the stiffs by fading boss Ted Drake, who favoured the patently less-qualified Bobby Evans and Mel Scott during the crucial period between 1960 and 1962, which ended in relegation. When Tommy Doc took over as boss, John was one of the few to survive the cutting of dead wood, becoming an ever-present in our rebound season (1962/3) and an elder statesman in that youthful squad right up until 1965 when he moved on to QPR for £8,000. Later, and for several lifetimes, he was assistant manager at Southampton. Happily, John is still spotted at Chelsea reserve matches – but in an official capacity as a scout or whatever, not as a fan.

JERRY MURPHY

Another late-1980s player who got stick from the fans. The difference with Jerry is he thoroughly deserved it. His primary contribution to our welfare in the 1985/86 season that saw him arrive from Crystal Palace on a 'free' was two goals that earned points away at Coventry and high-flying Everton. The twenty-five-year-old left-sided 'deceptive' (when given the benefit of the doubt) midfielder was hampered too much by injury early on to have a great impact in the Speedie–Nevin–Dixon era. As he was largely keeping the more popular Canoville and Hazard from the side, he didn't stand a chance. He wasn't the most popular figure in the camp either – one of only two or three players not invited to Tony Dorigo's wedding.

Towards the end of the 1987/88 season he was washed up at the Bridge, despite some years still to run on his contract. In an interview with ClubCall the Stepney boy announced he was sick of England and sick of English football, that he was off at the end of the season, and would look to make his name in Australia. Unknown to him, his manager Bobby Campbell listened to ClubCall every day. The next day Jerry was hauled before the Meat, paid up and booted out.

BERT MURRAY

'Ruby', after the 1950s American singer of the same surname. A former England Schoolboy and youth-team graduate to the senior side in 1960/61, Murray immediately revealed himself as a pacy, head-down bomber along the right wing. If there hadn't been a stand the other side of the greyhound track he'd have regularly ended up in the Fulham Road. He was more than just a sprinter however. His skills allowed him to convert reasonably successfully to midfield, and the fact that he ended up as a full-back (in place of injured Ken Shellito) in Tommy Docherty's treble-chasing Diamonds speaks volumes for his all round talents. Bert's goalscoring from the wing, though, was sensational. In 1964/65 his seventeen goals was the best haul from that position in three decades. A big pal of Terry Venables and Allan Harris, he would visit Butlin's each year with them, and was involved with Tel in the infamous Blackpool Incident. Bert is cited in some circles as being a decent emergency goalkeeper. Given that he was five feet seven inches-odd tall, emergency must have meant: 'if last person left standing'.

A few years after Doc sold him for £25,000 to Birmingham in 1966, Bert came back to haunt us, taking the throw-in that led to Brum's goal in the third round of the FA Cup in 1969. He now runs a pub in Peterborough. (Annual coach outings to Blackpool, no doubt.)

ANDY MYERS

1991's Young Player of the Year – 'Tyson' to his mates – is a lovely bloke and, as you'd expect from an FA School of Excellence graduate, a very good footballer. Left-back, centre-back, Andy would run through walls for the team, has the pace of a gazelle and the body of an ox. The problem is, he's accident prone and unlucky. Injury, and too-quick returns, have marred his career since his senior debut at seventeen against Luton in April 1991. Ligaments, broken bones, more ligaments... and the only surgery he really wanted was a gold-capped tooth.

Glenn's assistant manager Peter Shreeves used to say, 'The trouble with Andy is his second touch is always a tackle', and you knew what he meant, mean though it was. Yet he is honest and a true hundred-percenter. Maybe that's why even though he was capable of scoring the most fantastically stupid own goals he remains a player to rely on in a crisis.

Austria Memphis, 3 November 1994, was a case in point. Recovering from an ankle ligament operation he made his seasonal bow as a midfielder in an injury-hit Chelsea unit that needed a result to progress, having drawn a blank at the Bridge. Andy ran himself into the ground, and then ran again, frightening the Austrians with his power and directness. John Spencer may have been the goalscoring hero, but it was Andy that battled the opposition into submission.

A few seasons and serious injuries later he was to score a fantastic goal at Hillsborough, cutting in and firing an unstoppable shot from close range. When fit he remains the man you want to ride shotgun for you. Justifiably he was handed a bench place for our victorious FA Cup final in 1997, though he missed the cut for the following season's Coca-Cola Cup revelries, and earned his Cup Winners' Cup medal as a squad member rather than participant in the Stockholm final. And in that competition, just remember who was the least guilty, Luca apart, of surrendering to the conditions in Tromso.

Every club needs an Andy Myers. Chelsea should think themselves lucky and wrap him in cotton wool!

JOHN NEAL

John Neal was a great Chelsea manager who never saw through his master plan. Unlike their recent 'showbiz' appointments, Danny Blanchflower then Geoff Hurst, the Board at last decided to go to Middlesbrough for an experienced football manager, and hired John Neal, who along with assistant Ian McNeill, created a turnaround in his second season.

New chairman Ken Bates permitted the manager the luxury of spending scarce money on several astute purchases, overriding the youth policy that sustained the club to varying degrees for two decades.

In came the likes of Nevin, Dixon, Speedie, Spackman, McLaughlin, McAndrew, Niedzwiecki. Out went Locke, Driver, Chivers, Fillery and others.

In 1983/84 Chelsea achieved promotion with the chemistry of Nevin-Dixon-Speedie wreaking havoc in opposition defences.

And in the First Division Chelsea managed two successive sixth-place finishes in 1985 and 1986 as people began talking about the Chelsea swagger for the first time in a generation.

At a time when his simple strategies and intuitive understanding of individual footballers' psyches were really looking to reap dividends, and the chairman looked keen to invest in the manager's beliefs, John, a heavy smoker, was taken seriously ill.

It was clear that his life was in danger if he carried on with his regular duties. In the event, the softly spoken north-easterner was moved upstairs and John Hollins, who he had brought in to help out with coaching, was elevated to manager. From there on John Neal's elaborate project began to unravel.

As it is, the former manager required a quadruple bypass operation on his heart, and stress-free recuperation was vital.

He left the club and now resides in a modest flat in Wrexham. Happily he was able to hear the appreciation of supporters for the foundation he laid in the mid-1980s when he returned to the Bridge for the club's game against Southampton in 1997.

'That first season,' he recalled, 'was an unforgettable experience and something I'll always treasure. In fact, hanging on the wall as you enter my hallway there is a picture of me holding the Second Division Championship trophy with The Shed fans in the background. That was a great moment. But, in the end, although he (Ken Bates) tried to protect me at first, my heart was broken by what had been achieved and was destroyed.' He wasn't the only one.

PAT NEVIN

Pat Nevin arrived as a callow wee Scots youth in 1983, still intent on finishing his college course. He fell in with an arty crowd in London and adored the glamour of the capital. And on the pitch he shone. Oh how he shone.

A footballer who practised long and hard, studying tricks of others on videos and recalling some of the touches of his childhood hero Jimmy Johnstone of Celtic, Pat (he always hated the nickname Patsy) broke into the side in place of the fitful Paul Canoville as a number eleven, switching to the left after a few months, and soon became the hero of the terraces with his dazzling footwork and mazy runs.

An early triumph was the demolition of Newcastle. Already comfortable by half-time, Pat decided to turn on the style for the second period and was simply magical. Kevin Keegan singled the winger out at the end and personally told him how impressed he was. Typically, modest Pat was more impressed with Keegan's never-say-die approach when all was lost.

The wee man, who started his career with Craig Brown's Clyde, was fervently supported by his father, who would travel regularly to games from Scotland (he worked for BR) and spend time afterwards dissecting his game with his beloved son.

An unusual footballer in his lifestyle, conversation and approach to his career, Pat travelled to London games by public transport until a near-disastrous encounter with a Spurs skinhead on the Victoria Line. He was the original Chelsea Bohemian, one time arriving at a teammate's party in drag, to the open-mouthed amusement of the likes of Colin Pates. And he was accessible to fans who popped into one of the greasy spoon cafés he frequented around SW6.

Pat must rank as one of the best Chelsea players never to win any trophy worth winning. He was Player of the Year in 1984, his debut year, and 1987, the year John Hollins took over from Pat's great nurturer John Neal and destroyed his Chelsea career.

In July 1988 we got a trifling £925,000 for the brilliant winger, now a Scottish international regular, from Everton. There was little dispute where his heart lay, though – when he moved on to Tranmere, he returned to Goodison for the Chelsea game, and sat amongst the visitors... who noticed and exposed him!

Pat became a representative of the Professional Footballers' Association in 1995, then moved to Kilmarnock as a player once more.

And apart from his stunning ball skills and brilliant setting up of others for goals, what is he most remembered for? Why, the worst penalty in the world that he drizzled towards Manchester City's goal, of course.

EDDIE NEWTON

Steady Eddie. Scored on his senior debut aged twenty in May 1992 with a twenty-yarder at Everton. Scored twice at White

Hart Lane as an emergency forward. Gave away the first penalty against Manchester United at Wembley 1994. Adapted his game under Glenn Hoddle to become one of the best deep-lying midfielders in the country on the verge of England recognition in 1995. Delivered the killer penalty in the FA Cup shootout at St James' Park in January 1996. Broke his leg on Hitchy's knee in 1997 and has had two serious knee operations.

Our Newton didn't need an apple to land on his head to recognize what was happening all around him. An admirer of the Liverpool sides of the 1980s, and organizer of his own 'Edward Newton Soccer Academy' outfit for kids, he loved the revolution happening at the Bridge and has responded season by season when fit. After fourteen barren years at Chelsea, the Hammersmith boy found himself the proud possessor of an FA, Coca-Cola and Cup-Winner's Cup medal, playing in all three.

While still a player Ruud Gullit described Eddie as the 'silent force' of Hoddle's Chelsea, and that was true. The long-term injury though, will take a good pre-season before supporters are convinced the old Eddie is back for good. The old Eddie, mind, the one who made every Chelsea fan proud to be there to see him score the second goal at Wembley in 1997.

PETER NICHOLAS

A 1988 signing from Scotland who'd made his reputation at Crystal Palace, and, like Jerry Murphy proved a major disappointment. In truth he was nearing the close of a distinguished enough career, but his sluggishness contributed little to a struggling *fin de siecle* midfield that would come to miss the industrious Nigel Spackman, and his passing and general reliablity went unappreciated. Peter moved on from Chelsea into coaching.

EDDIE NIEDZWIECKI

'Steady Eddie' might have been a contender for greatest-ever

THE LAD'S A BIT EXOTIC-SOUNDING

Peter **BONETTI**

Roger **WOSAHLO**

Ken **SHELLITO**

Tore **ANDRE FLO**

Mark **FALCO**

Muzzy **IZZETT**

Tony **DORIGO**

Eddie **NIEDZWIECKI**

Celestine **BABAYARO**

Dan **PETRESCU**

Scott **MINTO**

keeper had it not been for the injury that prematurely ended his career in 1986. He was bought for £45,000 from Wrexham in May 1983, an unknown to all except sapient John Neal and his team of scouts.

Instantly displacing Steve Francis between the sticks, he was tall, solid on the ground, dominant in the air and consistent. Given Francis's evident shortness, his height was enough to commend him. It also helped that the defence had confidence in him, though he wasn't the greatest kicker, and the jitters at the back were banished.

Eddie's first game was a rewarding clean sheet – 5–0 over Derby. There would be fifteen more league shutouts for our ever-present custodian before the promotion-winning 1983/84 season was out.

He drew strength from that record to complete thirteen more blanks in 1984/85, including Chelsea's first four in a row since autumn 1980, to underpin a campaign that concluded in a sixth place finish in Division One, the highest since the 1960s.

By now Eddie was tipped to displace Neville 'The Bin Man' Southall in the Welsh goal, but remained his deputy until the QPR game in March 1986 when he suffered serious ligament damage after former Chelsea teammate Steve Wicks landed on him following an aerial tussle. Steve Francis, then Tony Godden stepped in, and although Eddie returned half-fit in winter 1986, his playing career was finished.

Happily, Eddie, a Bangor-born lad with a Scouser's wit, stayed on the coaching staff under successive management changes and has proved a vital member of Chelsea's staff who spy on opposition teams.

SEAMUS O'CONNELL

In October 1954 a strange thing happened. Firstly an amateur country boy made his debut at home for Chelsea and amazingly grabbed three goals against a fine Manchester United side. Secondly, Chelsea scored five and still lost that day – an all too familiar symptom of the Blues of the time.

Seamus was a burly native of Carlisle who didn't see the need to move from his beloved homeland (not for him the sophisticated attractions of the King's Road). He would train with local side United during the week (under the celebrated Bill Shankly), helping his father with a successful cattle-trading business, then grab the train south on the Friday afternoon and play the following day, returning to the far north-west a day or so later.

Inevitably his lack of availability was an issue. His performances certainly weren't. An instinctive finisher, as well as a neat player on the ball, Seamus hit a dozen goals from seventeen starts in barely one-and-a-half seasons.

Seamus was perhaps never likely to stick around SW6 for long. He drifted away from the Bridge to appear sporadically for amateurs Crook and Carlisle.

From his retirement home in the Costa del Sol, Seamus recalls his Chelsea days with affection. Then again, who else can say they scored a hat-trick against Busby's Babes on their debut?

TOMMY ORD

Some players are like Morning Glory – they bloom spectacularly one day, then disappear before most people have had a chance to see their display. In April 1973 trendy-looking nineteen-year-old Londoner Tommy, all long hair and 'Mungo' sideburns, broke into the first team midfield in the number ten shirt already worn that season by Huddy, Nobby Houseman, Chris Garland, Bill Garner, Johnny Boyle, Dave Webb and Steve Kember. Injury and in-fighting had robbed the King's Road swingers of their swagger and Tommy had only signed professional six months earlier from Athenian League side Erith and Belvedere. So when he scored a brilliant thirty-five-yard half-volleyed goal on his debut at home to Stoke (lost 1–3), the cynics were already resigned to a one-hit wonder. So it proved. Two poor further performances and he was packed off to Canada for the summer, loaned out to Bristol City and saddled up to Rochester Lancers of the North American Soccer League the following close-season.

PETER OSGOOD

Ossie is a living legend at the Bridge, one of the few 1970s heroes still to be involved on a weekly basis with his old club, and regularly called upon to give that era's perspective on the current side. To his credit, Ossie manages to balance measured criticism (he had his run-ins with Chairman Bates during the 1980s and was no fan of 'aloof' Rudi's management, and said so) with a delight in stylish players and aching desire for success that fans empathize with. 'We won the Cups but we never won the League,' he said recently. 'But with the squad we've got now I think the team of the 1990s can go one better than us and win the Championship.' How much more refreshing than some of the rancid stuff trotted out by some of his former colleagues.

Ossie's debut came in the League Cup fifth round replay against Workington on 15 December 1964. He was seventeen. Chelsea won 2–0 and the Windsor teenager scored both goals. The *Daily Mirror* had it thus: 'Lucky Old Chelsea – Third Division Workington Give Docherty's Wonder Boys The Fright

EURO STARS

The Blues' European campaigns have been intermittent, so relatively few have amassed large numbers of European games. To the end of the 1997/98 season, the tally was as follows:

Harris	27	Baldwin	14
Hollins	27	Tambling	14
Bonetti	26	Wise	14
Osgood	26	Hudson	13
Boyle	22	Newton	12
Hinton	20	Clarke	11
Webb	18	Graham	11
Cooke	17	Sinclair	11
McCreadie	16		

TOP EUROMARKSMEN

Osgood	16	Tambling	3
Baldwin	7	Venables	3
Vialli	6	Webb	3
Hollins	5	Birchenall	2
Zola	4	Brabrook	2
Di Matteo	3	Flo	2
Furlong	3	Hudson	2
Graham	3	Hutchinson	2
Greaves	3	Petrescu	2
Sinclair	3	Stein	2

Of Their £100-A-Week Lives', adding, 'New boy Osgood hits two late goals to save their face.'

Tommy Docherty has compared successive generations of new star strikers in English football with the young son of a builder he blooded as a teenager and found them wanting. According to Doc, he had everything: technique, passion, intelligence, pace, power and formidable skill. 'If Shearer can go for £12m,' said Tommy, 'then Ossie would go for £15 – or £20 – in today's market. He was that good.' Especially so before the injury (perpetrated by Blackpool's young Emlyn Hughes on 6 October 1966), that put him out for the best part of a year, removed him from our 1967 Cup final squad and forever transformed his casually elegant style. Up to that point Ossie had scored six goals in eleven starts and was being watched by England manager Alf Ramsey.

That was the first of his three extensive breaks from playing for Chelsea. The second arrived during the 1970/71 season when his indiscipline was punished by a then record-breaking eight-week suspension.

And the third was the hiatus away from the Bridge following a fall-out with Dave Sexton and a move to Southampton between 1974 and 1978 on the back of his first supporters' Player of the Year award in 1973.

The three may well be related. Ossie returned from his leg break a more casual and temperamental individual, not so bright and irrepressible. The young conjuror was heavier too, less able to practise the lithe, gliding movements of before.

The flair, though, remained. Dave Sexton introduced a deeper position for him too, where his excellent distribution could pay dividends. And in doing so, he developed more subtlety in his game and figured in the World Cup squad of 1970 as consistency if not work rate, increased in his game. Ossie was capable of blinding inspiration for spectacular goals. The Sexton side could murder a side and put the game out of reach in a spell of twenty minutes, when four of the key figures began to tick. Ossie was one of those players, along with Webb, Hudson, Cooke,

Hollins and Houseman, and he did it with style befitting the 'King of Stamford Bridge'.

The BBC once showed a slow-motion sequence of the striker weaving, spinning and feinting his way around three bewildered opponents, and set the whole thing to a wistful rendition of the Beatles ballad, *Something*: 'Something in the way he moves...' If Ruud Gullit talked about Chelsea playing 'sexy football', let's not forget Ossie's contribution to the same game in the early 1970s.

He epitomized the King's Road glamour of the Docherty–Sexton era though he lacked the hipness of Huddy and others, being a 'farmer's boy' from Windsor. Cocky, charming, he was associated with the likes of American pin-up actress Raquel Welch (though her appearance pitch-side during a game appears to have been part of a publicity stunt) and featured in the 'news' pages of the tabloids probably more than he would have liked. Today, he likes to downplay the 1970s image. Some hope.

He was self-confessedly one of the club's worst-ever train-ers after youthful exuberance had made way for mature evasion – he and several others like Marvin Hinton famously hid during cross-countries on the South Downs, rejoining the pack towards the conclusion of exertions, panting for all the world as if they'd completed the whole course. So it was perhaps no surprise that he and Sexton had fall-outs. On one famous occasion Chelsea fans demonstrated outside the Bridge with placards, demanding that Ossie be removed from the transfer list.

The people who would most have liked to see the back of Ossie were Palace fans. Beginning with the 1969 'scandal' when Ossie was alleged to have tricked the Palace keeper with a cry of 'Leave it John!', he was merciless home and away, grabbing four in a 5–1 demolition at Selhurst on one occasion and tormenting their defence on a number of occasions. The spell ended in 1973 when Eagles defender Jim Cannon crunched the waning Chelsea star out of the game. Needless to say, Ossie cites John Jackson as his favourite goalie.

Peter never managed a side, but he had tactical awareness (especially where his own position was concerned). For instance, he favoured a 4–2–4 after the successful switch to that formation won the European Cup Winners' Cup final replay against Real Madrid (4–3–3 was deployed in the first match). Ossie wanted to operate in the 'hole' behind Garland, Hutch or Garner ('They're two of a kind,' as he had it) and Houseman.

For his part Sexton just wanted more discipline and a higher work-rate from his star. He reckoned that if the Wizard of Os applied himself over ninety minutes like other players (Hollins being the prime example) he would have been the first choice for successive England managers. In 1966 he was overlooked, though many believed his lithe, callow unpredictability as much as his undoubted quality would have helped unlock some of the defences England struggled against in the opening skirmishes of the World Cup Finals. Perhaps it was his dip in form late in the season that turned Ramsey's mind; perhaps it was the distrustfulness, later also demonstrated by the hateful Revie, of a playboy prince.

Once relations with Sexton had stretched beyond the limits of elasticity, Ossie had to go. He earned another FA Cup winner's medal with Southampton, of course, and appeared to revel in the more laidback managerial atmosphere created by Lawrie McMenemy. He returned to Chelsea for a number of testimonial matches, including the emotional evening when Stamford Bridge bade farewell to Peter Houseman. That someone saw fit to scream an obscenity aimed at Ossie during the minute's silence revealed a sense of betrayal. Ossie was still a fine player.

By the time he eventually returned home in 1978, though, his effectiveness in the top flight had passed. He scored twice in his first season as a returnee, once in the 7–2 defeat at Middlesbrough and once against Manchester City (he always scored against them). But it didn't last. Both parties agreed that the reunion had been a bit of a mistake. Ossie had developed a taste for passing on his knowledge to the Chelsea kids, but it wasn't to be. He moved on.

Happily, after a number of money-making projects, some successful, some not, Ossie enjoys life as an organizer of golf events and as matchday host at the Bridge, milking the regular adulation of the fans.

ERIC PARSONS

Rabbit, as he was known (the affectionate nickname mysteriously evolved amongst Chelsea fans during his six-year tenure at the Bridge, and may or may not have had something to do with parsnips) dominated the old outside-right slot, or the wing to anyone under thirty-five, before and until shortly after our sole Championship season to date, 1954/55. When the trophy was raised at the Bridge, the supporters chorused for him to say a few words over the microphone. Choked with emotion, he was unable to say a word. It was no surprise to some.

His early career was blighted like so many by the Second World War and, of course, a misguided spell at West Ham United, so he'd just turned twenty-seven when he made his debut for the Pensioners. Like Peter Houseman a decade and a bit later he was a winger who incurred the wrath of sections in the crowd.

A cartilage operation was another knock, but the short and none too hefty son of Sussex returned with a vengeance to torment opposition backs with his tricky and intelligent play. With his craggy face, riven with laughter lines, Rabbit found goals relatively easy to come by and had an impressive return rate of nearly one goal in four in his near 500 wartime and postwar games; none more important than the two goals at home to Sheffield Wednesday that effectively sealed the Championship in Chelsea's jubilee year. None of that talented side could have imagined that more than forty years later we're still waiting for a repeat. Except, perhaps, those who sensed that finishing sixteenth the following season was hardly the way to herald the birth of a ruling dynasty. The following November, like so many of our favoured sons, Eric slipped off to Brentford.

COLIN PATES

Whatever happened to the Colin Pates who looked a million-pound player at the centre of the Chelsea defence? The YTS-schooled south Londoner had made 300 appearances by the age of twenty-five since his 1979 debut against Orient in Division Two. Comfortable on the ball, good in the air and able to marshal the defence with a maturity beyond his years, at twenty-four, he became one of the youngest captains in the First Division following promotion in 1984.

For two seasons, largely partnered by the more agricultural work of Joe McLaughlin, Colin's presence helped secure two consecutive sixth-place finishes. But injury and defensive lapses crept into his game against the new breed of pacy strikers and by 1987 he was being asked to play in midfield when available. In 1988 Colin, a popular, jesting presence in the dressing-room for almost a decade, moved on to Charlton for £430,000.

GAVIN PEACOCK

Serious-minded Gav's great claims to Chelsea fame are three-fold. Firstly, in his first year in our midfield he scored both the single goals that brought us the 'double' over champions Manchester United. Secondly, he scored both FA Cup semi-final goals against hapless Luton at Wembley, becoming the first Chelsea player to score a winning goal at Wembley in that competition.

The third happened in our third meeting with United of that 1993/94 season, the FA Cup final. He agonizingly hit the bar with a fantastic dipping shot in the first half dominated by Chelsea. Gav was something of an outsider at the club, quiet, likeable but practically humourless, and a devout Christian. As an attacking midfielder he was the one most threatened by the frenzied, mythical rumours of Matthew Le Tissier's imminent arrival any time between 1993 and 1996. Whether it was the insecurity that had him asking programme contributors who Chelsea were signing next or what, he was unfortunately an inconsistent performer and moved on to QPR in the summer of 1996.

DAN PETRESCU

There were several aspects to the acquisition of Dan Petrescu that indicated a sea change in the perception and fortunes of Chelsea. The Romanian wing-back announced that he actually wanted to play for Chelsea and Glenn Hoddle. 'We will be legends in yellow,' he predicted. The club hadn't had such a glowing thumbs-up from a world-class footballer in so long that it was almost embarrassing given how recent had been our turnaround under Glenn. And in his first game in autumn 1995, albeit a defeat at Leeds, the *X-Files* Mulder lookalike instantly had an impact. Like a new hi-tech addition to a chef's kitchen, though, it wasn't immediately clear how to use him to the best advantage. He would ghost into positions of threat, or suddenly appear next to a stuck colleague, like Superman gliding next to a tumbling Lois Lane, offering a way out. The shimmies and the dummies, the dinks and the slices soon became well known to his teammates, and although his defensive play was not built of the same steel as, say Stuart Pearce, the options he offers and the fluidity he contributes to our passing play has oiled the whole Chelsea machine, particularly since the arrival of the Italians.

Dan's experience has been another great benefit. European Cup, Italy, World Cup – games that may not have prepared him for a Vinnie Jones tackle, but they must have helped him retain his cool when he grabbed those memorable strikes against Newcastle at home in the League and Wimbledon away in the FA quarter-final, both in 1996.

His absence in the subsequent semi against Manchester

United contributed heavily to our demise at Villa Park. But his delightful pass put Vialli through for the earth-shattering third goal against Liverpool in the FA Cup 1997, and at Wembley Dan was able to win his first piece of English silverware. He made a direct contribution as it was his typically searching cross that reached Franco Zola, who side-flicked brilliantly for Eddie Newton's killer goal.

In Rudi's second year Dan found himself the most fre-quently subbed player on the pitch, sacrificed tactically when his performance on the right of midfield was perceived as not up to scratch. He didn't appear to like it. But it didn't stop him con-tributing his usual bagful of magic moments, none better than the fast-footed dribble and strike that ripped the heart out of Arsenal in the Coca-Cola semi-final second leg. Having professed to wanting to play the Chelsea way with Ruud Gullit, the Romanian international became 'Super Dan' under the Dutchman and his successor, winning his third cup winners' medal in 1998 and heading off to France 98 as one of eleven Chelsea participants. Dan knew what he was doing when he opted for the Bridge.

Following his winner (outwitting Graeme Le Saux) for Romania against England, Dan became Chelsea's all-time most capped international when he faced Croatia, surpassing the record of twenty-four set by Ray Wilkins between 1976 and 1979. He is a genuine Chelsea legend now, in yellow, blue or white.

JOHN PHILLIPS

'Teflon' to his detractors (nothing stuck), 'Sticks' to his pals, John was an outstanding though fallible Welsh international keeper, who would have had a fairer crack at the big time had he not been behind in the pecking order to one of the all-time Chelsea greats, Peter Bonetti. His father and grandfather both played for Shrewsbury, and the same club blooded the third Phillips at seventeen. A spell at Villa was concluded by the move to SW6 for £25,000 in August 1970. John was nineteen, and bought as cover for leg-break victim Tommy Hughes. His League debut two months later was little short of remarkable. 3–0 down to Blackpool at half-time, Chelsea rallied late on to win, Walker-powered, 4–3.

John was groomed as the long-term successor to the Cat. Indeed, he kept his place in the Cup Winners' Cup semi-final despite the number one's return to fitness. Nevertheless it was Peter who figured in the two matches of the final itself. John's misfortune was that Catty was so reliable, and had that little extra – command of his box – that John and others were unable to compete with. The two seasons in which he figured most prominently – 1973/74 and 1974/75 – coincided with unfortunate placings of seventeenth and twenty-first in Division One. In 1975/75 he became the only keeper to out-rank the Cat in appearances during twenty years, though, and Peter's contract wasn't renewed that May.

In pre-season 1975/76, though, jinxed John broke his leg and could only sit and watch as first Steve Sherwood emerged (fitfully) and then the now grizzled Bonetti was recalled from an American sabbatical to shore up the defence at the age of thirty-five.

Clearly none of the problems were John's fault, and the talismanic Putneyite was always a popular option and a great comforter in times of crisis.

In 1977/78, the first season back in the big time, a similar thing happened. Appearing in the first ten matches, including the memorable 1–0 win at Old Trafford courtesy Bill Garner, John was displaced for the rest of the season by his old spar Catty. The exception was one unfortunate Easter match at Upton Park when Sticks' cheekbone was fractured by Alan Taylor's boot. Bonetti resumed for the next game. (John might have been forgiven for expecting Peter to turn up and nick his fiancée from the altar, so regular and predictable was the Cat's upstaging.)

The perpetual understudy was a popular figure amongst the

players at the Bridge, organising some of their social occasions (one year including, would you believe, a satirical Christmas pantomime). John quit Chelsea in 1980, for Brighton, Crewe, Charlton and Palace, then set up a car parts business in London.

On his rare visits to Stamford Bridge these days he's shown himself a shrewd observer of the game, not to mention an intelligent and thoroughly likeable fellow with no trace of bitterness for the lack of first-team football.

PHYSIOS

There just aren't enough races between physios these days are there? They weren't always the fit young things you see hovering on the by-line when a Premiership player rolls around in agony.

Primarily they were ex-players rather than specialists in their field. The first man to wield the magic sponge at Chelsea was Jimmy Miller, a former Scottish international. He died midway through the club's second season and music hall comedian George Robey set up the first benefit game, all rewards to Miller's family, scoring a cracking goal from his inside-left position. It was the beginning of the club's association with showbiz, culminating in the film-star-packed dressing rooms of the early Seventies and the Keystone Kops defences of the late 1970s.

The first pitch-side medic many people remember is head trainer-cum-physio Harry Medhurst, partly because he looked as fit as a butcher's dog.

Bow-legged Harry, a former keeper who traded in his cap for a bucket and trained the first team at the same time (not literally, of course) from 1953, was the butt of players' jokes during the 1960s and 1970s. These were the days of a quick rub and 'You're all right, lad' – nothing like the masseurs and assorted specialists at the Bridge today. His interest had been kindled by wartime experiences helping his sister, a nursing sister, with air-raid casualties. On cessation of hostilities he was one of the seven who rolled up for the FA's first physiotherapist course.

The players got their own back for his ice cold water in the 'orchestra stalls'. The ageing, infinitely enthusiastic father of Norman (his successor in the treatment room from 1975–88) was an innocent in an increasingly smart game. Ossie recalls how, particularly during end-of-season tours the players would drag Harry into drinking games in which he was deliberately made the loser since he was so easy to make drunk and so entertaining when in that state. If the players treated him a little like a pub dog, to the fans Harry was an unorthodox hero. He is still probably the only physio to have his name chanted by the crowd: 'Med-hurst!... Med-hurst!'

After Norman's spell Bob Ward was the last of the 'old guard' of physio. The arrival of Mike Banks under Glenn Hoddle represented a more technical approach, not simply in terms of the scientific record keeping he ushered in, but also as a result of some of the hi-tech kit Ward had already ordered, augmented by the former Spurs assistant physio on his arrival. The new treatment room at Harlington was thus turned from a few weights and a psychiatrist's couch into a near state-of-the-art health spa. With the increased emphasis placed on massage under Ward, Terry 'Two Touch' Byrne answered a programme advertisement and landed a role on the medical staff. Having earned more different certificates than a dirty video Terry followed in Norman's footsteps and joined Glenn Hoddle's England medical team during the 1998 World Cup qualifiers.

More unusually, Glenn also ushered in alternative medicine. 'Tootsie', a West End reflexologist, diagnosed problems through players' feet. Eileen Drewery, the faith healer who rose to notoriety in the build-up to France 98, treated John Spencer, Frank Sinclair and club captain Paul Elliott. This kind of innovation, coupled with Glenn's unwillingness to cooperate with journalists, gave rise to the belief that the easiest way to get an interview with him was through a spirit medium.

POETS

F Douglas, Edgware Road, London, 1906:

Chelsea, you're the team to show 'em (when you're in the proper
*   vein),*
How to pass, and pass, and pass, to and fro, and back again,
Every pass is marked with science with, of course, a casual flaw,
Lor! How you do tease the half-backs, whilst the spectators guf-
*   faw*
Still, I often think (Beg pardon!), when I've paid my 'tanner'
*   toll,*
Extra shooting, now and then, might place more goals on the
*   scroll,*
And uplift you (where we want you), in the First Division roll.

Master Tony Byrne, aged eleven, Fernshaw Road, London, 1969

*   Peter Bonetti, greatest of all,*
*   Jumps up and down to hold the ball.*
*   He lands on the ground as though it's a mat,*
*   That's why we call him 'Peter the Cat'.*
*   He dives through the air for a spectacular catch,*
*   With speed and agility no-one can match.*
*   The greatest goalie of the century,*
*   That's why Peter's fantastic to me.*

Maria Carter, Bishops Road, London, 1973

*   I knew the dreaded day would come;*
*   I overheard Dad say to Mum*
*   'I'm going to decorate Maria's room';*
*   All day I walked around in gloom.*

*   With sad and heavy heart that night*
*   I told Chelsea of my plight:*
*   'Dear Hollins and Garland, Hudson and Osgood,*
*   I'll have to take you off for good!'*

They looked sad, too, as if to say
'We're sorry 'cos we'd like to stay!'
And so I slowly took them down
And tried my hardest not to frown.

At last each wall was stark and bare,
No trace of Chelsea anywhere;
Forlorn and sad, I crept to bed
To try to dream of them instead.

I looked around – a sorry sight –
No Chelsea there to say goodnight;
I found I could not sleep at all
Without the boys upon my wall.

But now my room's done and I'm glad
No longer will I feel so sad
'Cos now they're back for good –
Dear Hollins, Garland, Hudson and Osgood.

IAN PORTERFIELD

The wrong man in the right place at the wrong time. Sunderland's FA Cup goalscoring hero returned after a seventeen-month absence to manage Chelsea in 1991 saying, 'My aim is to win matches. Number two is to win by playing good, attractive football. But it is very important to win.' Nought out of two was a bad result.

His credentials appeared impeccable – at least to Chelsea fans – in that he had single-handedly beaten Leeds at Wembley in 1973. Lured down from Aberdeen in 1988 as assistant to Bobby 'the Meat' Campbell he was a popular and able performer. When he later left to become manager himself at Reading there was something of a popular revolt amongst players and fans that we'd lost him. People power isn't always

right, you see. Once Ken Bates had come to believe that
Campbell could take us no further in the top flight and brought
the Scotsman back from the Royals to replace him at the helm
in June 1991, the error of judgment was soon evident. Porters
was quite a good analyst tactically, but could be Quixotic in his
convictions. It was he, don't forget, who masterminded
Chelsea's first away League win at Liverpool in fifty-six years in
February 1992, correctly recognizing that Molby, as master dis-
tributor, was the key to Liverpool's attacking play. Cutting off
his supplies to the front frustrated the Scousers, and the sec-
ondary tactic of playing the ball quickly into channels, bypass-
ing midfield, also worked superbly. Nevertheless other results
under Porters around that time were less edifying, particularly
some feeble home performances at 'fortress' Stamford Bridge
throughout 1991–93 that planted us firmly mid-table. His judgment on some players appeared at odds with reality. He preferred Gareth Hall to Steve Clarke, didn't know how to get the
best from the immensely talented Graeme Le Saux, appeared to
dislike the promising Graham Stuart, and seemed determined to
see the able Erland Johnsen rot in the stiffs. We were still
enduring the 'dismantling years', and Porters proved as able to
deconstruct a decent side (one that had broken promotion
records reclaiming First Division status) and bolt on ill-fitting
spares as his immediate forebears.

The unsettled Tony Dorigo and vexatious Gordon Durie
were allowed to move on, understandably, but Ian neglected to
hire replacements of similar or better quality. Rated fellow Scot
Tommy Boyd never settled and looked frightened by the pace of
the English game; Geordie Joe Allon's major gift (apart from
being the second Chelsea player in recorded history to score with
his privates) was joviality in the dressing room. Other signings,
such as Willie Donachie, Vinnie Jones, Mick Harford and Clive
Allen smacked of desperate progress in no obvious direction
other than 'route one'. He was also guilty of the feeblest case of

mistaken identity when he signed the wrong Charlton full-back. Everyone was talking about Scott Minto. The press were linking Chelsea with him. So Porters bought Anthony Barness, perhaps the worst Chelsea debutant of the 1990s. Need we discuss the £2.1m Fleck, bought in 1992? Paul Elliott, however was a different matter. The big summer '91 signing instilled the leadership qualities required of a team largely composed of noddle-heads. Had his second season not been so unfortunately curtailed by injury, 'Jamaica' might have proved the lasting contribution of Ian Porterfield to the story of the Blues. As it is, his enduring legacy has been the blooding of some fine youngsters, including Frank Sinclair and Eddie Newton.

It all ended dismally. Two months without a win snapped the chairman's patience and he was sacked, a bitterly disappointed, even 'surprised' man, in February 1993, to be replaced by David Webb. The players, for the most part, liked him and missed him. The fans barely noted his passing. Similar work at home proved elusive for Ian. But he found gainful employment as coach of various emerging international sides, including that of Zambia, the cream of whose team was tragically destroyed in a plane crash in 1994.

GUSTAVO POYET

Coming from a land, Uruguay, where a law was required to ban clubs if they owe their players money at the start of season, where referees strike, fans are killed and financial strife is widespread, Gustavo Poyet must be grateful for a little stability in his life. He was perhaps the least heralded of the numerous summer '97 signings, despite a Blues connection. Such is the fate of the undersung free transfer.

The tall twenty-nine-year-old midfield all-rounder had been a member of the powerful Real Zaragoza side that knocked Chelsea out of the Cup-Winners' Cup three years earlier and went on to beat Arsenal in the final.

He immediately took the team by storm though. His strength in the air – plugging a perennial hole at both ends – work rate, intuitive interplay with others and subtle ability to convert saving tackle into swift counter-attack were quickly noted in the stands. By the time he broke the deadlock with an acrobatic header against Newcastle at home, he was a firm favourite, with three goals to his name. It would take more than six months for him to make it to five.

And had he not snapped a cruciate ligament in his right knee during training in October, he may well have gone on to figure in the end-of-season football awards.

'When I had the operation I thought for me the season was over,' he said later. 'I had never had any injury as bad as this before and I was told I should not expect too much. But we had already gone through the first round of the Cup Winners' Cup and I saw that the last game of the season would be the final and I just had a small dream I could play in it. I became Chelsea's biggest supporter, watching them go through every round, and I just worked as hard as I could to be fit in case there was any hope of being involved in the biggest match.'

Gus was a good patient, according to physiotherapist Mike Banks. Naturally lacking some of his usual loose-limbed exuberance, Chelsea's first ever South American signing perfected his English, travelled back home across the Atlantic for a while, and did what he was told. Around January rumours that he would be available in March circulated. They were premature, but not by much. When he reluctantly appeared on the pitch at half-time during one match, the ovation was deafening. He was deeply touched. And the supporters had even had time to think of a tune for him during his enforced sabbatical: 'Poyet... there's only one Poyet...'

'The moment came when it was decided I could play in a reserve match (in early April),' said Gus. 'And I was very happy because at least I knew I could play again but I still didn't know

ILLUSTRIOUS OPPONENTS

In Chelsea's first competitive match against European opposition, the Blues came up against **Frem** of Copenhagen, Denmark in the first round of the Fairs Cup on 30 September 1958. In goal for the Danes was **Bent Koch** and their only goal was scored by the undeniably mature **Gronemann**. Seven years on, in the same competition, Chelsea came up against the **Wiener Sportklub** of Vienna, Austria, and their centre-forward **Wolfgang Gayer** – not forgetting midfield schemer **Adolf 'Grassy' Knoll.**

Bigger names were to face Chelsea in later Euro ties. Against **AC Milan** in the Fairs Cup of February 1966, the Blues faced captain **Cesare Maldini** – now Italy manager, of course – international forward **Giovanni Rivera**, a substitute for Italy in the 1970 World Cup final, and **Amarildo**, who'd won the World Cup in 1962, scoring Brazil's equalizer in the final against Czechoslovakia. That same season, **Barcelona** fielded famed Portuguese forward **Torres**, who was just about to star in the 1966 World Cup.

In October 1968, in the second round of the Fairs Cup, the Blues lost on the toss of a coin to **DWS Amsterdam**. In goal was **Jan Jongbloed**, the unorthodox, slightly wobbly keeper who kept goal for the total football-playing Netherlands team that lost to West Germany in the 1974 World Cup final. His team-mate **Joop Burgers** did not play in the World Cup finals, but apparently tasted nice with chips.

about this (Cup Winners' Cup) final or whether, even, Chelsea would be there.'

Betis and Vicenza were successfully overcome and Gus's target became 13 May 1998, Stockholm. As a loosener, new boss Luca Vialli threw Gus on as a sub for young Jon Harley to tumultuous applause in the last half-hour of the traditional victory over the Spurs. He did enough to rekindle hopes of a Euro show,

By the time Chelsea reached the European Cup Winners' Cup final in 1971, **Real Madrid** were fading giants, but the legendary **Gento** and Spanish international **Amancio** still made appearances in both games. As defending champions, the Blues scored a record-breaking 21–0 aggregate victory over Luxembourg part-timers **Jeunesse Hautcharage**, who fielded the four **Welscher** brothers – **Eddy, Raymond, Jean-Pierre** and **Lucien** – in both legs, as well as **Guy** and **JM Thill.** Hautcharage is a small town. So you'd rather not be called **Jean-Pierre Poos**. That unfortunate played in the first leg at right-back.

Remember **Atvidaberg**? A lack of goals against the Swedes cost Chelsea the tie in the next round, but they did at least have **Ralf Edstroem** and **Roland Sandberg** up front, the international pairing who carried **Sweden** into the second round in the 1974 World Cup – and scored six of the Scandinavians' seven goals.

Coming forward to the 1994/95 Cup Winners' Cup, **Viktoria Zizkov** of the Czech Republic fielded **Karel Poborsky**, later of Manchester United infamy and Euro 96 quarter-final heroics, plus singing midfielder **Petr Gabriel**. **Austria Vienna** included **Franz Wohlfahrt** in goal, later to face Chelsea again in the Stockholm final of 1998, this time for **VfB Stuttgart**. And who was that pulling on a **Real Zaragoza** shirt in the 1995 semi-final first leg? None other than **Gus Poyet**, suspended for the second match.

especially with Di Matteo suspended. Within a week he was starting the Cup Winners' Cup semi-final second leg against Vicenza.

It all started appallingly. A defensive disaster gifted the Italians their early opener to make it 2–0 on aggregate. And for the opening twenty minutes Gus barely touched the ball and wondered whether his game would come together so soon at such a high level. As the match progressed though he grew in confidence and prominence. And on 20 minutes, he latched on to a wide knock-down from the keeper, slid sideways with consummate athleticism and fired the loose ball into the net. The technique was phenomenal, the finish incredible. It was his thirteenth start and his fifth goal of the season.

Franco Zola's header and Mark Hughes's brilliant run and volley completed the comeback and put the Blues in their first European final for twenty-six years.

But Gus's was the vital, brilliant one. His reward? After the game he was selected to produce a urine sample. He was dehydrated and couldn't summon a drop, so drank nearly a gallon of water. The result was no humiliating revelation except that he had to stop during his drive home to relieve himself at the roadside. It's not all glamour, is it.

In the final at Stockholm, Gus laboured and hassled, probed and passed, and was subbed by Eddie Newton within minutes of Gianfranco Zola's magnificent winning goal. He received a rousing appreciation from the Chelsea hordes. Another Cup Winners' Cup winner's medal to add to his collection, with the promise of a full season and more glory to come.

Unsurprisingly, the Chelsea experience turned out a good one for the likeable Uruguayan international. 'I am ready to make a big impression again,' he said as the season drew to a close.

R

SPOT ON

The most penalties scored in one season by a single player was thirteen, by **Graham Roberts** in 1988/89.

GRAHAM ROBERTS

Robbo was the type of clenched fist leader on the pitch the Chelsea team lacked for years when he arrived in August 1988 from Rangers. Instantly installed as skipper, the former Tottenham star's lofty belligerence, professionalism and dedication, not to mention heart-warming ability to convert a penalty (something of a problem over the years at the Bridge) were all widely hugely welcome. He galvanized a team still licking its wounds from unjust relegation and drove it towards record-busting promotion in May 1989. Though he was not so infallible in the top flight, and indeed lasted little more than half the season, there was one moment in the First Division that seemed to define his spirit better than any other.

The sadly missed David Speedie arrived at the Bridge with his new club Coventry to present a potentially irksome threat to Robbo and the Chelsea defence. With the skipper in commanding form, there was to be no happy return however. After yet another skilful snuffing out with the former Blues favourite snapping at his heels, Robbo publicly demonstrated his dominance by walking alongside Speedo, pulling out the side of his shorts and pointing towards it. The message: 'I've got you in my pocket, sunshine'.

Such was the confidence he brought to Chelsea at that time. Sadly it all dissolved into injury, then recriminations and litigation with the chairman over payments and alleged promises.

His last contribution was to score the goal that earned a point against Nottingham Forest in mid-February 1990. Chelsea finished fifth that season, the best position until 1998.

BILL ROBERTSON

Bill was the third and latest of the Blues 'family' Robertson to have played in the famous blue and white colours of Cadogan, and the second keeper. Born in Glasgow during the depression of the late 1920s, he was a well-built six-footer and starred in the small-time Arthurlie's side before coming south in 1946 at the age of eighteen, lured by the post-war soccer boom.

It took the youngster five years to step out of the reserves (there was no subs' bench in those days) and Harry Medhurst's shadow to make his debut. The timing was tricky.

With four games remaining of the 1950/51 season, Chelsea faced Liverpool with a relegation mountain to climb and a record of fourteen games without a win. His form for the reserves had been such that Chelsea actually won the Combination the same season (and the youth team the South-East Counties).

Confident Bill contributed to the victories of the last four games which maintained top flight status by the merest of margins.

It wasn't all good news. His back must have ached after picking the ball out of the net in the 1–8 debacle at Molineux in 1953, still Chelsea's record defeat.

Keepers are always pretty popular in such circumstances, but Bill still had to vie with others for the custodian's slot, making twenty-six appearances in the 1954/55 Championship season. He played in the Charity Shield at the Bridge in front of just 12,000-odd people that same year, but gradually drifted out of favour, making 215 appearances in total.

In September 1960, frozen out by Drake's renewal scheme and by the promise of the fledgling Bonetti, Bill sloped off to Orient for £1,000. He died in 1973.

JOHN TAIT ROBERTSON

Jackie was Chelsea's first player-manager in 1905/06 and our last before Glenn Hoddle. Now there's a thing. He was also the first of several Scots bosses. He built a team that blended experience and youth, passed superbly, was bulging with glamour and skill, and entertained wherever it went. He was succeeded by David Calderhead once promotion was won.

SIR GEORGE ROBEY

Perpetrator of the first recorded public joke at Chelsea's expense. George, a ludicrously popular music hall entertainer, signed London League forms with Chelsea to play as an amateur after a benefit game he had organized for dependants of the late Jimmy Miller ended with his name on the scoresheet. As it is, the signature was probably of more use to him than Chelsea. 'I only signed with Chelsea to keep them in the First League (Division),' he said onstage in Welham Green. And he only turned out for one reserve match, against Hastings. It is recorded that he played upfront and, with the goalkeeper sprawling and the ball at his feet four yards out, managed to concede a goal kick in his only chance of the game. (By the way, in case you didn't spot it, the 'joke' was two sentences ago. No need for a needle and thread to repair those split sides, then...)

DAVID ROCASTLE

By the time he arrived at Chelsea in 1994, carved up by knee operations and a problem foot, he was more a squinter than a sprinter (an odd habit he probably picked up at Leeds). In his time he won two Championships, but his time was past when we signed him as cover for injured midfielders and as an Englishman

EARLY DOORS

Chelsea's first goal was scored by player-manager **John Tait Robertson** in the club's second-ever game at Blackpool on 9 September 1905.

The first-ever debut goal was scored by **James Robertson** at Leicester Fosse on 30 September 1905.

The first man to score from a penalty kick for Chelsea was **Bob McRoberts** against Barnsley on 4 November 1905.

Jimmy Windridge scored the first Chelsea hat-trick against Hull City in Chelsea's first home game on 11 September, 1905.

George Hilsdon scored Chelsea's first-ever goal in Division One against Sheffield United at Stamford Bridge in September 1909.

The first goal in European competition was scored by **Jimmy Greaves** against Frem of Denmark on 30 September 1958 in the Fairs Cup.

Tom Priestley was the first, and last, player to wear a skull cap during matches.

The first long-throw specialist in the English game was **Sam Weaver** – the tactic was little used in the 1930s.

The first substitute ever used by Chelsea was **John Boyle**, who replaced **George Graham** at Fulham on 28 August 1965. He was also the first substitute to come on at the Bridge, for **Marvin Hinton** against Sheffield Wednesday on 15 September 1965.

who might be needed in Europe, given the restrictions of the time.

Rocky was a fantastic addition to the squad in terms of experience, personality and intelligent conversation. (He once revealed that when they won the League in 1991 some of the other Arsenal players were approached by fans saying, 'Can you shag my missus so she can say she's slept with a champion?' And yes, he knew all about the 'rumours' about him and dismissed them as disgusting slander.)

His passing and vision were fitfully evident, but his stamina was never really there. The former England international's finest moments were in the 1994/95 European campaign as he scored a cracking goal against Zizkov at home and ran his heart out in Vienna against Austria Memphis.

For four years he laboured in the reserves without complaint, before having his contract cancelled in 1998.

DENNIS ROFE

Fulham-born Dennis was signed for £80,000 in February 1980 from promotion rivals Leicester City at the age of twenty-nine.

Why?

Dennis, a nice enough bloke, tackler and professional, was made captain by manager Geoff Hurst, who really couldn't tell a thoroughbred from a tin of Pedigree Chum, and played fifty-four games on the trot (he couldn't canter). Passing was a problem. In the two and a bit years he was with us, he is rumoured to have passed to a Chelsea player on just three occasions, one of them after the whistle had blown for half-time.

New manager John Neal persisted for a while, then replaced him with Chris Hutchings, sending him off to the knacker's yard at The Dell.

Satisfyingly, Dennis's first act on returning to the Bridge in red-and-white stripes was to win the ball superbly ... and pass to a blue shirt.

He soon graduated to Saints' coaching staff, which is where he was last heard of.

DOUG ROUGVIE

Allegedly a very nice fellow, Scotland's footballer of the year arrived from Aberdeen with a bucketload of medals including two Championships, three Scottish Cup and one Cup Winners' gong. Whether it was just that we played the game differently down here, or it was that the twenty-eight-year-old brick outhouse was simply past his best, but his Chelsea career was peppered with frankly idiotic mistakes, penalty give-aways and other misdemeanours.

His earth-shattering tackles, towering headers and pacy, bow-legged runs won him a cult following on the terraces, but in the end most people simply groaned when this much-heralded defender appeared on the team sheet. There had simply been too many mistakes. In 1987, after three fitful seasons, he returned to Scotland and took up management.

FRED ROUSE

Chelsea's first £1,000 purchase was a panic buy in 1907 from Everton following a disastrous start to the first League season of three points from the first eight games (it was two points for a win, one for a draw at the time). The club had subtly announced it was 'hunting talent with an open cheque book'. The bustling, vibrant forward was bundled over in his first appearance at the Bridge. Some wag is said to have shouted, 'Blimey, there goes a thousand quid!' Fred was a versatile attacker and in two seasons and forty-two games hit the net eleven times. By February 1909 he had moved on to Brentford.

DEREK SAUNDERS

The third and final of the Chelsea 'family' Saunders, flame-haired Hertfordshire native Derek came to Chelsea's attention while playing for renowned amateur side Walthamstow Avenue, who had just won the FA Amateur Cup. In 1953 he signed up with Chelsea. The influential wing-half, five foot ten inches and strong in the tackle, had a bit of imagination about him too, and was able to move the ball around with confidence and vision.

Derek was an ever-present in our only Championship season – some achievement – and earned his caps as an English amateur international.

Perhaps his main failing was an inability to find the net. In his 223 games, he scored nine times. Six came in one season – 1956/57.

The following campaign, manager Ted Drake recognized his leadership qualities and appointed him skipper. The left-half retired from the game in 1959, worked on Chelsea's coaching staff at a time when the likes of Bonetti, Venables and Bridges were coming through, and then moved on to Westminster School before becoming a groundsman at Hampstead Cricket Club.

KEN SHELLITO

Remember the player, not the manager. Ken, who signed with the club the same day as James Greaves in 1957, was one of the greatest full-backs of his generation. As his first Chelsea manager, Tommy Doc, put it: 'If Kenny Shellito had never had that injury, George Cohen would never have put on an England shirt.' The man who would go on to be our youth-, then first-team manager, was dogged by a problem with his left knee that showed itself in the early 1960s, sporadically laid him off for weeks on end, and eventually ended his career in 1969. Ken remembers the moment in December 1963: 'It was just outside the Fulham Road end. I turned to chase a Sheffield Wednesday player and my knee locked. It was rigid for a week. The surgeon didn't want to operate when it was like that but in the end he had to. Complications arose and although I got back in the first team I wasn't happy with the knee, and needed more operations.' Four in total, over six years, to no avail.

From the late 1950s when he broke into the first team while still a teenager, until the mid-1960s when he earned his first – and last – full England cap, though, Ken was a revelation in the right full-back slot. His attacking style, skill, bravery and accuracy of delivery typified the new breed of young footballer. And once Eddie McCreadie had arrived on the other flank Chelsea boasted an approach that was the closest thing the English League had seen to Brazil's overlapping backs. (Blackpool's Armfield has laid claim to 'inventing' the overlap, but Shellito and McCreadie took it to new levels.) Sadly, he managed just 123 performances for Chelsea, scoring twice. Then as youth coach from 1969 Ken oversaw the production line of players like Steve Sherwood, Ian Britton, Gary Locke, Ray Wilkins, Garry Stanley and Brian Bason. In 1970/71, his side won an Easter tournament in Cannes, beating the locals, Torino of Italy and Feyenoord. They also lost narrowly, 1–0, to the Brazilian national youth team.

As a player Ken had flair. But as first team manager, appointed in July 1977 (coincidentally at the expense of his erstwhile partner McCreadie), he needed flares – the ship was soon sinking. In December 1978, bottom of the First Division and unlikely to extract themselves from the mire, Chelsea dispensed with the former hero's services. Ken, one of many East Enders of the era 'poached' by our brilliant youth-team spies, moved into management with QPR, Palace and then lower division sides.

JOHN SILLETT

The lesser of the two brothers made a bigger name for himself in management, stewarding Coventry to 1987's FA Cup victory over Tottenham. John was full-back like his older brother, though initially on the other flank, the left. He broke in to the side after the Championship win in 1955 and was a tough, if occasionally reckless, tackler. Once the inspirational Ken Shellito rose through the ranks at the dawn of the 1960s John's days were numbered. But he went on to a much bigger and better career in management. An amiable bloke loaded with anecdotes, he has also presented Central TV sports programmes with life-long friend Jimmy Greaves.

PETER SILLETT

Full-back Peter was tough as old boots (old boots being made of steel toes, elephant hide leather, high ankles and studs that were actually nailed into a wooden sole at the time). Not the most gifted of defenders, scarcely an athlete really, he nevertheless has two mighty claims to glory at the Bridge.

Firstly he kicked the ball harder than any Chelsea player since the war at a time when medicine balls and footballs – when wet – were distinguishable virtually only by the protruding laces on the leaden soccer variety. Frequently, though not exclusively, his hefty kicks were to the benefit of the team.

Free-kicks to the Blues were welcomed almost as much as more recent, Zola-powered ones. But there was no subtlety about Peter's dead-ball work. His free kicks were like the act of a firing squad: ready, aim, fire. Occasionally the middle element appeared to have been overlooked and the missile would sail off into the crowd, though he once scored direct from just inside the opposition's half.

The second cherished memory is the penalty goal at home to Wolves in 1955, since it's often cited as the goal that clinched the Championship.

There was some debate over who should take our penalties before this crunch game with skipper Billy Wright's celebrated team but when centre-back Wright punched a goal-bound Seamus O'Connell shot over the bar, the full-back stifled all debate. He stepped forward and delivered a low drive that has been measured (not scientifically, admittedly, but with a blue-tinted velocimeter) as the hardest penalty of all time. It was reckoned that if keeper Bert Williams had got in the way Peter's blast would have taken him with it into the net.

Tiny Wolves winger Johnny Hancock nearly stole Peter's thunder (having given him the runaround all game), managing to hit both posts with one line-hugging shot, before Chelsea custodian Chick Thompson could paddle it away.

Peter scored the majority of his thirty-four goals from free-kicks and penalties in a way that Stuart Pearce could relate to. It was this special asset that overcame his lack of pace and allowed him to vie with John Harris for the right-back berth.

The height and size of rock-jawed Harris, swarthy keeper Bill Robertson, the two gaunt Silletts – especially sporting those rugged old boots – gave the impression that opponents were up against Frankenstein's defence.

But in those late 1950s Chelsea weren't as frightening as they should have been. Two more incidents will give a flavour of life in the Chelsea team post-Championship. The first was a comedic own-goal donated to Everton. A long-range effort from one of the Toffees squeezed under England international keeper Reg Matthews' body and towards the goal. Peter, with a view to helping the tidying up operation, raced goalward to cover. Unfortunately, Reg reached the ball first. And instead of picking the ball up, he elected to kick clear, turned on a sixpence and whacked the ball powerfully into the midriff of his onrushing centre-half, who collapsed holding his stomach as the ball rebounded into the net.

Later on, it was Peter who broke the startling news to the

players that the next opponents, relegation-haunted Nottingham Forest, had offered a bribe for the Blues to throw the match. Typical Chelsea: the principled players rejected outright the money... and lost anyway.

Bought for a song from Southampton, for eight seasons Peter was a superb servant, a golf partner to manager Ted Drake and a wonderful character at the club. As a new recruit Terry Venables was shocked to be warned not to train so hard as he was showing the older players up. 'Don't run faster than me,' barked Peter, 'or I'll smash your chest in.'

Jimmy Greaves relates that Peter could drink pints of beer like water – even Greavesie couldn't keep up with his mate. In 1962 Peter was given a free transfer to Guildford City. He continued to work in football, as manager or administrator, at various clubs and was still a great friend of Jimmy and others. Sadly, after a short illness, Peter died of cancer in 1998.

ALAN SIMPSON

One half of the famous Galton & Simpson comedy writing team, Alan impressed in a trial for Chelsea as a teenage keeper in early 1947, but contracted tuberculosis before the season started and was not able to sign. He met Ray Galton while recuperating and the fruitful partnership was born. Chelsea's loss was Hancock's and *Steptoe and Son*'s gain.

FRANK SINCLAIR

Frank. Frankie! Oh Fra-a-nk!! Chelsea's son of Lambeth has divided fans since his graduation from YTS to first teamer in April 1991. He has his 'Mad Frank!' fanatics. He has his '****ing Sinclair again!' detractors. And he is rumoured to be the only Chelsea player to soil his shorts while playing. Poor old Frank or good old Frank – take your pick. He will be remembered for an inadvisable pass back at Selhurst Park in January 1993 that stopped almost comedically in a puddle, allowing sole possession of the ball to a Palace striker. Chelsea lost 3–1. He will be remembered for that bewildering fancy 'flick-out' against Leicester at the Bridge, where the ball got caught between his legs and dribbled over the line. He'll be remembered for the celebration following his first League goal away at Villa in 1992, where the celebration lasted as long as the game. Chelsea lost 3–1. He'll be remembered for being replaced by Andy Myers in 1991's defeat at Nottingham Forest. Chelsea lost 7–0. And he'll be remembered for dropping his shorts after scoring a fantastic full-back's goal at Coventry on the season's opener in 1997. Chelsea lost 3–2. But mainly he'll be remembered for his opening headed goals in the almighty matches against Vicenza in the Cup Winners' Cup (won 3–1) and Middlesbrough in the Coca-Cola Cup final (won 2–0) in 1998.

Frank was Chelsea's most improved player over the period 1996–98. Chided for not working on his game enough and for an overactive social life off the pitch by Ruud Gullit, a man he respected, Frank responded with more serious, concentrated performances. His pace, athleticism, strength, bravery and improved touch – if not always his decision-making or delivery into the box – were often vital. And he appeared to be one of the few defenders capable of making the tactical switch from five to four at the back with relatively little difficulty. In fact, he started as a right-footed left back, played left midfield once under Porterfield (lost 3–0), switched flanks to right-back, then back to left, before, under Hoddle, finding himself on either flank, or in anywhere in the centre of defence. Rudi recognized that wing-back was not Frank's greatest slot since creativity was paramount and his strength was best utilized in defensive situations. So in a back five he was better deployed as a stopper in the central three. In seeking to prove himself in the suddenly star-studded company of Zola, Vialli, Petrescu, Di Matteo, Flo et al Frank vies for that berth, or right full-back, in the side. His new-found ambition was recognized when the Jamaica Football Federation approached him to join the squad in preparation for France 98, and he was duly capped as Chelsea's first Jamaican international in spring 1998, playing all three World Cup Finals matches.

The culmination of all this had been the powerfully executed header from Dennis Wise's cross that gave Schwarzer no chance at Wembley, April 1998. Cup winner! Naturally, his fellow 'Blues Brother' Eddie, scorer of the second goal in the FA Cup Final, was among the first to mob him. 'Funny,' says Frank. 'We seem to do things in twos, me and Eddie. We've been together at the club a long time and the first thing he said to me was "I can't believe you've had to go and copy me, scoring a goal the year after!" He's as happy for me as I am, and last year it was vice-versa.'

When Frankie first broke into the first team, he confidently asserted, 'Some people want to call me the new Paul Parker but I'd rather people spoke of the new Frank Sinclair.' It took a while, but maybe he is now recognized as the new Frankie.

NIGEL SPACKMAN

Spackers was a grand servant for the Blues in his two spells at the club. Initially signed by John Neal from Bournemouth in 1983, he scored a cracker on his debut which set everyone imagining the goalscoring feats to come from the midfielder.

Ah well.

In the early days he was a rosy-cheeked galloper around the pitch, harrying and carrying for a team that had previously struggled to dictate matches. Now Spackers did it for them. Without the extravagant skills of Nevin or the clever distribution of Mickey Thomas, he maximized on effort, and was hugely influential in the Blues' rise from Second Division to fifth in the First.

He was popular too, as hundred-percent ninety-minuters tend to be, earning the affectionate tribute of his surname being sung to the theme from TV's *Batman*.

He was a big loss when Liverpool surprisingly stepped in for him in 1987, then QPR and finally Rangers recruited him for his new-found versatility and reliability. The accrued experience of Championship victories and European adventures was something he never tired of relating to his Chelsea teammates when he returned for £485,000 in 1992 at thirty-one. Spackers had an odd sense of humour and was frequently provocative, but was more often a fun, thoughtful bloke to have around the dressing room.

By the time of his return, though, a prolonged back problem limited not only his game but also his appearances. His legs less rampant, he adapted his game to the holding midfield role or even sweeper once Glenn became manager. His old head was simply invaluable during the European campaign of 1994/95, particularly in Austria, and justifiably he finished runner-up to Erland Johnsen as Player of the Year.

His second stay lacked the impact of the first but was worthwhile for both parties.

After four years of his second stay Spackers had shown enough to be offered the player-coach job at Sheffield United, later succeeding Howard Kendall as manager, then resigning from a club in turmoil in 1998. He observed games for Glenn Hoddle in the build up to France 98.

DAVID SPEEDIE

Speedo, Scottish international and mouth almighty, could be a prickly customer. It took Pat Nevin, who roomed with him on Scottish expeditions, several hours 'counselling' to come to terms with the brilliant little forward's testy behaviour. He was one of the close season signings by manager John Neal that transformed Chelsea from Second Division also-rans into First Division Championship pretenders within two seasons.

Fans who'd been dismayed at his signing from Darlington were soon won over by his combative hassling style and excellent technique. He got into trouble with refs and opponents, but he was right at the heart of mid-1980s Chelsea. No taller than five feet seven inches, his spring-heeled challenges in the air and quick feet on the ground helped seal an instinctive link play with Pat Nevin and Kerry Dixon.

After just a few games the twenty-two-year-old displaced the experienced Bryan 'Pop' Robson and sealed his place with two goals against Oldham on his debut. There would be more than sixty to come in over 200 fiercely competitive performances from the Scotsman.

Always game, he even popped up once as an emergency goalie. Enthusiasm was one thing. Being lobbed from forty yards was another. He was, after all, a shortie no matter how well he got up for headers.

Coventry bought David in 1987 as the 1982 trio was broken up. When he returned with them to the Bridge, the now light-hearted Speedo smiled and dropped his shorts to the Chelsea faithful. He moved on to Liverpool, Blackburn and Leicester before becoming a players' agent. (Wouldn't fancy negotiating with him, would you?!)

DICKIE SPENCE

The Yorkshireman was a tricky outside right in the 1930s who delighted crowds with his skills and earned two England caps. After the Second World War he was to play a significant role in establishing the fruitful youth development scheme of Billy Birrell's era.

JOHN SPENCER

If mouths were inches, five-foot five-inch Spenny would have been a giant. The gangsta rap-loving, *Bravo Two-Zero*-reading, wise-cracking, infuriating striker was the loudest thing at the Chelsea training ground after the tractors that mowed the grass.

Irrational, hilarious, boisterous and moody, he was a mass of contradictions; a Glaswegian Catholic who supported Rangers

THE LAD'S A TOP SALE

Up to May 1968, the Blues' top ten biggest sales were as follows:

1 **John Spencer** to QPR for £2.5m, November 1996
2 **Gordon Durie** to Tottenham for £2.2m, August 1991
3 **Andy Townsend** to Aston Villa for £2.1m, July 1993
4 **Danny Granville** to Leeds United for £1.6m, June 1998
5 **Paul Furlong** to Birmingham for £1.5m, July 1996
6 **Tony Dorigo** to Leeds United for £1.3m, May 1991
7 **Neil Shipperley** to Southampton for £1.2m, January 1995
8 **Graham Stuart** to Everton for £950,000, August 1993
9 **Pat Nevin** to Everton for £925,000 in July 1988
10 **Gavin Peacock** to QPR for £900,000 in 1996

(he'd become the first of his tradition to play for the Protestant club as a kid); a short-legged man who was one of our fastest sprinters and a big-headed bloke lacking confidence.

Spenny's finest spells, in between the regular hamstring injuries inevitably resulting from his physiology and vigour, were in a position suggested by manager Glenn Hoddle that he initially rejected. Years later, he admits he was wrong to blow up when Hod tried to play him at the front of the diamond. What he doesn't say is that when Hod later needed to play him again as an out-and-out striker, the role he'd previously favoured, Spenny was equally annoyed!

The £450,000 August 1992 signing will be remembered for two contributions. Significantly, alongside Mark Stein he proved that a fast-footed, sharp-shooting twin short-house strikeforce was a viable prospect against the leviathans of opposition central defences. And then there is the small matter of one of the greatest goals in Chelsea's European history, the sensational eighty-yard sprint from just outside his own box to elude panting Austrian defenders, ignore the equally impressive run from Eddie Newton, and coolly slot the ball past goalie Wohlfhart (later to be beaten by an equally superb goal from Franco Zola in the 1998 final of the same competition.)

He'd previously shaved his head in tribute to the Andy McNab SAS book he was reading and proclaimed he was 'going behind enemy lines'. It proved prophetic.

A steadier personality and sounder body would have contributed more regularly to the Chelsea of Hoddle's era than did the unfortunate Spenny. His league total of thirteen goals in 1995/96 made him top scorer but it wasn't enough. With the arrival of Gianluca Vialli and form of Mark Hughes there was little point in his sticking around. QPR took him in 1996, and he moved on to Everton the following season, still knocking 'em in when fit.

GARRY STANLEY

Possessor of a rocket of a shot, mop-topped Garry was a shooting star of our midfield between 1975 and 1978. Unfortunately, we're talking unguided missiles rather than Exocets. He once participated in a 'hardest shot' competition at White Hart Lane, and he was easily the most powerful of those on show. As happened in his career, he missed the target and failed to register an 'official' velocity. Likeable Garry, who moved on to Swansea, is still a semi-regular visitor to the Bridge.

MARK STEIN

There were several good reasons to like Mark Stein. Firstly, he'd ripped Manchester United apart as a Stoke striker in the League Cup in 1992/93. Secondly, he still holds the Premiership record for consecutive goal-scoring – eight in seven games on the spin in 1994 achieved in a prolific spell at the beginning of that year, just three months into his Chelsea career. A classic goal area poacher, Steino's vicious target-finding was a delight to watch; his decisive penalty in the riveting 4–3 defeat of Spurs is one of the most emphatic spot-kicks seen at the Bridge.

Frozen out by the arrival of Mark Hughes in 1996 and different, more technical style of football, Steino languished in the Reserves under Gullit and Vialli, moving to Bournemouth in June 1998.

GRAHAM STUART

Nicknamed 'Bobby', as in Charlton, since he was our first graduate of the Lilleshall national school of excellence, Graham was a gifted, technically excellent midfielder-cum-forward whose inability to find consistency could be maddening. At his best he could run games, rampage past strings of opponents, as he did at Hillsborough in August 1992. In that game he ran from box to box as Robert Fleck and Mick Harford surged on decoy runs, body-swerving his way through the Owls' midfield, then dribbling through their defence before drilling the ball past the then England keeper Chris Woods.

Some people (including David Webb when he managed us) wanted Chelsea to build a team around Bobby and other promising homegrown youngsters.

However, Stuart was never given that much faith, and wasn't allowed to make the kind of mistakes to be expected of a twenty-one-year-old. With rumours of big-money interest from Arsenal (he scored the superb winner against them at the Bridge), and impatient for first-team football, he left for Everton in a rumoured dispute over money – as joint top scorer – at the end of the 1992/93 season.

His shot that hit the bar in the 1996 FA Cup Final led to Everton's winning goal against Manchester United. But in 1997 he was lured across the Pennines to Sheffield United. It could have been so different.

RON SUART

Ron spent the first part of his football life in the north and served Blackpool for ten years before switching Lancashire clubs for Blackburn Rovers, where between 1949 and 1955 he played 187 League games at full-back. A switch to management, eventually with Blackpool, ended when Tommy Docherty called him up as assistant manager in April 1967. Curiously, seven years earlier Ron had tried to lure the Doc from Arsenal as player-coach for the Seasiders. Tommy had opted for the same position at Chelsea instead. At Chelsea, Ron was required to look after the reserves and carry out some scouting and other tasks. It was he who watched and reported on many potential signings. Unheralded Ian Hutchinson was one of Ron's discoveries, as was Micky Droy. Unfortunately so was Derek Smethurst. So it wasn't that much of a winning streak.

Once Dario Gradi was hired in January 1971, his responsibilities were increased and he was made assistant manager. Sir Alf Ramsey saw enough in his man-management to put Ron in charge of an Under-23 European tour and a League representative XI's six-week sojourn down under. Ron was the natural choice as gaffer when Dave Sexton was relieved of his duties in October 1974, a post he'd already temporarily experienced at the end of Tommy Docherty's reign, shortly before the Sexton appointment. But the side, riven by player factions, unmotivated and distracted by financial matters off the pitch, failed to respond to Ron's understated management style. He'd been a friend to most of them, and he wasn't able to turn the screw in order to avoid relegation. He opted for experience, recalling Peter Bonetti over Phillips, dropping the promising Ray Wilkins and trying positions out on Steve Kember like a desperate salesman in a cheap clothes shop.

The drop was confirmed by a 2–0 defeat at Spurs in April 1975. Ron stood down to make way for his ambitious young assistant, Eddie McCreadie, and became general manager, then coach until leaving the club in 1983. More recently Ron has found work with Wimbledon.

KENNY SWAIN

Kenny was one of the most laid-back players in Chelsea history, perhaps because he knew that football wasn't his only option. Rejected as a teenager by Bolton Wanderers because he didn't get on with the chores of being an apprentice, the Scouser left school with eight 'O'-levels and two 'A'-levels and a place at teacher training college in Surrey. Wycombe snapped him up from college football, then Dario Gradi invited him to Chelsea for a trial and Dave Sexton signed him. He had to write a letter of apology to the school he was supposed to teach at when the season started.

At Chelsea Kenny's career took off during the 1975/76 season, when he, Garry Stanley and Ray Wilkins formed a bridgehead of youth into the ranks of oldsters. Eddie McCreadie's one-touch protégés settled superbly in a Second Division they were too good for, and Kenny, playing wide left as a paceless but deftly skilled winger, became a hero of the promotion-winning side. Though his work rate was of the old Cooke–Osgood school, his talents, in crossing, passing and beguiling opponents were equally in that mould. An unsettled period followed Eddie Mac's departure and Ken Shellito's succession, in Kenny's mind and in team selection. Pace and incisiveness down the left could now be found in Clive Walker. Kenny, finally bitten by the bullet of ambition, appeared disinterested in the mundane goings-on at the Bridge. It didn't help that Shellito decided to drop the otherwise exemplary midfielder for turning up ten minutes later than usual for a home match in February 1978 (Kenny claims he was stuck in traffic).

It was no great surprise when ten months later temporary manager Frank Upton, in virtually his only substantial contribution at senior level, flogged Kenny off to Aston Villa for a paltry £100,000. He was twenty-six and in his prime. At Villa Park Kenny replaced ultra-pacy, England international right full-back John Gidman, of all people, who was then in dispute with his club. Under Ron Saunders' guidance, Kenny won the Championship in 1981 and the European Cup the season after. Nevertheless, Kenny maintains friendships with Chelsea FC and his old teammates, and is always happy to talk about his goals against Fulham in front of no less than 55,003 or Southampton in November 1976, when a strong run was met by Ray Wilkins' cross and a side-foot home for a memorable victory.

BOBBY TAMBLING

They were big boots to fill, but Bobby was up to it: Jimmy Greaves departed in a blaze of goals on the last game of the 1960/61 season, and the youngster who stepped in finished his career with a record-busting 202 goals from 370 competitive first-team matches. Had Jimmy stayed, it's unlikely Bobby would hold the position in Chelsea history that he does.

Things began inauspiciously. Signed up as a fifteen-year-old in July 1957, Bobby was immediately homesick for Havant, his home near Portsmouth. In another eighteen months, though, he was making his League debut for Ted Drake's side against West Ham as outside-left. He scored the first, fellow debutant Barry Bridges nabbing the second, in a 3–2 win. Unsurprisingly he was part of the 1960 Chelsea side that carried aloft the FA Youth Cup. Two years later, with Greaves and Drake gone, Bobby notched thirty-seven, albeit in the Second Division, including a sequence from October to November 1962 of six games (all won) reaping 12 goals and four out of the seven against Portsmouth that confirmed promotion. He benefited hugely from the support of those around him. Early on there was the experienced, unhurried Harmer. Then there were midfield bosses Venables, Cooke and Hudson. As partners he was lucky to have the likes of Bridges, Osgood and Graham.

By the mid-1960s he'd earned three England caps, though he was never to prove himself at that level. The League was a different matter. He scored four goals four times (including a brilliant performance against Sunderland in his last full season, 1968–69), a hat-trick on three occasions, and a brace in no fewer

FA CUP MARKSMEN

The goals have come thick and fast in the FA Cup over the past few seasons (even in the 1998 3–5 shocker against Manchester United). But **Bobby Tambling** remains far and away the Blues' top FA Cup goalscorer. Of course, as everyone knows, **Peter Osgood** was the last player to score in every round (from the third, when the big guns come in). The top twenty-one marksmen are:

1 **Tambling**	25		11= **McNichol**	7	
2 **Bentley**	21		11= **Mills**	7	
3 **Osgood**	19		11= **Smith (Bobby)**	7	
4 **Houseman**	10		11= **Turnbull**	7	
5= **Bridges**	9		15= **Cock**	6	
5= **Gallacher**	9		15= **Hutchinson**	6	
5= **Hilsdon**	9		15= **Thain**	6	
5= **Whittingham**	9		15= **Thomson (Bob)**	6	
5= **Peacock**	9		15= **Webb**	6	
5= **Hughes**	9		15= **Wise**	6	
10 **Dixon**	8				

than twenty-two games. Five goals in a 6–2 win at Villa Park in 1966 were even more significant when it is remembered that three were with his 'swinger', his right foot. Arsenal were another side Bobby seemingly had it in for – he scoring four of a total career ten against the Gunners in one away game in 1963/64.

That rare commodity, a Tambling header, also sticks in the mind, the excellent winner in the FA Cup third round clash at Anfield in 1966. 'When you get the goal that knocks Liverpool out of the Cup and silences the Kop,' he later recalled, modestly, 'that's really something.'

He played a full part in Europe during the Fairs Cups of 1965/66 and 1968/69, scoring twice in the first campaign that saw Roma, Milan and Munich beaten. When he notched his 100th goal, he sported a shirt with the number emblazoned in huge white figures on his back, but you got the impression that the idea was not his.

Bobby's thrusting, foraging style suited the hectic mode of Docherty's Chelsea. His left-footedness gave balance to the team too. He could hustle in from the wing, ghost through between centre-backs who towered over him, and was a deadly body-swerver in one-on-ones. Unassuming, hunch-shouldered, apt to stick his fingers through his parted hair as he lined up for kick-off after one of his 202 goals, Bobby was a superb servant and a great sportsman. His misfortune was to be at his peak in a side that was great without being good enough to win the major honours, though his seven goals in the victorious League Cup campaign of 1964/65 were vital. He also scored in the 1967 FA Cup final defeat by Spurs, but was quite possibly the most disappointing player on the park.

With Venables, supplier of the early 'channel' balls he and Bridges loved, departed and Charlie Cooke a different kind of midfield schemer, Bobby's star faded towards the end of the decade.

He moved on to Crystal Palace in 1971, and on Easter Saturday returned as an opposition player to receive an illuminated address from his former employers and generous vocal support from the Shed end. 'The Directors, Management and Staff,' read the address, 'are unanimous in expressing congratulations to Bobby Tambling on his fine accomplishments which have enhanced the proud record of Chelsea in the world of football.'

Bobby, who became a Jehovah's Witness towards the end of his career, moved to Waterford in Ireland where he was still dominating matches at the age of 37 in 1978.

ANDY TOWNSEND

'Eyes to the left, nose to the right', was the joke about the Irish international on the terraces. In one match Andy was whacked on the conk and our worst fears were confirmed – it had nearly been straightened.

The South Londoner was also famous for swallowing his tongue, if not holding it. Andy was just as likely to joke about such matters himself as tease others, dubbing Kerry Dixon 'The Wig' for his fabulously teased blond coiffure, grabbing the ClubCall microphone to force Graham Stuart to explain himself over some training room misdemeanour, or painstakingly, hilariously announcing his 'Ugly XI' for the PFA team of the season (no, it didn't include himself).

The Irish international was a great signing – for two and a half of his three seasons with the club. The Republic's star of Italia 90 cost Chelsea £1.2m that summer as the club surged back into the First Division, and his midfield work was inspirational, whether wide left or playing through the middle, whether providing 'killer' balls into the danger area with his cultured left foot, shooting accurately on the volley or swivelling and dribbling at pace with the ball at his feet.

His swerving, dipping strike against Queens Park Rangers in spring 1991, the best possible reply to a 'cleared' corner, was typically instinctive.

Linking up with fellow new boy Dennis Wise, Andy was a virtually unanimous Chelsea Player of the Year in his first season. In his second he added goals to his game in a more advanced role. He third top-scored with six in that campaign, and perhaps already set his sights on a move when Chelsea finished a disappointing fourteenth in the First Division, losing to lower Division opposition in both Cups.

1992/93 was just as bad, beginning well enough with a high league slot and progress in the League Cup up to Christmas, then all falling apart in one January week, out of the FA Cup to

Middlesbrough, out of the League Cup in the quarter-final at rain-sodden Selhurst Park to Palace (Andy's goal providing scant consolation in a dreadful 1–3 result) and losing 2–4 to Manchester City. Turmoil reigned for the rest of the season, and Andy looked disinterested. It was as if the cornflakes he favoured before a game were drowned in sour milk.

Perhaps unfairly, he has been tagged as a 'mercenary'. He was quoted as saying that Chelsea weren't ambitious enough and that he was determined to win something before his career was over. Glenn Hoddle tried to persuade him to stay, but the deal was done.

Andy won the League Cup with his new team Aston Villa, then moved to Middlesbrough, where he was virtually bypassed in the League Cup final of 1998 by a far superior Chelsea midfield.

BOB TURNBULL

Known as 'Turnbull-at-the-Gate' in the era of cumbersome nicknames. In 1925/26 he was also known as the bloke who got all the goals, notching up a sensational twenty-nine League goals. Chelsea had recently been relegated from Division One largely through failing to trouble the scorer enough, so his presence was doubly welcome. The arrangement was fleeting as he was replaced in 1927 by Jimmy Thompson, a taller and more imposing centre-forward. Signed from Charlton, Bob's mobility, opportunism and ability with both feet were his prime assets.

FRANK UPTON

Perhaps football management's only genuine caretaker, since all he did was look after Stamford Bridge overnight. That was in between the sacking of Ken Shellito and the laughable appointment of Danny Blanchflower in 1978.

Frank had been part of the coaching staff, a position he'd held for some time having returned to Stamford Bridge after his playing career ended in the mid-1960s. Defender or wing-half, Frank had been vital in the 1962/63 promotion campaign, described by Brian Glanville at the time as a player able to 'wreak devastation, as though he were at play in a bowling alley and his opponents so many skittles.' Frank is now on the coaching staff at Derby County.

TERRY VENABLES

Terry Venables, the 'new Duncan Edwards' and a product of the Chelsea youth scheme, was midfield general and captain for both legs of the League Cup Final against Leicester in 1965, scoring one of the goals from the penalty spot in the 3–2 aggregate win.

Many fans would credit the cheery East End playmaker with our finest ever goal. Or at least the cheekiest. The occasion was the Inter-City Fairs (now UEFA) Cup match against AS Roma. It was Stamford Bridge's first big European night, watched by 32,000 people, and they weren't starved of incident. Eddie McCreadie was sent off for punching one of the querulous Italians, but ten-man Chelsea stormed into the next round with a 4–1 win (and an incredible 0–0 draw amid the most violent and intimidating crowd scenes Terry ever knew in Rome). Terry scored a hat-trick on the night, but one of those would be remembered forever. A free-kick was given just outside the Roma box, and the defenders were not removed the stipulated ten yards. With theatrical histrionics, Terry paced out ten yards from the ball, meeting and breaking through the wall around eight yards away. Then he suddenly screamed, 'Now John!' and Johnny Hollins pushed the ball through the hole in the wall for Terry simply to turn and slot it past the bewildered keeper. The Chelsea players collapsed with laughter. The Romans exacted their revenge by hacking him so hard he was off the pitch for ten minutes.

It was typical of the fun time, tinged with danger, that marked the Docherty era. Almost up until the Blackpool Incident Tel was the Doc's favourite son. But Venners' influence on his teammates was perceived by the manager as undermining his own authority. Terry's advice to Marvin Hinton to ignore the boss's instructions and drop back as sweeper when required in the return leg against Roma was the final straw. Young Ron Harris was appointed skipper in his stead in 1966 and he was replaced in the team by Charlie Cooke before being packed off to Spurs unceremoniously and reluctantly.

The following season, Terry was in Tottenham's FA Cup final team that beat Chelsea 2–1 in 1967. Frequently linked with a return to the club that set him on his stellar career Terry took another Chelsea old boy, Allan Harris, part of the way on his managerial tour that culminated in the England job.

GIANLUCA VIALLI

Gianluca Vialli, fresh from lifting the European Cup as Juventus' skipper in 1995, arrived at cosmopolitan Chelsea as a former acquaintance of newly installed manager Ruud Gullit.

His dream to 'become a Chelsea legend' materialized only after a mild nightmare of a first season, in which his forward partnership with Mark Hughes didn't always click, he found himself warming the bench (with or without the occasional cigarette) and performing heroics only in cameos, as in his two-goal display in the Cup comeback against Liverpool, while another Italian, Gianfranco Zola, teamed up with Sparky and grabbed most of the headlines. So much so that when Rudi gave the centre-forward his five-minute run-out in our 1997 FA Cup Final victory, it was assumed it might be his last appearance in a Chelsea shirt.

As it was, the hero returned for his second season refreshed and re-energized, a changed man, as Rudi noted with satisfaction.

The hard running, intelligence and experience, good technique and persistence returned to his play, coupled with consistency. He was our hero in displays in Barnsley (a four-goal limb-loosener), Tromso (scoring two vital goals in the Arctic snow), Bratislava (a stunning strike of his 'khyber'), and countless other matches.

Then in February his life turned upside down. Rudi was dismissed and he was asked to take over as player-manager. He instantly accepted with grace and set about raising morale, beginning with a 3–1 turn-around of the first leg 1–2 deficit in the Coca-Cola Cup semi-final with Arsenal, leading by tireless example on a night for heroes.

With the Coca-Cola Cup won, Luca and his acknowledged partner and assistant Graham Rix set about winning Chelsea's first European trophy for twenty-seven years. Betis overcome, Vicenza's first leg lead was 1–0. On the return at the Bridge, another famous night, Luca's boys overcame an early shock goal for the visitors to triumph 3–1, Luca himself setting up the second, Franco Zola's header, with a brilliantly sneaky run and cross.

Blackburn manager Roy Hodgson was bowled over by Luca's performance. 'That was the ultimate display of centre-forward play,' he oozed. 'He chased everything, harried defenders, won the ball and made run after run himself. Every attack, he was either in the box or providing the crosses from out wide himself. The cross he put in for Zola's goal was absolutely superb, perfect.'

Then the Cup Winner's Cup final in Stockholm. Chelsea and the player-manager outshone the Stuttgart players without scoring. Then a substitution, by Graham Rix. Franco for Tore Andre Flo. Seventeen seconds. Goal!

In little more than three months of trying, the wealthy Italian had become one of the most successful managers and players in Chelsea history.

How much of this is down to Luca's luck? Some people in football are lucky.

As the player-manager prepared for a challenge on the

Championship in 1998/99, Colin Hutchinson secured on his behalf the services of Brian Laudrup, Marcel Desailly, Albert Ferrer and Pierluigi Casiraghi. It felt like yesterday when Dennis Wise, Paul Elliott and Andy Townsend were hailed as just the job to fit in with Kerry Dixon, Kevin Wilson, John Bumstead, Kenny Monkou and Dave Beasant.

Like so many other movements in the last few years, Luca's appointment seemed a natural progression as we eased into football's top drawer.

CLIVE WALKER

It could have been 'Super Clive' – he scored some super goals, including two memorable strikes from distance against Champions Liverpool in January 1978's 4–2 FA Cup shock assault.

It could have been 'Walker the Wizard' – some of his incisive wing play was amongst the most effective in that position since Charlie Cooke and Frank Blunstone. But no. History records his nickname as Clive 'Flasher' Walker. I don't know, you reveal yourself to one passing schoolgirl...

Oxford-born YTS graduate Clive had lightning pace, great dribbling skills with his left peg, and a fierce shot. His failings were his inconsistency and inability – particularly in one-on-ones – to capitalize on his own brilliant opening-up of defences.

His mercurial skills were best revealed by his one-man-shows, particularly against Bolton. In October 1978, eighteen months after his League bow as a nineteen-year-old, the winger was brought on as sub on the left flank with just over fifteen minutes remaining. Visitors Bolton, 3–0 up, looked set to leave the Bridge with the full quota of points. The micro maestro's impact was unlike any seen at the ground for years. In no time he was tearing the shell-shocked Lancastrian defence apart, setting up Langley and Swain and scoring himself to bring the scores level. The last-minute Sam Allardyce own goal that sealed a remarkable reversal has often been attributed to Clive, so inescapable was his contribution.

Again at the close of the 1982/83 season Clive saved Chelsea, this time from possible relegation to the old Third

Division, by scoring one of the most important goals in our history, an inspired twenty-five-yard winner at Burnden Park.

At his best Clive electrified people. The referee at that first Bolton game stated that he'd never heard an atmosphere like it. Flasher had that effect.

Sadly, injury interrupted Clive's career in 1983 just as he began to play a less erratic, more measured game. Our loss has since been the gain of Brighton, then non-League cup giant-killers like Wycombe. Clive was still playing top-flight non-league in 1998 at the age of 40.

BEN WARREN

One of the most tragic Chelsea stories belongs to the England half-back who had the world at his feet but saw it all fall apart. Renowned for his fitness and sportsmanship on the pitch and his generosity and kindness off it, Ben came from Derby in 1908 and was outstandingly brilliant for three seasons until first injury, then lengthy illness struck. This was, of course, pre-NHS, and he had no health insurance. Distressed by the effect the sickness was having on his finances and his family, Ben became mentally ill and was confined to an asylum leaving his wife and children unsupported. A benefit fund was established and generously supported by all sections of the football community but Ben died the same year, 1914.

DAVID WEBB

A £40,000 buy (plus exchange for Joe Kirkup) from Southampton in February 1968, Webby went to see his potential new colleagues play at Liverpool and was so taken by the idea of playing with the likes of Cookie and Ossie that he took a pay cut to join. Such was the fun, spirit and joy coursing through that team. His previous boss at Leyton Orient had been Chelsea's recently appointed gaffer, Dave Sexton, and the Saints seemingly underrated him.

He proved a fortuitous signing, one of those catalysing

players who seem to make things happen, for better or, occasionally, worse. His debut was at Old Trafford, Webby helping inflict on the Reds their first home defeat for nearly two years and thirty-seven games.

The Blues were grateful for Webby's appearances in the FA Cup and Cup Winner's Cup finals, if only for his defensive qualities.

The sparky East Ender made sure everyone knew about it too: 'Don't worry lads, we'll win the Cup now, just as we won the replay in the FA Cup last year after I did the same.' What 'DJ' had done was to clear off the line in extra-time of the first encounter of the final. Naturally, he must have also harboured thoughts that, as in the famous replay at Old Trafford in 1970, he would be the cup hero with the winning goal. It wasn't to be: Demps and Ossie put us 2–0 up after less than forty minutes. Even though Real Madrid pulled one back through Fleitas with a quarter of an hour to go, and that he had to sweep away a last-minute loose ball after one of The Cat's saves, there was no need for a repeat of the brave headed challenge, latching onto a flicked-on long throw, that saw Webby bring home the bacon against Leeds. For six years he represented the heart and soul of the club. His playfulness with the crowd was always warmly appreciated, and his versatility (he played in every shirt, including number one one Boxing Day, except eleven) as unbelievable as his determination to do well whatever he was asked to do. He had footballing ability on his side, of course, and strength. When manager Dave Sexton asked him to move forward to create a bit of mischief and maybe salvage a point or two, he always seemed to be successful. He even started games as centre-forward and, having a decent skill level, acquitted himself well.

Webby was unique. Only he could get dropped for growing a beard; equally, only he could fall over in a muddy goalmouth, pretend to swim, and get away with it. It was the carefree pause for a little showbiz that endeared him to the crowd.

Another favourite moment was the time when he fluffed a

decent shooting opportunity, gazed skywards, and proceeded to dig an imaginary hole with an invisible spade, and jump into it. Wonderful.

Something about his upbringing made him both opportunist and practical. His father died young and he found many ways to supplement his family's meagre income. Football brought him rich rewards, but as one commentator put it, if he'd have grown up in the Bronx he might just as easily have been a prize fighter. A detached mock-Tudor home in Chigwell for he and wife Jackie, bought on his signature to Chelsea, was laughingly justified to the press: 'What's good enough for Bobby Moore is good enough for me.'

Webby's arrival coincided with the rise of our great late-1960s team. And in a way he exemplified the Sexton sides: stylish, capable of beating anyone on his day, but occasionally alarmingly off-colour – though not so much as, say, Cookie – but, overridingly, resourceful.

One attacker described his tackling as like 'running full tilt into a brick wall'. Dave Sexton commended his '150 per cent' effort, adding, 'he can play a bit, you know.' The first was more visible than the second in the Wembley final, Eddie Gray tormenting the imperturbable right-back. When Webby swapped to centre with Chopper handling Gray in the replay, it was almost inevitable that he would redeem himself for the previous display. The header couldn't have been scored by a more deserving man.

The Cup victories (and loss in the League Cup, 1972), were peaks in a contribution to the team's well-being that's often underplayed. When those scornful hacks declaimed his 'modest' ability they ignore the diverse roles he played at Chelsea: swashbuckling defender; competent goalscorer; clown prince and occasional keeper (the famous Boxing Day victory over Ipswich when no other custodian was available). When Chelsea needed something – a last-gasp tackle, a surge of adrenalin… a goal, Webby was there to deliver more often than not.

DJ was there when it all went wrong too: like others who made their reputation at the Bridge and in bars along the King's Road in those days, he was sold off by the manager in 1974, joining QPR. Relations with the manager had begun to strain when he grew his hair and a thick beard, emulating hirsute James Bond actor George Lazenby who he'd seen 'getting all the birds' around a Caribbean hotel pool, and Sexton dropped him. 'The Chelsea fans keep sending me razor blades in the post,' he joked, mockingly pronouncing himself 'The Rasputin of the Stiffs'.

After a period as manager at various lower league clubs, Webby was called in 'like Red Adair' as he put it, to salvage Chelsea's woeful 1992/93 season from the depths of the late Porterfield era, turning things round only to be replaced by Glenn Hoddle at the end of term. Great bloke, Webby. Great Chelsea legend too.

ROY WEGERLE

What is it with Chelsea and white South Africans? Like Derek Smethurst and Colin Viljoen before him, Roy largely provided another good reason for the boycott on South African sportsmen, even those who are naturalized Americans. We were promised a kind of 'George Best of the Veldt' in the guff that surrounded his transfer from Tampa Bay Rowdies. And it's true there were glimmers of brilliance from Roy. He notched a few goals in the opening spell following his signing in June 1986, including one well-taken effort against QPR (the club where he would later arrive and make his name). Overwhelmingly, though, Roy was enthusiastic, talented but, in the strictest sense of the word, unprofessional. Though eager, he lacked the discipline and application required at the level he found himself at. Too exotic and ambitious for our reserves he moved to Luton in 1988, then Loftus Road, where they still talk about the sublime goal of the season he managed against Leeds (if not his work rate and fearlessness in the tackle). Roy moved on to Coventry and Blackburn, then retired from Premiership football after struggling for peak fitness. He now plays Major League Soccer in the States.

KEITH WELLER

Face it. Keith was signed so no-one else could have him. Or maybe because all the women fancied him. Why else was he permitted so few outings with a talent like his? The pacy, glamorous striker was twenty-four by the time he made his Chelsea debut in August 1970. He was a relatively expensive signing (£100,000) at a time when Chelsea were optimistically looking to build on eight years of top-flight football and a recent, first FA Cup success. He was the sort that divided fans. Not as classy or wholehearted as others, but capable of superb action from dead-ball situations and possessed of a powerful right foot that earned four England caps. In his spells at Tottenham and Millwall (from where he had signed in the close-season of 1970), his robustness and eye for goal from distance had mostly been deployed through the centre of midfield. His distribution of lovely weighted passes was also noted. With Ossie, Hutch and Tommy Baldwin still favoured men at Chelsea, Keith was asked to attack from wide on the right. He was popular with the players, though – definitely 'one of the lads' with the tastes of a lary Islingtonian. So he settled in off the pitch, if not on it.

Following the 13–0 defeat of Jeunesse Hautcharage in the first round of our defence of the Cup Winners' Cup in autumn 1971, Dave Webb bumped into Jimmy Bloomfield at the Bridge, who told him he was taking Weller to Leicester for £100,000. Webby says he knew that was the end of an era. The team would be broken up and all the quality sold off. Webby may have had some of Keith's famous European performances fresh in his mind. Although he failed to score in any of the nine European matches he figured in, Keith's direct play had consistently worried foreign opposition throughout the successful 1970/71 campaign and he went close on a number of occasion with deft flicks and blockbusters. It was in fumbling his indirect free-kick that the inexperienced Manchester City goalkeeper Healey notched an own-goal in the decisive second leg of the European Cup Winners' Cup semi. (If the keeper had let it go in untouched, it would not have counted. Keith, who had come off the bench that night, could not be credited with the goal as a result.) Following a rewarding period with Bloomfield at Filbert Street Keith joined up with several of his old Blues teammates in the North American Soccer League.

COLIN WEST

Short, Middlesbrough-born Chelsea youth product whose impact as a goalscorer five minutes into his debut at Highbury was never followed up with anything permanent. Pacy but lightweight, he carved out a career for himself at Dundee (moving there in 1990) then Hartlepool United.

BOB WHITTINGHAM

This sharp-shooter from Bradford is best remembered for the formidable potency of his shot. The grass-scorching rockets petrified goalkeepers, apparently. One custodian commented that he'd 'rather face his Satanic majesty than Whittingham'. (Surely Cantona wasn't playing in 1910/11?) But there was more to this well-built inside-forward's game than blistering drives. For instance, there was the build-up to them... Bob was apt to pick the ball up in midfield, hare diagonally off with the ball towards the wing, then suddenly turn and shoot from thirty yards into the corner of the net. It was frequently as much a surprise to the fans as the opposing goalie. He scored thirty-two goals in 1910/11, thirty in 1911/12. War intervened and Bob guested for Stoke, where he ended up permanently shortly after cessation. Unfortunately his health soon deteriorated and he died of consumption in 1919.

STAN WICKS

With the same birthplace, surname and stature, it would be no surprise for middle-aged readers to discover that Stanley and Steve Wicks, separated by twenty years but united by their positions in the Chelsea first team, were related. They're not.

Stan, with half an inch more height than his six-foot two-inch namesake, arrived in January 1954 to rejoin team manager Ted Drake from Third Division Reading, where his toughness at the back had been noted over more than 200 games. Drake had of course stewarded the Royals before assuming control at the Bridge. With Ron Greenwood settled in the centre, he didn't turn to his trusty twenty-six-year-old until November, midway through the Championship campaign. His sturdiness and composure were enough to ensure swift England 'B' representation, as well as becoming vital to Chelsea's occasionally nervy run-in

THE LAD'S A BIT NAUGHTY-SOUNDING

Jack **COCK**

Murdoch **DICKIE**

Alan **DICKS**

Charles **DYKE**

Peter **FEELY**

RUUD Gullit

Colin **HAMPTON** (had he married into the **WICKS** family)

George **HORN**

Joe **KIRKUP**

Terry **PHELAN**

Seth **PLUM**

Stanley **PROUT** (well, it sounds rude)

George **RODGER**

Dave **SEXTON**

John **SITTON**

Sidney **TICKRIDGE**

Peter **TUCK**

Kingsley **WHIFFEN**

Jimmy **WINDRIDGE**

Eric **CANTONA** (well, it's a dirty word round our house)

to the silverware during spring 1955. In the summer, with Ron long gone and the Blues celebrating our first League title, Stan retained his place for the Charity Shield win over Newcastle (at Stamford Bridge) to usher in what turned out to be an ultimately disappointing defence of the Championship, thirteen places behind the leaders, Manchester United. He went on to play superbly in over forty-two games (well, the season did include four fourth round replays against Burnley – Chelsea eventually won 2–0) and would no doubt have been a near ever-present fixture again during 1956–57 had it not been for a knee injury that terminated his career. He was twenty-eight and on the verge of full international recognition.

Sadly, Stan died in 1983. At Chelsea, though, he'll always be remembered as the right man in the right place.

STEVE WICKS

The tall central defender was sold off to Derby in 1979 by cash-strapped Chelsea. By that time, in his four years of first-team football, he had proved himself a tough tackler, dominant in aerial challenges and a pretty good passer too. His best partnership was with David Hay in the promotion-winning team of 1975/76. With Hay's removal he formed one of Chelsea's tallest-ever central defences alongside Micky Droy.

After Derby Wicksy moved on to QPR, then Palace, before returning to the Bridge in 1986 a shadow of his former self. (What had QPR done to him?)

His young son Matthew was the subject of a celebrated tug-of-war between Manchester United and Arsenal in 1996. Arsenal won – and let him go two years later.

GRAHAM WILKINS

The alphabet and Wilkins family christenings must be the only instances where Graham has been named ahead of his brother Ray. Defender Graham was either damned unlucky or plain garbage. For an amazing nine seasons between 1972 and 1981 the slender, ball-playing brother of star man Ray battled against the boo-boys, not helping himself with the occasional feeble challenge, bad back pass or own goal.

RAY WILKINS

In August 1979 Danny Blanchflower sold off one of our greatest-ever youth products. It brought a dream to an end. Ray was the brightest prospect in the mid-1970s teams, an England player to be proud of. While he was around, Chelsea was still a name to respect.

He forced his way into a star-studded side lacking motivation and morale, just after his seventeenth birthday in 1973. The side would soon be relegated, but Ray was outstanding, orchestrating games with his delicate skills, faultless technique and incisive passing. There were brilliant goals too, like the precision lob from distance against Hereford in January 1977, or the brilliant slide-in from Swain's cross into Southampton's net in 1976, before a lack of confidence towards the end of his Blues career inclined him to safer sideways passing.

There was always a sense of throwing him in the deep end, and perhaps it eventually took its toll on the exceptionally gifted central midfielder.

In 1975, aged eighteen, he became Chelsea's youngest-ever skipper. Two years later he overtook Bobby Tambling's 1963 record as the club's most youthful captain to win promotion. He was simply magnificent at the hub of that buzzing, zesty young side, taking free-kicks, making all the goals, doing virtually everything. Sides cottoned on and he was man-marked, but 'Butch' adapted his game and turned it round again.

Relegation in 1978/79 was always going to be a wrench. When Ray left, something died at the heart of the club.

Players like him don't come round very often. Our misfortune was that he arrived at a time when his presence simply

INTERNATIONAL BRIGADE

At the close of the 1997/98 season, the leading totals were as follows:

1 **Ray Wilkins** (England)	24
2 **Eddie McCreadie** (Scotland)	23
3= **Andy Townsend** (Republic of Ireland)	22
3= **Kevin Wilson** (Northern Ireland)	22
5 **Dmitri Kharine** (Russia)	21
6 **Craig Burley** (Scotland)	20
7= **Joey Jones** (Wales)	19
7= **Dan Petrescu** (Romania)	19
7= **Vic Woodley** (England)	19

wasn't enough. Ray moved on to Manchester United, then Milan, Paris St-Germain, Rangers and QPR.

This phenomenal Chelsea youth product also made eighty-four England appearances, his twenty-four while in the Chelsea fold establishing him as the club's most-capped player until surpassed by Dan Petrescu during France 98.

STAN WILLEMSE

Moon-faced Stan is right up there on the A list of the Bridge's Boy's Own heroes, and not least because of his background as a Royal Marine vet. At thirty, in his sixth and best season in West London, he was still raiding superbly behind enemy lines with the zest and derring-do that had fans in raptures.

A left full-back who was an uncompromising tackler, he is best remembered for those skilful lunges forward, where it was quite usual for the well-built Brighton native to take on and trounce five opponents on his way into the box. The occasional penalties that resulted were always useful.

In a way, the former England schoolboy and 'B' international provided the blueprint for the type of left-back that has been Chelsea fans' preferred incumbent ever since. Once he left for Orient in 1956, the next great headline-maker in that position was Eddie McCreadie, a similarly brave, hard and attack-minded player. And it's not a short leap of the imagination to the current team's star, Graeme Le Saux.

When frequent returnee Stan makes his appearances on the pitch, he is remembered for the vital role he played in helping seal the Blues' defences at the back and ripping into the opposition when steaming full ahead, he gets such a great reception.

ANDIE WILSON

Succeeded and exceeded Jack Cock in the hearts of the crowd. People talked of his 'art and subtle grace'. Blimey. He was perhaps the first in that line of tricky Scots ball-players leading on to Charlie Cooke and Pat Nevin. The Scots international centre forward and sometime skipper (twenty-three caps) was bought from Middlesbrough in November 1923 for £6,000 to stave off relegation. Unfortunately even the popular Andie, converted to inside-forward at the Bridge, couldn't stop the drop. It meant that he would spend six years of the prime of his playing career in the Second Division and just three in the top flight with the Blues. Andie was the supreme ball artist, all twinkling toes, cat-and-mouse temptations and deceptive moves. His lack of pace was more than compensated for by a barrel-load of crowd-pleasing tricks. This was no head-down winger. He was more than capable of a telling pass from one flank to the other. All this despite losing the use of one arm during the First World War (some said it made him harder to read!). He wasn't a mighty goalscorer, though fifty-nine was a decent haul from the 238 games he played, considering the number of openings he made for his colleagues. When he moved on in October 1931, having put on some weight over the years, it was first to QPR then, curiously, Nîmes. A spell in management was followed by a new career in international bowls.

KEVIN WILSON

Kevin's signing from Ipswich had to be settled by tribunal, which in turn would set the level of the player's wages. On the way back from the hearing, though, Chairman Ken Bates revealed that 'Willo' should ignore the tribunal amount and he'd be seen right with an improved wage offer.

Unfortunately, word of the augmentation got out, and Chelsea were forced to pay more to sign the forward!

With his for-goodness-sake-shave-it-off moustache, Kevin played more than 150 matches for Chelsea during the turbulent years of 1987–92. Persistent as a midge round fruit on the pitch, with fine shooting from any range, and a popular figure in the dressing room despite his notorious meanness with money, he made a good second-stringer to the likes of Kerry Dixon and Gordon Durie.

Capable of playing just behind or as a part of the forward line, the Northern Irish international wasn't tall enough, or possessed of good enough first touch, to perform as a target man. His scoring rate was variable, but many of those chances he did convert were match winners.

Following his move to Notts County, he played for Walsall and is currently Northampton's player-coach.

JIMMY WINDRIDGE

In a game that was at the same time more graceful (or slower) and more physical (or harder) than currently, Brummie inside-left Jimmy could be a master of the pitch, as he demonstrated with a hat-trick in Chelsea's first home League match against Hull in September 1905 at the age of twenty-one.

Bought for £190 before our election to the League, Jimmy was unsettled in his home town since he wanted guarantees of

SPORTING ALL-ROUNDERS

Jimmy Windridge, the club's first ever inside-left, played football for England and cricket for Warwickshire CCC.

Willie Foulke, the club's first goalkeeper, played county cricket for Derbyshire.

Ron Harris played cricket for England schoolboys.

Arthur Sales was an athlete who ran 100 yards in 10.5 seconds in the 1920s.

Max Woosnam, who won a full international cap for England in 1922, played Davis Cup tennis for Great Britain.

John Jackson, the Scottish international goalkeeper, became a golf professional after he left Chelsea.

Frank Mitchell, born in Australia, was on the staff of Warwickshire County Cricket Club for many years.

Reg Weaver took part in the famous pre-war Powderhall sprints.

Joe Payne played Minor Counties cricket for Bedfordshire.

first-team football they weren't prepared to give. Chelsea officials met him and found him 'quiet-spoken, pleasant and willing to come to Chelsea' which in most people's books already makes him a top geezer. In no time he was 'Windridge the Wizard'. *Football Star* called him 'one of the best inside-forwards in the country'. Two seasons on and he was England's inside-left, eventually forming an incredible international trio with Hilsdon and Woodward.

For his dribbling and control, he has been rated as the best in his position for the first fifty years of Chelsea's life.

Elusive of the type of 'sandwich' challenges that two nasty opponents might manufacture, the ball magnetically attracted to his dancing feet, eagle-nosed Jimmy, a decent county cricketer for Warwickshire too by all accounts, was an unpredictable player.

Deft in his passes, penetrating with his runs, he provided plenty of ammunition for George Hilsdon, and contributed in no small measure himself – the two almost single-handedly fired Chelsea to First Division promotion in 1908. Jimmy died in 1939 at the age of fifty-six.

DENNIS WISE

Manager Ruud Gullit observed his thirty-year-old skipper in 1997 and commented: 'Wise is now in the most important phase in his career. He seems more responsible and I am pleased to see it. But he has changed because of the whole new environment at the club and not just because of me.'

A word to the Wise. And an observation that the England international midfielder, perennially described as the cheeky chappy, had exorcized some of the demons that had sometimes marred a brilliantly consistent run of form since his arrival from Wimbledon in the summer of 1991.

The chirrupy midfielder was a Cup winner before he signed for the Blues, with Wimbledon, of course, and it was perhaps his misfortune to be associated for so long with the Plough Lane brand of football. Chelsea had finished fifth the previous season, and were looking to better that with such relatively high-profile purchases. There were segments of our fans who had to be convinced that there wasn't still something of the Crazy Gangster about him still.

Dennis, always comfortable with the technical side of the game, grew into a thinker and a leader too. Under Bobby Gould he'd been a steal-a-yard-and-get-a-cross-in winger. Chelsea wanted to bring out the more subtle elements of his game, the visionary passes, the intelligence, the match-winning runs.

In his time he has played all over the Blues midfield, out-lasting and out-motoring younger and supposedly more illustrious colleagues and opponents. Always hard-working but liable to flare up and be absent through such indiscipline, he was asked by Glenn Hoddle to add composure to his game, as well as to adapt to the demands of the various formations and availability of players. He successfully adapted, for example, to the requirement for a defensive midfielder when Nigel Spackman or Eddie Newton were unavailable. And he began to read the game superbly, knowing when to press for things and when to let the foot off the pedal. If, especially under Glenn and Rudi, the goalscorer in him faded, the understated leader emerged strongly, especially in knockout competitions. His seering twenty-five-yard strike against Viktoria Zizkov will be remembered for its timeliness as well as its beauty.

Whether the transformation had anything to do with his ill-advised tussle with a taxi driver is open to question. He always claimed he'd learned from the infamous episode and its aftermath. It seems that he was never confident of Glenn's friendship from that moment on; it was the situation that led to his temporary removal from the captaincy. Dennis's assertions about where his manager was going wrong during his first winter – too much pretty-pretty stuff, not enough graft was the gist of it – has had wider ramifications. As 'The Rat' predicted, he has had no call-up for England since Glenn's accession to national manager.

None the less, Dennis gave his all throughout. In 1994 there was no more disappointed man than he after the Wembley defeat. But none more determined to end the twenty-six-year lack of meaningful silverware afterwards.

Sometimes, as in the potential banana-skin visit to Portsmouth and the even more daunting semi-final battle against his old club en route to the 1997 final, it often seemed that Dennis was so focused there could be no other result than victory.

He's become a towering presence in big matches, sorely missed when he's out, suspended or injured. While enemies love to highlight his 'temper', the regular acts of thoughtfulness pass almost unremarked.

He's always the first to invite a star-struck youngster onto the pitch at the end of a significant victory. And which other player would have insisted that new manager Luca be presented with the Cup at Wembley? Bates's favourite player was determined that he would not be remembered as a medal-winner with the Dons, convinced that he would lead Chelsea to glory. So it proved. And, finally, after seven year's underrated toil, he was named Player of the Year in 1997/98.

DARREN WOOD

Pacy, strong and capable of deft skills, though sometimes lacking concentration, the hundred-percenter from Scarborough had already played 200 times for Middlesbrough by the age of twenty when he was reunited with former boss John Neal at the Bridge in September 1984. A former England schoolboy comfortable in midfield or on the flank but most accustomed to right full-back, unsung Darren made 178 appearances (including the bizarre 5–4 Full-Members' Cup victory over Manchester City in 1986) before moving on to Sheffield Wednesday in 1989 for a sizeable £350,000.

VIC WOODLEY

When Scots international keeper Jackson was signed in summer 1933 he might have expected a decent run in the 'Tartan Chelsea' side of the day. However, he injured himself in diving at the feet of a Huddersfield forward and Vic, who'd arrived two years earlier, stepped into the fray. So impressive was the improvement in his form after that 'let off' that he soon established himself in the England team that had to face the likes of the mighty Austrians. The two vied for top-dog slot for several seasons, trained together without enmity.

So Chelsea enjoyed the luxury of having present incumbent

international goalies in the first and reserve team. The situation almost repeated itself in the 1970s with Phillips (Wales) and Bonetti (England) and 1997/98 with Kharine (Russia) and de Goey (Netherlands), though not to the same degree.

At six feet the former Windsor and Eton amateur was three inches taller than his Scots rival. But it was his safe handling, mobility and concentration that created the edge.

He had glamour too, despite – or maybe because of – the largely rearguard battle he fought maintaining Chelsea's top-flight status. His polo-necked image on cigarette cards was one of the most sought after in England.

After the Second World War Vic's swansong was a penalty save in the celebrated Moscow Dinamo match. A few months after that he was released to Bath City aged thirty-five, opening a public house in the area on his retirement. He died in 1978 aged sixty-eight, but still held two Chelsea records: most international caps for a goalie (nineteen); and most consecutive appearances, seventy-seven between October 1935 and April 1937.

VIVIAN WOODWARD

Fifteen games into the 1909/10 season, Chelsea boasted a mere ten points and were placed fourth from bottom. Newspapers were full of 'What's Wrong With Chelsea' stories. Well, the simple answer was that there were seventeen on the injured list, but since when has fact got in the way of a good slagging? It was the time for a hero. Happily one existed, and he'd always promised that if Chelsea were really desperate he would answer the call. The ultimate amateur – a gentleman architect with looks to swoon for and a debonair sportsmanly air – he turned out for Tottenham and England's non-professional internationals, but had made it clear that if Chelsea needed him he would make the switch across London. He actually lived closer to Chelsea than Spurs.

Viv is rated one of the greatest inside-forwards of all time.

He was loved by the footering public. A native of Essex, he played a cultured game, sometimes running half the length of the field lithely evading tackles with the dip of a shoulder or feint of the hips, othertimes sweeping a majestic, meticulous pass out to the wing. His speed and freedom of movement were prime assets, and he was never known to react badly to a tackle or perpetrate fouls himself. For a while he completed the England trio at the heart of Chelsea's attack: Hilsdon, Windridge and himself. The problem was that international call-ups meant that the Chelsea followers saw them fewer times than appears reasonable.

Viv's career at Chelsea stretched gloriously into the First World War and one final act of chivalry. In 1915 Chelsea reached the famous 'Khaki Cup Final'. Allowed home on leave from the RAF (of course) Flight Lieutenant Woodward accepted the club's invitation to be there but dispatched a reply (underlined) that he did not want to play, since the likes of Bob Thompson had got the Blues to the final, and they should be the ones to represent Chelsea at English football's most celebrated day. (Maybe he had a feeling Sheffield United were going to win anyway.) He never played for Chelsea again, but became a director in 1922 and held that role until 1930. He died in 1954.

YOUTH

It is manager Billy Birrell we should be thanking for the youth scheme that has served the club so well over the years. He ushered in a new era of cost-effective player acquisition in 1947, initially under the guidance of ex-players Dick Foss and Albert Tennant. Foss became Chelsea's first youth team manager, succeeded by another former Blues star Frank Blunstone in 1965. Retired flying right-back Ken Shellito took the helm in winter 1969, assisted by ex-Blue Eddie Heath, followed by Frank 'The Tank' Upton. Throughout this period the youngsters' trainer was onetime Chelsea winger Dicky Spence.

In 1979 'Mr Chelsea', current assistant manager Gwyn Williams, took over, the first of the new era of former schoolteachers to add pastoral care to nurturing in the art of football.

The only triumphs in the FA Youth Cup came under Dicky Foss in 1960 and 1961. The web of scouts who brought the best players to Chelsea's attention should not be overlooked. One of the most colourful and successful was ex-player Jimmy Thompson, a larger-than-life figure with false teeth and a jokey cloak-and-dagger manner the kids loved, and who coaxed several of the East End's brightest prospects away from the clutches of West Ham and Spurs. Among them were Jimmy Greaves, Terry Venables and Ron Harris.

The success of the 1970s youth policy is more difficult to measure because our brightest either struggled in a poor side or were sold off before they had reached their peak. But the names of Gary Locke, Ray Wilkins, Steve Wicks and Garry Stanley indicate that the youth schemers were doing their jobs.

In the 1980s there were John Bumstead, Colin Pates and Keith Jones followed within a few years by the likes of Eddie Newton, Frank Sinclair, Gareth Hall, Jason Cundy, Dave Lee, Graham Stuart, Muzzy Izzett, Andy Myers, Michael Duberry, Jody Morris, Nick Crittenden, Jon Harley... Rhys Evans next?

It was a measure of the success of the 1990s YTS set-up that no less than fifteen of the star-studded, double trophy-winning 1997/8 squad learned their early craft under Chelsea's guidance. Another Chelsea youth product, Craig Burley, helped win the Championship as skipper of Celtic.

With a football academy on its way before the Millennium, the future looks assured.

Z

GIANFRANCO ZOLA

Franco joined Chelsea from Parma during the 1996/97 season on 15 November. Such was his impact that he was made Footballer of the Year having played just six months of the campaign. He was the first Chelsea player to win the honour.

'When Franco first arrived we did a keep-ball session,' said assistant manager Graham Rix. 'Dan Petrescu and other players are not too bad at this to say the least. But on the first morning Zola was head and shoulders above the rest. No-one could get the ball off him or even get near him.'

Franco Zola arrived after a chase on Chelsea's part that extended back deep into the Hoddle era. The name Gullit may have been the key that unlocked the little Sardinian's attachment to Serie A, or perhaps the timing was simply right for him and Parma.

He had won the Scudetto in his first season with Napoli in 1990 alongside Maradona, moved to Parma for £1.4m in 1993 and won runners-up medals in the Cup Winners' Cup, Scudetto and the Italian Cup. His genius helped Chelsea to a first major trophy in twenty-six years.

The enchanting five-foot six-inch Sardinian, for whom the summer of Euro 96 had been all about a missed penalty, was an instant hit with his precise free-kick against Everton, but it was the four magical strikes in three matches (West Ham, Villa and Sheffield Wednesday) over Christmas 1996 that had fans in ecstatic admiration.

We were lucky enough to have another player of genuine greatness in our midst, in a team that already had Ruud Gullit, Robbie Di Matteo, Dan Petrescu and Luca Vialli.

SHORT AND SWEET

Up to the close of the 1997/98 seasons, six players had made just a single substitute appearance for Chelsea. Of these, the shortest Blues career must be that of forward **Joe Sheerin**, who came on at Wimbledon for a limping **Gianfranco Zola** on 22 April 1997 in the ninetieth minute – and did not touch the ball. He remains on the professional staff, so there's still time for him to improve his figures. The same applies to **Steve Hampshire**. The other four names are **Roger Wosahlo** (1966/67), **Jimmy Clare** (1980/81), **Steve Livingstone** and **Gerry Peyton** (1992/93) – the latter was on loan from Everton at the time.

Another forty-two players have made just a single start for the club. Of these, **Neil Clement** and **Nick Colgan** were still on the books at the end of 1997/98. There have been some odd ones down the years.

Colin Court played just once – in Chelsea's first ever European tie at Frem of Copenhagen on September 30 1958.

Amateur full-back **James Fletcher** made a single appearance in 1905/06 – but the history books record that he never registered with

His relaxed, jocular manner fitted easily into the Chelsea dressing room. The English players dubbed him 'The Fonz'. (The Italians, like the English with the Welsh, simply joked about the Sardinians' liking for goats.)

There were so many moments of breathtaking brilliance in that first season: the dazzling trickery in scoring a phenomenal early goal against Manchester United at home; the curling stinger in the comeback against Liverpool in the FA Cup; the unbelievable drag back and swivel in the semi-final against Wimbledon. Even his deft, instinctive flick back for Eddie Newton's killer goal against Middlesbrough in the 1997 final had the Football League.

Goalkeeper **Stanley Macintosh** let in six in his only game at Derby on 6 December 1930.

Les Fridge let in five in the last game of the 1985/86 season against Watford.

Murdoch Dickie's one game at outside right was the 4–7 defeat at Liverpool on 7 September 1946.

Michael Pinner's single appearance in goal was a 4–5 home defeat by Wolves in April 1962.

Centre-half **Frank Wolff** and outside-right **James Toomer** played their only first-team games in the 1–7 defeat by Crystal Palace in the 1905/06 FA Cup – Chelsea had to field a weakened team because a League match had been scheduled for the same day.

William Sinclair and **James Smart** both arrived from Morton at the same time and both played just once for the Blues – in a 2–6 defeat at Burnley on 24 April 1965.

Alex Cyril Stepney, who played over 500 times for Manchester United and won a European Cup winner's medal, played just once for the Blues, in 1966/7, after **Tommy Docherty** signed him for £50,000 – then a record fee for a goalkeeper.

flair where a lesser player might have looked awkward.

They said he had happy feet. In the second campaign they said he had a disappointing season. Not if you look at the statistics. The number of assists were immense, the completed passes above other people's standards.

Even if Italy didn't think they needed him for France 98, Blues fans knew the value of the smiling Sardinian, especially in the European Cup Winners' Cup games.

He was stubbornly defiant in the face of press criticism in England, his relegation to the bench in March and increasing evidence that Cesare Maldini saw him as surplus to requirements (despite his history-making winning goal against England at Wembley).

There had already been his astonishing hat-trick against shell-shocked Derby in November. In March, the smouldering Italian caught fire. Two goals in a 6–2 rout launched a stiletto into Crystal Palace's heart and consigned them to relegation. Then a stunning header converting Luca Vialli's fierce cross levelled the semi-final score against Vicenza.

The Cup Winners' Cup final kicked off with Franco as sub. Yet the goal he scored against Stuttgart on that famous night in Stockholm will go down in the Chelsea annals as one of the all-time greats. He had occupied the bench somewhat morosely for most of the game. The first piece of action he saw on replacing Tore Andre Flo was a skirmish in which he lost the ball, which rebounded to the lurking Dennis Wise. Franco spotted the opening, darted between two opposing defenders and raced onto Dennis's perfectly weighted lob. As the ball bounced on the edge of the Germans' box, Franco adjusted his run and blasted a rising shot into the roof of the net giving Wohlfahrt no chance.

By his own admission the celebration wasn't one of his better efforts, but perhaps all the more charming for the simplicity and spontaneity of it. There was something so apposite about that moment. The assister, the scorer, the manner of the execution, the fact that the ball had 'winner' written all over from the moment it scorched off his right boot. It was worthy of winning any match anywhere. But the fact that it was Zola, the man we loved, the man who would miss out on Italy's France 98 squad but win his third medal in eighteen months at Chelsea; that was what made it so meaningful. And he had been on the pitch just seventeen seconds.

His contract might keep him at the Bridge until 2002. 'We are playing great football and making it possible to challenge for the title,' he said in 1998. 'But you have to work all the time – if you are top of the League, you have to be even better. Chelsea is going well, but the work, the opera, is not finished.'

There have been so many Blues heroes, from one-appearance wonders to old troopers. Here's a list of those not featured in the A-Z, along with their years of service:

David Alexander 1939-45, Clive Allen 1991-92, Les Allen 1954-59, John Allister 1949-52, Joe Allon 1991-93, Len Allum 1932-39, Sylvan Anderton 1959-62, George Anderson 1927-29, James Ashford 1920-25, Jimmy Bain 1945-47, Joe Bambrick 1934-38, George Barber 1930-41, Eddie Barkas 1937-39, Darren Barnard 1990-95, Anthony Barness 1992-96, William Barraclough 1934-37, Fred Barratt 1920-27, Sid Bathgate 1946-53, Tom Baxter 1919-20, Dr John Bell 1920-23, Walter Bellett 1954-58, Walter Bennett 1922-24, Paul Berry 1953-60, Sidney Bildewell 1937-46, Edward Birnie 1906-10, Sid Bishop 1928-33, George Biswell 1928-29, Micky Block 1959-62, Michael Bodley 1985-89, Gordon Bolland 1960-62, AG Bower 1923-25, Jimmy Bowie 1944-51, Andy Bowman 1951-55, Terry Bradbury 1957-62, Jim Bradshaw 1909-10, Billy Brawn 1907-11, Ron Brebner 1906-07, William Bridgeman 1906-19, Harold Brittan 1913-20, Micky Brolly 1971-74, John Brooks 1959-61, Dennis Brown 1962-64, John Brown 1912-15, William Brown 1924-29, William Y. Brown 1911-13, John Browning 1919-20, Peter Buchanan 1936-46, Robert Buchanan 1911-13, Harry Burgess 1935-45, Robert Bush 1906-07, Dennis Butler 1960-63, Geoff Butler 1967-68, Michael Byrne 1905-06, David Calderhead (Jr.) 1907-14, David Cameron 1920-26, Jock Cameron 1907-13, Bobby Campbell 1947-54, John Carr 1928-31, Robert Carter 1929-33, William Cartwright 1908-13, Len Casey 1954-58, Sid Castle 1923-26, Laurent Charvet 1998, Alex Cheyne 1930-31, 1934-36, Wilf Chitty 1930-38, Gary Chivers 1978-83, James Clare 1977-81, Neil Clement 1995-present, David Cliss 1956-62, John Coady 1986-88, Nick Colgan 1992-1998, Michael Collins 1951-57, John Compton 1955-60, Davie Copeland 1905-07, James Copeland 1932-37, Peter Corthine 1957-60, Colin Court 1954-59, Allan Craig 1933-39, James Craigie 1905-07, John Crawford 1923-34, Nick Crittenden

1997-present, James Croal 1914-22, Stan Crowther 1958-61, George Dale 1919-22, Seamus D'Arcy 1951-52, Alex Davidson 1946-48, Gordon Davies 1984-85, Alan Dickens 1989-93, Murdock Dickie 1954-46, William Dickie 1919-21, Alan Dicks 1951-58, William Dickson 1947-53, Perry Digweed 1988, Jim Docherty 1979, George Dodd 1911-13, Billy Dodds 1986-88, Hugh Dolby 1909-12, Len Dolding 1945-48, Charles Donaghy 1905-07, Alexander Donald 1930-32, Angus Douglas 1908-13, Andy Dow 1993-95, Sam Downing 1909-14, Phil Driver 1980-83, Sam Dudley 1932-34, Bernard Duffy 1923-27, Charlie Dyke 1947-51, Robert Edwards 1951-55, Sid Elliot 1928-30, Timothy Elmes 1980-82, Robert Evans 1960-61, Norman 'Norrie' Fairgray 1907-14, Mark Falco 1982, Peter Feely 1970-73, Christopher Ferguson 1927-30, Edward Ferguson 1920-23, Willie Ferguson 1921-33, Jim Ferris 1920-22, William Finlayson 1920-23, James Fletcher 1905-06, Harry Ford 1912-24, Craig Forrest (loan) 1997, Steve Francis 1982-87, Charlie Freeman 1907-1920, Jim Frew 1922-26, Les Fridge 1985-87, James Frost 1906-07, Lee Frost 1976-80, Jim Gallon 1919-21, John Galloway 1946-49, Derek Gibbs 1955-60, George Gibson 1933-38, Michael Gilkes (loan) 1992, Ray Goddard 1946-48, Joe Goodwin 1905-06, Danny Granville 1997-98, William Gray 1949-53, Robert Gregg 1933-38, Robert Griffiths 1931-41, Kevin Hales 1979-83, Harold Halse 1913-21, Ian 'Chico' Hamilton 1968, Colin Hampton 1914-25, Alfred Hanson 1938-46, Gus Harding 1906-13, Jon Harley 1997-present, Mike Harrison 1956-63, Charlie Harris 1905-09, Jack Harwood 1912-13, Jack Harrow 1911-36, William Haywood 1921-24, George Henderson 1905-09, Tom Hewitt 1911-13, Frank Higgs 1928-30, Walter Hinshelwood 1951, Frank Hoddinott 1921-23, Arthur Holden 1908-10, Pat Holton 1959-60, Jim Hope 1930-32, David Hopkin 1992-95, George Horn 1909-13, Jack Horton 1933-37, Terry Howard 1984-87, Harry Hughes 1951-52, Paul Hughes 1994-present, Tommy Hughes 1965-71, William Hughes 1948-51, Derek Johnstone 1983-85, Paul Parker 1997, Ian Pearce 1991-93, Gerry Peyton (loan) 1993, Terry Phelan 1995-97, Michael Pinner 1961, Seth Plum 1924-26, William Porter 1906-07, Tony Potrac 1970-73, John Priestley 1920-28, Tom Priestley 1933-34, Peter Proudfoot 1906-07, Stanley Prout 1932-34, Ernie Randall

1950-53, John Rankin 1930-34, William Read 1911-12, Ernie Reid 1937-39, Edward Reilly 1908-09, Peter Rhoades-Brown 1979-84, Fred Richardson 1946-47, Graham Rix 1993, Jim Robertson 1905-07, William H Robertson 1945-48, Arthur Robinson 1908-10, Bryan 'Pop' Robson 1982-83, Tom Robson 1965-66, George Rodger 1924-31, Robert Russell 1944-48, Wiliam Russell 1927-36, Arthur Sales 1924-28, Robert Salmond 1938-45, John Saunders 1948-54, James Saunders 1909-10, Mel Scott 1956-63, Buchanan Sharp 1919-23, James Sharp 1912-15, Colin Shaw 1961-63, Duncan Shearer 1983-86, Joe Sheerin 1997-present, Jack Sherborne 1939-45, Steve Sherwood 1971-76, Neil Shipperley 1992-95, Joe Simner 1947-49, William Sinclair 1964-66, John Sissons 1974-75, John Sitton 1977-80, Doug Smale 1937-45, Jim Smart 1965-66, Arthur Smith 1938-45, George Smith 1921-32, Jim Smith 1951-55, Philip Smith 1910, Bobby Smith 1950-55, Steve Smith 1920-23, Dennis Sorrell 1962-64, John Sparrow 1974-81, Miles Spector 1952-53, Joe Spottiswood 1919-20, James Stark 1907-08, William Steer 1912-18, Willi Steffen 1946-47, Alec Stepney 1966, George Stone 1924-28, David Stride 1976-79, Fred Taylor 1909-20, Albert Tennant 1934-53, Albert Thain 1922-31, Jimmy Thompson 1927-29, Charles 'Chick' Thomson 1952-57, James Thomson 1965-68, Robert Thomson 1911-22, Sid Tickridge 1951-55, Ron Tindall 1953-61, James Toomer 1905-06, John Townrow 1927-32, Peter Tuck 1951-54, Robert Turnbull 1925-28, Edward Tye 1914-15, Colin Viljoen 1980-82, Andy Walker 1913-20, Colin Waldron 1967, Tommy Walker 1946-48, Joe Walton 1906-11, Joseph Ward 1920-22, Robert Warren 1948-51, Ian Watson 1962-65, Jim Watson 1905-06, Reg Weaver 1929-32, Sam Weaver 1936-45, Kingsley Whiffen 1966-67, Alex White 1937-48, Ben Whitehouse 1906-08, Robert Whiting 1906-08, Jack Whitley 1907-14, Richard Whittacker 1952-60, William Whitton 1923-26, Harry Wilding 1914-28, Arthur Wileman 1909-11, Ernest Williams 1909-10, Paul Williams 1980-83, Reg Williams 1945-51, William Williams 1927-28, Clive Wilson 1987-90, Daniel Winter 1945-51, Frank Wolff 1905-06, Max Woosnam 1914, Roger Wosahlo 1964-67, Allan Young 1961-69

SOURCES

Scott Cheshire. Chelsea – An Illustrated History (Breedon Books) UK 1994

Scott Cheshire/Ron Hockings. Chelsea Players Who's Who (Breedon Books) UK 1989

Rick Glanvill. Rhapsody In Blue – The Chelsea Dream Team (Mainstream Publishing) UK 1995

Jimmy Greaves. This One's On Me (Coronet Books) UK 1979

Ron Hockings. 90 Years Of The Blues – A Statistical History Of Chelsea Football Club 1905–1995. (self-published) UK 1995

Stephen F Kelly. Back Page Football – A Century Of Newspaper Coverage (revised edition) (Aurora Publishing) UK 1997

Tommy Lawton. Football Is My Business (Sportsmans Books) UK 1961

David Prole. Football In London (Sportsmans Books) UK 1963

David Sawyer. Keeping Up Appearances – A History Of Chelsea Goalkeepers (self-published) UK 1996

Albert Sewell, Ed. The Chelsea Football Book No.1 (Stanley Paul) UK 1971

Albert Sewell, Ed. The Chelsea Football Book No.2 (Stanley Paul) UK 1972

Terry Venables and Neil Hanson. Venables – The Autobiography (Penguin) UK 1994

Miscellaneous matchday programmes 1905–1998

Miscellaneous newspaper reports 1905–1998

The Chelsea Internet mailing list

Pub talk in Chelsea Ram, Ferret And Firkin, Jolly Maltsters, Cock etc.